MAJOR BATTLES AND CAM...

WORLD WAR II IN THE
MEDITERRANEAN

1942–1945

MAJOR BATTLES AND CAMPAIGNS

John S. D. Eisenhower, General Editor

MAJOR BATTLES AND CAMPAIGNS

WORLD WAR II IN THE
MEDITERRANEAN

1942-1945

By Carlo D'Este

Lieutenant Colonel
United States Army (Ret.)

With an Introduction by
John S. D. Eisenhower

ALGONQUIN BOOKS OF CHAPEL HILL

1990

✓

Published by
ALGONQUIN BOOKS OF CHAPEL HILL
Post Office Box 2225
Chapel Hill, North Carolina 27515-2225

a division of
WORKMAN PUBLISHING COMPANY, INC.
708 Broadway
New York, New York 10003

LIBRARY OF CONGRESS CATALOGING-IN-PUBLICATION DATA
D'Este, Carlo, 1936–
   World War II in the Mediterranean, 1942–1945 / by Carlo
D'Este; with an introduction by John S. D. Eisenhower.
      p.   cm. — (Major battles and campaigns; 2)
   Includes bibliographical references.
   ISBN 0-945575-04-1 : $22.95
      1. World War, 1939–1945—Campaigns—Mediterranean
Region.   I. Title.   II. Title: World War 2 in the Mediterra-
nean, 1942–1945.   III. Title: World War Two in the Mediter-
ranean, 1942–1945.   IV. Series.
   D766.D47   1990
   940.54′23—dc20   90-19
                                                                CIP

10   9   8   7   6   5   4   3   2   1

First printing

905572

CONTENTS

LIST OF ILLUSTRATIONS

LIST OF MAPS

INTRODUCTION

by John S. D. Eisenhower

GREAT HISTORICAL EVENTS need reevaluation from time to time. Though we usually know the basic facts of any world event in rather short order, interpretations of them change with the passing of time. And, of course, new information becomes available. New facts, though not many, appear. But with the passage of time we receive more information regarding the viewpoints of the participants after they have had time to reflect or, in some cases, as they feel more free to express their true opinions. Thus it is incumbent on all of us interested in history to maintain open minds and be ever ready to consider new challenges to the "accepted wisdom" that often perpetuates historical myths.

This book, by a prominent military historian, Lieutenant Colonel Carlo D'Este, United States Army (Ret.), comes at a natural time for a reevaluation of the Allied campaigns in the Mediterranean. Forty-five years have gone by since World War II ended. A new generation of writers, Colonel D'Este among them, can now examine the old shibboleths, free of the supposed truths on which we were raised. And he is just the author to do it—experienced, educated in the U.S. Army's best schools, and irreverent enough to examine every idol with a skeptical eye.

The Mediterranean theater of war, World War II, can benefit to an unusual degree from such a new look. As a secondary theater during the later stages of that conflict, the Mediterranean has been given less attention than the more celebrated OVERLORD, the invasion of Northwest Europe. The cross-Channel invasion, from D-Day on 6 June 1944 until V-E Day, has been written about again and again. (D'Este himself is the author of a notable book on the Normandy campaign.) Every detail of the conduct of OVERLORD has been examined and reexamined. The war in the Mediterranean, on the other hand, has been neglected, its contemporary mythology virtually unchallenged. This book is therefore extremely timely.

It is ironic that the Mediterranean has been relegated to the back shelves of the military libraries of World War II, for it was secondary only in comparison to OVERLORD. In the U.S. Fifth Army in Italy, during only one campaign of the Mediterranean, battle deaths among Americans, British, and French amounted to an astonishing 32,000 men. That staggering figure almost equals that of the 33,000 American troops killed during the entire Korean War (1950–53). It even compares to the number (47,300) killed in the ten-year Vietnam conflict (1963–72). The hardships endured in the Italian campaign were, by and large, more severe than those in Northwest Europe, and the psychological strain on its participants far more devastating. By no means do these figures denigrate the traumas undergone by our soldiers in other conflicts; they merely explain our wonder at how such a large campaign as the Mediterranean could be treated as "secondary."

Colonel D'Este has done a masterful job in telling this story. He has struck a fine balance between evaluating the high-level direction of the war and describing the horrors of the fighting. He brings to life the difficulties both sides experienced in moving tanks, artillery, and supplies through the mud of the Apennines. One finishes reading this book with the feeling of actually having been there, at the Factory on the Anzio beachhead, in the comfortable Fifth Army headquarters in Caserta, or in a vulnerable glider being towed through enemy and friendly fire to indistinct drop zones in Sicily. Whereas some accounts keep the reader in the sterile atmosphere of the army operations room, while others concentrate entirely on the sufferings of the Mauldin-type Willies and Joes, D'Este shows the reader both, and with admirable balance.

It is, however, in the realm of the generals that any war book can spark controversy, and this book provides more than its share of that. The author's treatment of those very human and vulnerable men who were entrusted with such crushing and awesome power is sympathetic but unfettered by common American views and prejudices, and the reader may be in for some surprises.

The three main specimens who come under Colonel D'Este's microscope are two British generals, Sir Harold R. L. G. Alexander and Bernard Law Montgomery, and one American, Lieutenant General Mark Wayne Clark. All three eventually attained the highest rank their respective countries had to offer. That fact, however, spares none of them from the author's critical pen.

Of the three, the picture of Clark differs least from the accepted view. Clark, known as "Wayne" in the U.S. Army, was a young, energetic, aggressive, and extremely ambitious officer. A master of army politics, Clark found himself thrust into combat for the first time as commander of the U.S. Fifth Army at the nearly disastrous Allied landing at Salerno (9 September 1943). The reader—at least this one—is taken aback to learn how very inexperienced the self-assured Clark was when it came to real fighting; the techniques he had learned in army politics were useless on that precarious beachhead. But Clark learned. And even though he is rightly faulted by the author for his thirst for publicity—and for his near paranoia when it came to imagined British infringement on his own rights, the text shows that Clark grew to the point where he was ultimately able to function in concert with the rest of the Allied team.

Incidentally, much credit must be given to British Prime Minister Winston Churchill for recommending Clark to be the 15th Army Group commander (in place of Alexander) in the latter days of the war, for in that position Clark had under his command the famed British Eighth Army. The gesture also illustrates the extent to which Clark had grown in the course of the year's fighting in Italy.

In a way, Colonel D'Este's evaluations of Alexander and Montgomery are even more interesting than his handling of Clark, because the way he rates them is exactly opposite to the accepted American view. American accepted wisdom has depicted Montgomery as abrasive, egocentric, ruthless, cautious, and incompetent. D'Este agrees that his personality was abrasive, but argues forcefully that there was nothing incompetent about Monty. According to these pages, Montgomery was right far more often than he was wrong when it came to tactical disagreements. In fact, Monty appears in these pages to be close to infallible. Particularly with the onset of preparation for the invasion of Sicily, Monty seems to have been the only high-ranking Allied officer who was remotely interested in what was being planned. He had definite ideas as to how forces should be disposed, and he carried his points by dint of his personal force and determination. The story of Monty's cornering Eisenhower's Chief of Staff, Walter Bedell Smith, in an Algiers latrine may be overplayed, but it illustrates the point.

Montgomery irritates the Americans in these pages, but he is not the villain. To the author the villain is Alexander, and here Colonel D'Este's opinion diverges from the conventional view to the greatest degree. Harold Alexander was the Americans' favorite British general. He was reputed to be Churchill's favorite as well. The author admits this, but he attributes the real basis for Alexander's popularity to laziness and incompetence rather than to military ability. His easygoing amiability, the author argues, helped establish Alex's rapport with the Americans, not his abilities.

But Alexander's shortcomings, even from an American point of view, go further. For in these pages we see an Alexander who holds American troops in contempt and employs them in difficult, critical places as seldom as possible. In so doing he renders his own countrymen a disservice by making them carry the brunt of the heavy fighting—and at a time when British manpower reserves are scraping the bottom of the barrel.

Admittedly there have been rumblings about Alexander's shortcomings long before this book was written, especially after Alex published his own memoirs (an unfortunate project) in the late 1960s. But never has the case against Alexander been made so definitively. Whether or not one agrees with Colonel D'Este completely, his views are worth careful consideration.

By no means, however, are the author's characterizations of the command levels confined to the three officers mentioned above; far from it. In these pages one will find excellent descriptions of others, particularly on the German side. Here German Field Marshal Albert Kesselring is (rightly) the hero, towering in comparison to the more famous Erwin Rommel. Worthwhile evaluations are made of Jürgen von Arnim, who was left to surrender 250,000 men at the end of Tunisia, and the lesser known German generals von Vietinghoff and von Senger, both of whom seem to have maintained an unusual independence of thought, even in the Nazi regime.

Back to the Allies. Major General Lucian K. Truscott, of the U.S. 3d Division, stars. So does Ernest Harmon, of the 1st Armored. Patton is also characterized in a balanced way. (Eisenhower scarcely appears.) And worthy of mention is the author's fairness to the hapless major generals Ernest J. Dawley and John P. Lucas. They have awaited their just due for too long.

That the Allies ultimately succeeded in ousting the Germans from the Mediterranean was due to many factors: greater manpower, superior resources, control of the sea, and (from mid-1943 on) control of the air. Whether the expenditure in resources was worth the results remains a matter of controversy—one that this book leaves the reader to conclude for himself. But even though the fighting in Italy became of secondary importance to the Allied war effort after OVERLORD, there was nothing second class about it for the men who slugged it out with the skilled soldiers of the German Wehrmacht in mountainous terrain cruelly favorable to the defense.

No observer reviewing the Allied military effort in Tunisia, Sicily, Salerno, Cassino, Anzio, or on the Po River will be struck by the brilliance of the Allied strategy. Carlo D'Este certainly is not. But one attains a sense that the Mediterranean campaigns were necessary, that they were the best the Allies could do at that stage of the war, and that their command structure developed both in competence and in the harmony between forces of different nationalities. And the fighting in the Mediterranean, as the Allies learned, had far more than its share of drama. Such is the story that Colonel D'Este tells, and tells very well indeed.

COLONEL D'ESTE BRINGS IMPRESSIVE credentials to this work. He graduated magna cum laude from Norwich University in 1958, attained a master's degree at the University of Richmond in 1974, and was an honor graduate of the U.S. Army Command and General Staff College. He retired from the U.S. Army in 1978, on the completion of his twenty years' service, to assume his writing career. His previous books include *Decision in Normandy* (1983) and *Bitter Victory: The Battle for Sicily, 1943.* He is currently writing a book about the Anzio beachhead and plans a biography of General George S. Patton, Jr., as his next work.

THE
MEDITERRANEAN THEATER
OF
OPERATIONS
1942

EIRE

DEN

GREAT
BRITAIN

London•

HOLL

BELGIUM

Fr

•Paris   LUX.

FRANCE

•B

SW

•Bordeaux

Annecy•

Lyons•

Marseilles

PORTUGAL

Lisbon•

•Madrid

Barcelona•

CORSICA

SPAIN

BALEARIC IS.

SARDINIA

CENTRAL
TASK FORCE
(Fredendall)

EASTERN
TASK FORCE
(Ryder)

WESTERN
TASK FORCE
(Patton)

Tangier•   •Gibraltar

SPANISH
MOROCCO

Oran Mostaganem Algiers

Bizerte

•Port
Lyautey

Rabat

Bône

Tur

•Casablanca

FRENCH MOROCCO

ALGERIA

Tebessa
•

•Marrakesh

El Guetta
•

Kasser

TUNISIA

•Safi

```
0      200    400    600    800    1000 Kilometers
|———————|———————|———————|———————|———————|
0   100   200   300   400   500   600 Miles
```

Mareth Li

TF

AUTHOR'S INTRODUCTION

THE BRITISH VICTORY BY General Bernard Montgomery's British Eighth Army over Field Marshal Erwin Rommel's Panzerarmee Afrika—first at Alam Halfa in August 1942 and again two months later at El Alamein— was the turning point of the war in the West. After two years of successful campaigns during which all of Europe and a large portion of Russia had fallen, it was also the first visible signal that Hitler's self-proclaimed thousand-year Reich was not invincible after all.

For the British the war had been a calamitous series of setbacks ever since Dunkirk. Norway, Greece, Crete, Burma, Hong Kong, Dieppe, and Tobruk had all earned permanent places in the annals of British military disasters. In Malaya the worst defeat ever handed the British ended with the surrender of the 85,000 men of Lieutenant-General* Arthur Percival's Tenth Army in Singapore in February 1942. Less visible but equally deadly was the battle of the Atlantic. There the Allies were steadily losing the struggle, and German U-boats were sinking Allied shipping faster than it could be replaced. From December 1941 through August 1942 Axis submarines sank 931 vessels, totaling 4,762,928 tons. Many were lost within sight of New York harbor and other East Coast ports.

When Hitler unleashed Operation BARBAROSSA—the surprise attack against Russia in June 1941—more than three million German ground troops, supported by 3,000 tanks and 2,000 aircraft, swarmed over a front extending from the Black Sea to the Arctic, catching the Red Army flat-footed. The two unlikely bedfellows, Britain and Russia, had made their cause a common one, and both were now on the defensive across the breadth of Europe and in the Mediterranean. Russian tenacity, the dreadful cold of winter, and Hitler's miscalculation that the war in the East

---

*British officers' ranks are always hyphenated in this book, according to the custom in the British armies; American officers' ranks are rendered here without hyphens, and German officers' ranks are anglicized except where there is no corresponding U.S. equivalent.

would be quickly won combined to provide the Red Army with the opportunity to continue the fight in 1942. German blunders at Stalingrad and later at Kursk ultimately ensured that Germany would lose the war.

In the West, the dramatic reversal of British fortunes took place near a windblown and fly-infested railroad siding on the Egyptian border with Libya. There, in the bloodiest battle of the desert war, a little-known British general led a revitalized Eighth Army and defeated Rommel, the celebrated Desert Fox. Thereafter the names of both El Alamein and Montgomery were immortalized, and an exultant Churchill could later proclaim, "Before Alamein we never had a victory. After Alamein we never had a defeat." Part of the credit for the British success at Alamein belongs to Rommel, who, despite the warnings of his superior, Field Marshal Albert Kesselring, was lulled into unjustified overconfidence. The bloody nose his panzerarmee gave Eighth Army at Gazala and Tobruk led Rommel to believe that Cairo was his for the taking.

Some of the later campaigns of the war, Normandy in particular, were the result of brilliant planning and audacious execution. Others, such as the Battle of the Bulge and Arnhem, were the result of serious Allied miscalculations. Most campaigns, however dramatic, represented the conservative approach to warfare that characterized the Anglo-American alliance. The exception was the first joint Allied venture of the war, Operation TORCH, the invasion of northwest Africa in November 1942. Inexperienced in amphibious operations and yet to fight their first battle, U.S. forces nevertheless plunged undaunted into the campaign along with equally green British forces in one of the world's most inhospitable regions. For the first time Britain and her ally, the United States, were to challenge Axis control of the Mediterranean.

With the exception of the invasion of Anzio in early 1944, where audacity was replaced by military folly, there was a notable absence of boldness in subsequent operations in the Mediterranean. The campaigns in Sicily and Italy were the result of strategic compromises between two allies with very different concepts of defeating Germany and Italy. Ironically, the Allied campaigns in North Africa in 1942–43 were the direct result of the lone British success of the war up to then.

In early 1941 Hitler sent an expeditionary force under Rommel, then a relatively junior general, to North Africa to bolster the sagging fortunes of his Italian ally, whose Tenth Army had suffered a crushing defeat in Cyrenaica at the hands of a small British force commanded by Lieutenant-General Sir Richard O'Connor. For the next eighteen months the British had little else to sustain their morale as the Eighth Army fought a series of losing battles against the Afrika Korps across the vast North African desert. The British were humiliated at Gazala and Tobruk, and by July 1942 Eighth Army was defending the final Axis obstacle to the conquest of Egypt: Alam Halfa.

Churchill had already removed General Sir Archibald Wavell as Commander-in-Chief, Middle East, in 1941, and in August 1942 he did the same to General Sir Claude Auchinleck. It was the arrival of General Sir Harold R. L. G. Alexander and Montgomery that heralded a new era of British success in North Africa.

El Alamein had strategic results far beyond its immediate significance. Rommel himself was the first senior German commander to foresee the long-term implications. By late 1942 Rommel had concluded that continued Axis presence in North Africa was a futile gesture, and he urged Hitler to withdraw German forces while there was still time. His blunt assessment was that there was no hope of victory and "the abandonment of the African theater should be accepted as a long-term policy. There should be no illusions about the situation; . . . if the Army remained in North Africa it would be destroyed."

Rommel's warning was given a chilly reception by Hitler, who throughout the war repeatedly failed to comprehend that the price of reinforcing failure was inevitably military disaster. The Führer flew into a rage and declined to acknowledge the growing plight of his forces in North Africa, who were seriously deficient in manpower, weapons, food, and fuel. Despite mounting evidence that the desert war had turned in favor of the British, Hitler, even though he never considered North Africa anything more than a sideshow, spurned Rommel's counsel. When the Allies invaded Northwest Africa in November 1942, Hitler reacted by creating a panzer army in Tunisia under General Jürgen von Arnim. Some 100,000 additional troops, among them several of the Wehrmacht's finest formations, arrived in time to join the battle for Tunisia.

The aim of this book is to recount the strategy and tactics whereby the Anglo-American alliance fought the campaigns in the Mediterranean theater of operations. The leadership on both sides knew that the decisive battles of the war would be fought on the soil of Europe, not along the shores of the sunny Mediterranean. Although a secondary theater of war and always regarded by the American leadership as little more than a diversion, the Mediterranean campaigns nevertheless are a vital part of the history of the Second World War.

What began on a relatively small scale in Tunisia eventually grew to an Allied endeavor of enormous proportions as the American commitment to the war increased. The path leading to the liberation of Europe in 1945 began in the desolate hills and plains of the French colony of Tunisia, where the first major Allied campaign of World War II was fought.

ONE

Lighting the "Torch"

AMERICA'S FORMAL ENTRY INTO WORLD WAR II in December 1941 had done little to alleviate the plight of the British in the Middle East. Although Britain now had an ally, her army continued to fight a series of mostly losing battles across the far-flung empire as the United States began gearing up to join the fighting sometime in 1942. Until that day came, the war in the African desert pitted the British Eighth Army against Rommel's German-Italian panzer army.

From the outset the American focus had always been on defeating Germany by the most direct means, irrespective of political considerations. At the Arcadia Conference in Washington in December 1941 the Americans and British had agreed to place priority on the defeat of Germany first, rather than Japan in the Pacific.

General George C. Marshall, the architect of American strategy, wanted no part of a U.S. commitment to the Mediterranean. He believed that the decisive campaign of the war would be fought in Northwest Europe. To this end he relentlessly pursued the development of sufficient forces and equipment in the United Kingdom, from which a cross-Channel invasion of France could be mounted at the earliest possible moment.

By the summer of 1942, however, there was no agreement as to what the Allies would do nor where they would do it. An invasion of Europe in 1942 was not even remotely feasible, and Marshall began backing plans for such an operation in 1943. President Franklin D. Roosevelt was more concerned that a suitable role be found for American combat forces as quickly as possible and was unwilling to tolerate a delay into 1943.

Heated Anglo-American negotiations throughout the summer of 1942 resulted in a compromise: In return for an American commitment to

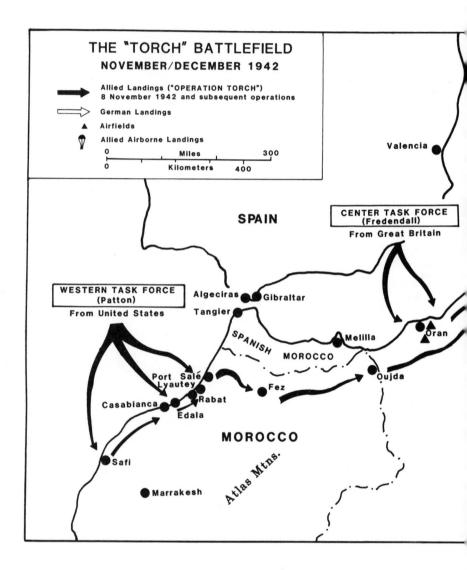

THE "TORCH" BATTLEFIELD
NOVEMBER/DECEMBER 1942

Allied Landings ("OPERATION TORCH")
8 November 1942 and subsequent operations

German Landings

▲ Airfields

Allied Airborne Landings

Miles   300
Kilometers   400

SPAIN

Valencia

CENTER TASK FORCE
(Fredendall)
From Great Britain

WESTERN TASK FORCE
(Patton)
From United States

Algeciras   Gibraltar
Tangier

SPANISH   MOROCCO
Melilla
Oran

Port Salé
Lyautey   Fez   Oujda
Casablanca   Rabat
Edala

MOROCCO

Safi

Marrakesh   Atlas Mtns.

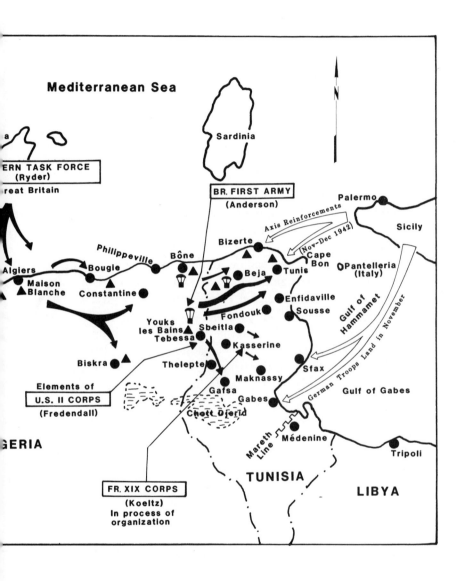

Mediterranean Sea

Sardinia

ERN TASK FORCE
(Ryder)
reat Britain

BR. FIRST ARMY
(Anderson)

Palermo

Axis Reinforcements
(Nov–Dec 1942)

Sicily

Bizerte

Philippeville

Bône

Cape
Bon

Pantelleria
(Italy)

Algiers

Bougie

Beja

Tunis

Maison
Blanche

Constantine

Enfidaville

Sousse

Gulf of
Hammamet

Fondouk

Youks
les Bains
Tebessa

Sbeitla

Kasserine

German Troops Land in November

Biskra

Thelepte

Sfax

Maknassy

Gulf of Gabes

Elements of
U.S. II CORPS
(Fredendall)

Gafsa

Gabes

Chott Djerid

GERIA

Mareth
Line

Médenine

Tripoli

TUNISIA

LIBYA

FR. XIX CORPS
(Koeltz)
In process of
organization

military operations in the Mediterranean, the British agreed to a massive buildup of American forces in Britain for a cross-Channel operation in 1943.

Marshall was compelled to accept the reality of an American commitment to the Mediterranean, which initially called for a joint Anglo-American operation to seize French North Africa as a stepping-stone to further Allied operations. This North African venture was scheduled for November 1942 and was given the code name TORCH by Churchill. Separate invasion forces from the United States and Britain were to rendezvous off North Africa, where three task forces would go ashore simultaneously on the morning of 8 November 1942. As a concession to induce U.S. participation in TORCH, Churchill agreed that an American officer should command Allied forces in the Mediterranean. The logical choice was a virtually unknown junior major general named Eisenhower.

Dwight David Eisenhower's rise to fame and high command was easily the most dramatic of any American officer of World War II. In 1940 Eisenhower was a lieutenant colonel commanding an infantry battalion. By December 1941 he had reached the grade of brigadier general before being summoned to Washington immediately after Pearl Harbor. There he soon became the head of the War Plans Division of the War Department. By 1942 he was a two-star general and had so impressed George Marshall that he was sent to London in April 1942 to coordinate U.S. planning with Churchill and the British Chiefs of Staff. The Prime Minister took an instant liking to the personable, outgoing American who displayed such uncommon enthusiasm for the Anglo-American Alliance. When the decision to invade Northwest Africa was finally made, Churchill's only suggestion among the Americans for the command of Operation TORCH was Dwight Eisenhower.

The Allied task was formidable: to land and seize nine important objectives along a nearly one-thousand-mile coastal front from (French) Morocco's capital of Casablanca to Oran and Algiers in Algeria. Once the vital port cities of Algiers, Oran, and Casablanca were secured, the Allies were to thrust quickly into Tunisia to capture Bizerte and Tunis before the arrival of Axis forces.

The Western Task Force, commanded by Major General George S. Patton, Jr., sailed from the eastern United States and seized Casablanca, Safi, and Port Lyautey on the Atlantic side of French Morocco. There were two other task forces—a U.S. force of 39,000 men commanded by Major General Lloyd R. Fredendall which sailed from Scotland and landed at Oran, and a similar Anglo-American force of 23,000 British and 10,000 U.S. troops under Major General Charles Ryder, a Kansan who commanded the 34th Infantry Division, which seized Algiers. In all, 117,000 troops were committed to TORCH, 75 percent of them American.

The situation in French North Africa was complex and beset with intrigue and a confusion of loyalties among the French military, some of whom were loyal to Marshal Pétain's Vichy regime. To complicate matters, many French held a legacy of bitterness toward the British for the incident at Oran's main port of Mers-el-Kebir in July 1940, when the Royal Navy attacked the French fleet to keep it out of the hands of the Germans, and over 1,200 French sailors perished. The reaction of the French to an Allied invasion of their North African colonies was uncertain and fraught with the danger that their forces might bitterly resist Operation TORCH.

Less than three weeks before the invasion the Allied commander-in-chief, Lieutenant General Dwight D. Eisenhower, dispatched Major General Mark Clark at the head of a small team that landed secretly by submarine near Algiers. There, aided by diplomat Robert D. Murphy, President Roosevelt's personal representative in North Africa, an attempt was made to rally French support for TORCH. The talks with a sympathetic group of French officers was inconclusive but later led to an Allied invitation to General Henri Giraud to take control of all French forces in North Africa. Giraud was one of the few French officers sympathetic to the Allied cause whose reputation was not tarnished by association with Vichy.

Giraud's involvement came too late to influence TORCH, but Murphy, on the eve of the invasion, made a last-ditch attempt to avert bloodshed by trying to enlist the support of Admiral Jean Darlan. Darlan, the Commander-in-Chief of all French forces and Pétain's deputy, was by chance in Algiers visiting his ailing son.

Darlan procrastinated, and the TORCH landings commenced with the Allied commanders still uncertain about what they would encounter. It was not until Clark arrived after the fall of Algiers that the Frenchman was persuaded to issue a cease-fire directive to all French forces, which averted further bloodshed. However, what became known as the "Darlan Deal" came too late to avert bitter resistance at Oran, where battles raged for two days before French forces there surrendered to Major General Terry Allen's U.S. 1st Infantry Division.

The TORCH landings were hastily organized and carried out under very difficult sea conditions. Not only were the troops inadequately trained, but the planning was more theoretical than practical; as one historian later noted, "Losses in landing craft were heavy due to the high surf, and had it not been for the sporadic nature of French resistance, the landings could well have failed." Major General Lucian K. Truscott, who later commanded the 3d Infantry Division, also called TORCH "a hit-and-miss affair that would have spelled disaster against a well-armed enemy intent on resistance." Eisenhower subsequently admitted that before TORCH he had prayed harder than he had ever prayed in his whole life.

Virtually every mistake possible occurred during the landings; inadequate communications, mechanical failures, engineers left stranded on troop transports, and the wrong priorities for landing equipment were among the problems that plagued the TORCH commanders.

After the landings and according to plan, Lieutenant-General Kenneth N. Anderson assumed command of British forces under the banner of the British First Army, while American forces came under the control of Lloyd Fredendall's II Corps. George Patton's Western Task Force remained in Morocco, engaged in training.

The Allies were quickly and roughly initiated into the reality of the immense task confronting them. The distance from Algiers to the Tunisian battlefront was vast, and the road net was extremely primitive. Along the Mediterranean ran the only railroad, originally built by the French and in uncertain condition. In all, the North African theater of operations encompassed nearly a million square miles of some of the bleakest terrain on earth. Resupply was to become the single most difficult problem facing the Allies during the Tunisian campaign.

As if logistics were not headache enough, the Allies soon had a new problem to contend with—furious Axis resistance. Hitler quickly lost his indifference toward operations in the Mediterranean and ordered the immediate reinforcement of Tunisia. His object was to prevent the Allies from obtaining the key ports of Bizerte and Tunis, which they could utilize to mount an invasion of southern Europe. German and Italian troops began arriving in Tunisia in a steady flow in early November. The Luftwaffe made Allied movement costly on land, while at sea German U-boats sank Allied shipping with distressing regularity.

To the east, Eighth Army continued the pursuit of Rommel's Panzerarmee Afrika as it executed a deliberate retreat toward the Tunisian border. Despite Montgomery's stunning success at El Alamein, his critics complained, often vehemently, that his failure to initiate a more determined effort to catch Rommel was a squandered opportunity that later permitted the Axis army a new life in Tunisia.

Within the hierarchy of the Royal Air Force (RAF) there existed a considerable division of opinion over the air tactics being employed against Rommel. Proponents of close air support such as Air Vice-Marshal Harry Broadhurst (who later succeeded Air Marshal Sir Arthur Coningham as the commander of the Desert Air Force in February 1943) favored a more aggressive use of RAF tactical aircraft, while others, particularly Coningham, were far more restrained. Combined with a breakdown in relations between Montgomery and Coningham, who bitterly resented the torrent of publicity accorded the Eighth Army commander after El Alamein, this was the other principal factor which benefited Rommel.

After chasing the Panzerarmee Afrika across the Libyan desert, Montgomery's troops were exhausted and his army was stretched out over nearly a thousand miles of desert. His critics, both then and later, charged that he forfeited an opportunity to defeat Rommel once and for all by cutting off his retreat. Montgomery naturally saw the situation differently and was quite unwilling to risk a setback from Rommel, whom he considered as dangerous a foe as ever. It was not until mid-November, as the TORCH forces were struggling to establish a fully operational front in western Tunisia, that the Eighth Army reached Tobruk, the scene of its dreadful defeat six months earlier.

THE FIRST DAYS OF THE TUNISIAN campaign in November 1942 saw limited combat between Allied and Axis forces. The real contest was a race to determine which of the two forces would solidly establish itself in Tunisia first. In mid-November General der Panzertruppen Walther Nehring, who had previously commanded the Afrika Korps and had been wounded at Alam Halfa, arrived to assume command of XC Corps, an ad hoc Axis force which grew to about 25,000 by month's end. Some of his reinforcements were German units that had been in reserve in Italy, France, and Germany; others were originally destined as replacements for the depleted Afrika Korps. Nehring resourcefully improvised a bridgehead to delay the Allied advance and defend Bizerte and Tunis with a disparate force of infantry, airborne, artillery, and Italian units, supported by some seventy panzers, of which twenty were the new 88-mm Tiger model.

The senior German commander in the Mediterranean* was Field Marshal Albert Kesselring, a wily Luftwaffe veteran whom the Allies came to regard as one of the outstanding German commanders of the war. Kesselring was a former artillery officer who had risen quickly and without fanfare to the rank of major general in the post–World War I Reichswehr before transferring to the new air wing in 1933, where he became one of the architects of its rise to prominence. He played a major role in the effectiveness of the Luftwaffe during the Polish campaign of 1939 and in France and Norway in 1940. In 1942 he was rewarded by Hitler with a promotion to field marshal and assignment to the Mediterranean. Kesselring's genius lay in his ability to understand and effectively employ both air and land forces. One of his few flaws was an almost incurable sense of optimism, which became the source of his nickname, "Smiling Albert."

Kesselring had long urged the establishment of a new front in Tunisia, and OKW† was obliged to react to TORCH by ordering three divisions there: 10th Panzer and the Hermann Göring Division from southern France, and a new division, the 334th Infantry, along with an Italian corps headquarters and two divisions.

Kesselring believed it essential for Nehring to block Anderson's advance on Tunis, while Rommel was urged to continue his withdrawal toward Tunisia as deliberately as possible. Nehring's task was to protect at all costs the Axis front in Tunisia during the reinforcement phase. The objective of the Axis reinforcement was not only to resist the Allied invasion of North Africa but to destroy these forces in Tunisia. The stage was thus set for the first major campaign of the war in the West by the Anglo-American Alliance.

AS THE FIRST ALLIED VENTURE INTO coalition warfare, TORCH became a classroom where many difficult lessons were learned. The original aim of Allied operations in Tunisia was, first, to secure the ports and lines of communication, and, second, to trap and destroy Rommel's army in Tripolitania between the advancing Eighth Army and Anderson's First Army. However, Eisenhower soon found that his most pressing task was not strategy but overseeing a complex logistical lifeline that began with

---

*As Commander-in-Chief, South, and Luftwaffe commander in the Mediterranean theater.

† *Oberkommando der Wehrmacht*, the German Armed Forces High Command headquarters, located in Berlin.

the organization of a transportation system between Algeria and Tunisia. Algiers was five hundred miles from Tunis, and combat operations could not be sustained in Tunisia without the food, fuel, and ammunition which are the lifeblood of any army in combat. Nearly two-thirds of the TORCH combat forces were still in western Morocco and unavailable for commitment because of the inability of the fledgling logistical system to resupply a large force to the east.

The responsibility for capturing Tunis was given to Anderson, whose British First Army then consisted only of Major-General Vivian Evelegh's 78th Division and Task Force Blade of the 6th Armoured Division. In mid-November Anderson launched a two-pronged offensive in an attempt to grab Tunis before the Axis did. Evelegh's 36th Infantry Brigade thrust along the Bône-Tunis highway toward Bizerte, while Blade Force followed Evelegh's 11th Infantry Brigade, which advanced into Tunisia along an inland route toward Beja.

The first engagement of the campaign was a sharp exchange on 17 November between Brigadier A. L. Kent-Lemon's 11th Brigade and paratroopers of the 11th Parachute Regiment, part of the German battle group that Nehring had sent to anchor the western end of the Tunis-Bizerte defenses. The Germans' outposts along the frontier were anything but firm, and had the British drive been concentrated instead of widely dispersed, the Axis flank might well have collapsed. Under the prodding of Kesselring, however, Nehring's defenders successfully thwarted the British advance.

The first round of the battle for Tunisia was an unequal struggle won by the Axis, whose ground forces were aided immeasurably by the sudden surge of strength in Luftwaffe tactical aircraft. By early November German air strength was 445, nearly double the previous month's strength. The Luftwaffe's objective was to buy time for Nehring by disrupting and delaying the Allied advance in western Tunisia. It was one of the few times during the war in the West that the Luftwaffe could claim success.

The Allied air forces attempted to counter the Luftwaffe by establishing forward airfields in Tunisia. An improvised U.S. airborne operation at Youks-les-Bains by the independent 509th Parachute Infantry Battalion gained the Allies a foothold in western Tunisia on 15 November.

Allied shortcomings, however, quickly became evident. There were not enough squadrons, supporting equipment, or services. The closest all-weather airbase was at Bône, over 120 miles from the front lines. In contrast, the Luftwaffe was able to operate with virtual impunity from all-weather fields that were often as close as 5 miles from the battlefield.

The most serious Allied deficiency, however, was a grave misunderstanding of the fundamentals of close air support of the ground forces. The exceptional cooperation in the Western Desert between Eighth Army and the Desert Air Force was an example that simply was not yet understood by the airmen in Tunisia, most of whom were fresh from England or the United States. Moreover, as the RAF historian John Terraine has written, "As the Allied air forces began their advance eastward towards Tunis, one of the earliest lessons of the Desert war was distressfully relearned—this, too, was a 'war for aerodromes.'"

The Allies quickly found that the Luftwaffe held all the aces. The Germans were adept at shifting their aircraft to cope with conditions on the ground, and the aggressive pilots took full advantage of the open terrain to bomb and strafe Allied convoys and airfields. In later campaigns German troops would curse the absence of the Luftwaffe over the battlefield. In Tunisia it was Tommies and GIs who did the cursing. Whenever he visited the front Eisenhower would hear an endless and familiar lament: "Where is this bloody air force of ours? Why do we see nothing but Heinies?" Thus the battle for Tunisia became in equal measure a contest for domination of the air as well as for control of the ground. On both counts the Allies failed in 1942.

The initial Allied offensive in western Tunisia was doomed to failure from the start. Not only were their ground forces woefully understrength and spread too thinly, but the employment of "penny-packet" tactics was an outmoded form of warfare. Originally introduced by the British, the concept of task forces (usually a reinforced brigade) fighting separate battles without benefit of mutual support had been employed for too long in North Africa. These tactics were banished by Montgomery as one of his first acts upon assuming command of Eighth Army. Until the arrival of Alexander and Patton, however, the inexperienced Allied commanders in Tunisia elected to use them, with disastrous results.

Attack by task forces was precisely the British plan for capturing Tunis, and it was easily thwarted by the combined Axis air-ground effort. By the end of November, Anderson and Evelegh were obliged to acknowledge that their effort had failed. Like it or not, there would have to be a pause to permit a buildup of ground forces and air units at forward bases. Although Anderson made one final attempt in December to capture Tunis with a French-American-British force, it was severely mauled by XC Corps at Longstop Hill overlooking the Gulf of Tunis. The battle, which lasted four days, threatened to unhinge the Axis in Tunisia and was bitterly contested by German forces, who launched a powerful counterattack supported by tanks on Christmas Day. Although losses on both sides were high, Allied forces suffered the heavier casualties.

The battle for Longstop Hill was a microcosm of the problems in both planning and execution that the Allies faced in Tunisia. Reconnaissance was inadequate, as was air and artillery support. Allied troops and airmen were not lacking in courage, but their inexperience and the results of their first ventures in coalition warfare left no doubt that there would have to be considerable improvement before they would be an equal match for the veteran German troops in Tunisia. On the advice of Anderson a dejected Eisenhower made a bitter decision to cancel further Allied offensive operations in Tunisia in 1942.

For nine months of the year North Africa is a dry and parched land, so inhospitable that it is one of the most sparsely populated places on earth. From December to March the rains fall with a suddenness and fury that turns the ground into sticky mud with the consistency of tar. The race for Tunis also became an attempt to beat the winter weather. The Allies lost.

FOR THE RECENTLY FORMED Allied Force Headquarters (AFHQ) and the Anglo-American expeditionary force engaged in its first combat against an experienced and stubborn enemy, the first months of the Allied experience in Northwest Africa following the TORCH landings were as dismal as the weather. Unlike the veteran Eighth Army, the troops of the British First Army and the U.S. II Corps were untried in battle, and, as the next six months were to demonstrate again and again, Tunisia was a testing ground where the harsh lessons of combat were taught. The appalling weather left the Allies mired in the mud of the cold Tunisian winter, barely able to move and with their tenuous logistic lifeline all but shut down. At times conditions were so dreadful that a vehicle leaving the road or an aircraft that accidentally strayed off the temporary runways sank irretrievably into the mud.

After the debacle in late December at Longstop Hill left Tunis and Bizerte firmly in Axis hands, Allied strategy had to be abandoned.* This less than auspicious start came at the very moment when Hitler was not only spurning Rommel's counsel but, to emphasize his determination to

---

*The dismal weather and repeated setbacks led Eisenhower to write candidly to a colleague that military operations in North Africa "have violated every recognized principle of war, are in conflict with all operational and logistic methods laid down in text-books and will be condemned, in their entirety, for the next twenty-five years."

hold North Africa, was placing all German forces in Tunisia under the command of the veteran Colonel-General Jürgen von Arnim, who was summoned at short notice from the Eastern Front to assume command of Fifth Panzer Army and take control of the Axis defense of Tunisia.

This powerful Axis reinforcement doomed TORCH's timetable and required a major revision of Allied strategy to ensure that Tunisia would be won by early spring, so that the invasion of Sicily could take place in June, a program both Churchill and Roosevelt had insisted on at the Casablanca Conference in January 1943. The problem was that the winter rains prevented the resumption of full-scale offensive operations in northern Tunisia until at least the end of March. The winter stalemate prompted the Chief of the Imperial General Staff, General (later Field-Marshal) Sir Alan Brooke, to orchestrate the assignment of Harold Alexander to assume overall command of the ground campaign in Tunisia.*

At all levels Americans and British were learning with difficulty to live with each other's strange customs and differing concepts of waging war. Anglo-American brawls in clubs and bars were common. Those who knew Eisenhower well were never deceived by his infectious grin and sunny outer façade, behind which lay a fiery temper and an iron determination that nationality in his command was to be irrelevant. More than one American staff officer at AFHQ earned relief for calling his counterpart "a *British* bastard." One unwitting American colonel who broke this commandment was stunned when Eisenhower shouted at him, "There are no British, American, or French . . . bastards at this headquarters. There are certainly bastards aplenty and I'm looking at one." †

Although there was little overt friction, the commonality of language could not obscure the fundamental differences between the traditions practiced in the British army for centuries and the rawness of a peacetime American army suddenly thrust into a global war. Harold Macmillan, Churchill's representative at AFHQ, described the British as "the Greeks in this American empire," and counseled a newly arrived officer that "We must run AFHQ as the Greeks ran the operations of the Emperor Claudius." In British eyes, one of the culprits promoting Anglo-American friction was Eisenhower's then deputy, Mark Clark. Recently elevated to lieutenant general, Clark was generally regarded as an "evil genius," a disruptive force within AFHQ, and an intriguer who

---

*In February 1943 Eighteenth Army Group was created to control the operations of First and Eighth armies and the U.S. II Corps. Alexander's role was that of both an army group commander and deputy commander-in-chief to Eisenhower.

†Quoted in David Schoenbrun, *America Inside Out* (New York, 1984).

caused immense irritation. His habit of issuing direct and often contradictory orders to the staff caused great concern among the American officers.

The considerable disorganization and indiscipline in the rear areas so discouraged Eisenhower that Marshall feared for his health. When the Chief of Staff toured American supply and service units in February 1943, he was so irate at what he observed that, at his instigation, several senior officers were relieved and the word went out, in Marshall's words, that there would be no more "goddam drugstore cowboys standing around."

There was little love lost between Anderson and Fredendall, or between Fredendall and his subordinate commanders. Anderson's cold demeanor came across to American officers as patronizing and left the impression that he had no confidence in them. Although he had commanded a division in combat, Anderson soon began to generate a similar lack of confidence among the British hierarchy. Montgomery, as usual, was outspoken in his criticism of Anderson, whom he termed no better than "a good plain cook."

Nor was Montgomery the only high-level critic of Anderson. Not long after his appointment to head the British army in the dark days of 1941, Brooke had noted that "it is lamentable how poor we are in Army and Corps commanders; we ought to remove several but Heaven knows where we shall find anything very much better. . . . The flower of our manhood was wiped out some twenty years ago and it is just some of those that we lost then that we require now." Anderson was one of those Brooke had in mind as unfit for army command.

As Eisenhower would soon learn, all was not well within II Corps. Fredendall's disdain for Anderson was only exceeded by his contempt for the French and for the commander of the 1st Armored Division, Major General Orlando W. Ward. It was the worst possible moment for a leadership crisis.

EXCEPT FOR A SMALL PLAIN AROUND Bône and the eastern coastal plains, Tunisia is largely dominated by mountains. South of Tunis two subsidiary hill masses called the Eastern and Western Dorsals form the shape of an inverted Y. The Eastern Dorsal runs from the vicinity of Gafsa in the south to a point west of Enfidaville in the north, while the Western Dorsal runs southwest from the same point toward Kasserine and Thelepte. In January 1943 the Fifth Panzer Army's defense of Tunisia was anchored along the Eastern Dorsal from Gafsa in the south to the Mediter-

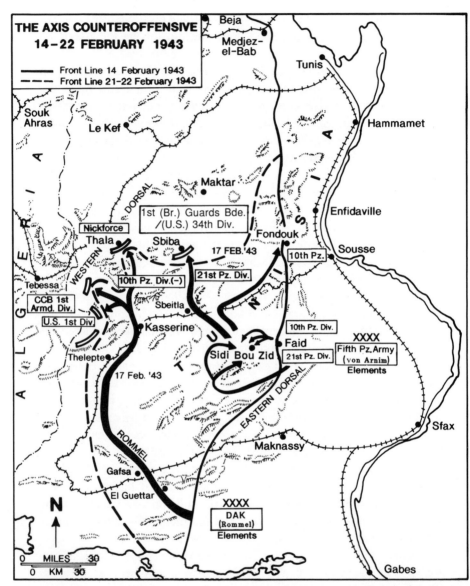

THE AXIS COUNTEROFFENSIVE
14–22 FEBRUARY 1943

——— Front Line 14 February 1943
– – – Front Line 21–22 February 1943

On 14 February the 10th and 21st Panzer divisions attack U.S. forces at Sidi Bou Zid. After attacking Sbeitla, von Arnim splits his force, sending the 21st Panzer toward Sbiba and the 10th Panzer to Fondouk. Rommel's Afrika Korps (DAK) sweeps away all opposition but encounters stiff resistance at Kasserine Pass where TF Stark delays the German advance. Von Arnim disobeys orders and sends only part of the 10th Panzer Division to Rommel. The Germans fail to press their advantage and Nickforce contains the 10th Panzer at Thala, while another Anglo-American force stops the advance of the 21st Panzer Division at Sbiba. By 22 February Rommel orders the Afrika Korps to withdraw.

ranean west of Bizerte. All of the passes leading to central and western Tunisia were under Axis control. Although von Arnim never received the full complement of six to seven divisions promised by Hitler, he did have three veteran divisions guarding the Eastern Dorsal, along with Italian units securing the passes, and the 10th Panzer Division near Tunis as his mobile reserve strike force. By month's end von Arnim had over 100,000 veteran German troops, and with the arrival of Rommel's army from the east the number rose to about 170,000. By the end of the campaign Axis forces in Tunisia would exceed 250,000.

Allied forces in Tunisia were seriously understrength; their 250-mile-long front along the Western Dorsal was manned with only three corps: one British, one French, and one American.* In the south Fredendall's II Corps guarded a vast area between the Eastern and Western Dorsals from Gafsa to a point midway between the Faid and Fondouk passes.

The inability of the Allies to support additional troops in Tunisia had not only left valuable manpower idle in Morocco; it had also resulted in the fragmentation of American forces in order to plug gaps along the front. The weakest link was the French sector, which Anderson—until Alexander's arrival the senior Allied ground commander—ordered reinforced with regimental combat teams from the U.S. 1st and 34th Infantry divisions plus the 1st Guards Brigade, with Combat Command B of the U.S. 1st Armored Division in reserve. General L. M. Koeltz's French XIX Corps was strong on determination and grit but handicapped by antiquated World War I–vintage tanks and equipment.

In the British 5th Corps sector the two infantry divisions and one armored division were backed by the 18th Regimental Combat Team of Terry Allen's U.S. 1st Infantry Division. This dispersal of American troops to plug the gaps in other sectors left II Corps dangerously undermanned along a hundred-mile front covered by only two combat commands of the 1st Armored Division and the French Divisione de Constantine, with Combat Command D in corps reserve.

The December battle at Longstop Hill had left no doubt that the British were incapable of sustaining a further offensive in the north. Instead, Eisenhower's planners turned their attention to Operation SATIN, an offensive designed to split the Axis defenders by means of a right hook by U.S. and French forces through the Eastern Dorsal to the coast at either Gabes or Sfax. With stronger and more experienced troops such a ma-

---

*Although designated First Army, Anderson's command never amounted to more than the equivalent of a corps.

neuver might have been successful, but the British objected strongly when they learned of the proposed plan at the Casablanca Conference, and it was shelved. Both Brooke and Alexander believed such an attack had no chance against the experienced panzer divisions opposing them. Although obliged to cancel SATIN, Eisenhower directed Fredendall to exert an "aggressive defense" in the Tebessa sector, thus positioning the U.S. 1st Armored Division to repel a German attack into central Tunisia.

By early February the German commanders were aware that their efforts had earned them a brief respite from the final confrontation with the Allies. Eighth Army's logistical tail stretched clear back to El Alamein, and Montgomery decided that the capture of Tripoli signaled a moment when his troops must rest and refit before tackling Rommel, whose army had retreated westward into the formidable Mareth Line. Rommel knew an attack from Montgomery was forthcoming, but he worried more about an Allied attack into his rear from the direction of Gafsa and was determined to eliminate the threat by striking first. Moreover, Rommel understood that he had no chance whatever to defeat Eighth Army, but by defending the Mareth Line with minimum forces a final opportunity existed to defeat the inexperienced Allied force in southwestern Tunisia.

Having anticipated the projected Allied right hook, the German leadership was determined not only to spoil those plans but also to improve their own positions along the Eastern Dorsal in the process. Both Rommel and Kesselring recognized the opportunity to strike a blow that could split the Allies in two and threaten their overextended lines of communication from Algeria into Tunisia. Rommel's plan was the exact reverse of SATIN; he envisioned a full-blooded thrust to shatter Allied forces by driving a wedge through the Western Dorsal to the Mediterranean as far west as Bône. The attack, to be delivered by all of the panzer strength left in the Afrika Korps and Fifth Panzer Army, would center around Gafsa and be aimed at destroying the untested and understrength American II Corps.

From the German standpoint, the problem was that there was insufficient armor available to mount the attack. Rommel could not spare the 15th Panzer Division from the Mareth Line, and von Arnim refused to release either of his panzer divisions to support Rommel. Little dependence could be placed on the Germans' Italian allies. Relations between the two were already dismal, with the Italian high command (Commando Supremo) openly opposed to any attempt to place Rommel in command of Axis forces in Tunisia. To make matters worse, there was little love lost between the aristocratic Prussian von Arnim and Rommel, and even less cooperation between them.

Von Arnim and Rommel could scarcely have been more different. Where Rommel was daring and unconventional, von Arnim was orthodox and disinclined to take risks. Where Rommel had learned to exist on what at times was a near starvation diet of supplies, von Arnim seemed unduly concerned by the mounting shortages. Rommel was an offensive-minded commander; von Arnim never viewed the Axis offensive as anything more than a defensive spoiling operation to improve his positions in the Eastern Dorsal.

The result was a fragmented plan which left no one in overall command. The scenario called for von Arnim to strike at Sidi Bou Zid between 12 and 14 February with 10th Panzer. Rommel's blow was to fall on Gafsa with a battle group (Kampfgruppe DAK), an armor-heavy task force assembled from the Deutsches Afrika Korps that included elements of the Italian Centauro armored division. If successful in destroying II Corps, Rommel was prepared to exploit his success and move on Tebessa, using the 21st Panzer Division, which von Arnim was to release to him to bolster Kampfgruppe DAK.

Through ULTRA,* the AFHQ intelligence officer (G-2) was aware of the large German buildup behind the Eastern Dorsal and expected an offensive soon, but it was believed that Rommel would attack farther to the north at Fondouk, with secondary attacks at Faid and Gafsa. On this premise Anderson realigned the combat commands of Ward's U.S. 1st Armored Division to meet this anticipated threat.

American forces guarding the passes through the Eastern Dorsal were pitifully outgunned. The men of the 1st Armored were not only inexperienced but were employing equipment that was simply no match for the superior German armament. The U.S. Stuart tank, with its tiny 37-mm gun, and the outmoded Grant tank were hopelessly inadequate when pitted against the German dual-purpose 88-mm field guns and the first of the infamous Tiger tanks, which OKW had sent to Tunisia for field-testing.†

---

*The top-secret intelligence mechanism that enabled the Allies to decode even the Axis powers' most closely guarded communications.

†Although the Grant tank mounted a 75-mm gun, it lacked a turret and was restricted to only a few degrees of traverse. The appearance of the American-made M-4 Sherman as the standard battlefield tank of the Allies did little to redress their inability to do battle on anything approaching an even match with the more versatile and heavier-armed German panzers. To make matters worse, the Allies had no com-

The Allied commanders made the Axis task easier by their faulty dispositions, which left almost no capability for mutual support. When Giraud learned of Rommel's presence in Tripolitania, he urged Eisenhower to shift Major General Ernest N. Harmon's 2d Armored Division from Morocco to the Tebessa sector. His anxiety was based on the simple premise that "one never feels too strong facing an adversary like Rommel." Although sympathetic, Eisenhower was at the mercy of his logisticians, who insisted that additional combat forces could not be supported in Tunisia at this stage of the campaign.

In the early morning hours of 14 February a powerful German tank-infantry force of the 10th Panzer, backed by Luftwaffe dive-bombers, surprised the American force guarding Faid Pass. The hapless defenders—Combat Command A and the 168th Regimental Combat Team— were quickly overwhelmed, with enormous losses. These two forces were positioned out of supporting range of each other on adjoining *djebels* (hills), but after the attack began were refused permission by Fredendall to withdraw to a common line.

The American ordeal had only begun when 21st Panzer attacked from the south through Maizila Pass. By noon the defenders of Sidi Bou Zid were crushed between two panzer divisions which debouched onto the sandy plain of Sbeitla. An American colonel reported to his commander at Sidi Bou Zid that the front had cracked and that GIs could be seen abandoning the battlefield. He was disbelieved and told that they were merely "shifting positions." The officer retorted, "I know panic when I see it."

Wishful thinking on the part of American headquarters was climaxed by a futile and costly counterattack by the reserve force of Combat Command C, a task force of light tanks, infantry mounted on half-tracks, self-propelled artillery, and tank destroyers. Valiant as it was, the attack played directly into the hands of the Germans. At noon, with no idea of what opposition they were facing, this force sped to the rescue and straight into the jaws of the two panzer divisions, in a modern-day re-enactment of the ill-fated Charge of the Light Brigade.

American losses at Faid were over 2,000, of whom 1,400 were cap-

---

parable weapon to the German 88-mm gun, which was famous for its tank-killing ability. Moreover, in Tunisia the Shermans were still gasoline driven, and they became death traps for their crews until replaced with diesel engines. Throughout the war the inadequacy of Allied armor never permitted a successful frontal attack against German tanks. Instead, the more dependable Shermans used wolf-pack tactics by attacking from the flank, where the panzers were more vulnerable.

tured, including Patton's son-in-law, Lieutenant Colonel John Waters, who commanded an armored regiment. Only 300 American troops managed to evade capture. Equipment losses were equally staggering; the battlefield was littered with the smoking ruins of 94 tanks, 26 self-propelled artillery pieces, and 60 half-tracks. By the evening of 14 February the fighting was over and the Germans were in control of Sidi Bou Zid and threatening to thrust through to Sbeitla.

The seeds of this disaster had been sown two weeks earlier, when an ineptly led American counterattack failed to regain Faid Pass after its French defenders were overwhelmed by tanks of the 21st Panzer Division. The American effort had not only failed but had exposed to the Germans the poor coordination between armor and infantry forces. Moreover, the dispersal of the 1st Armored Division exacerbated an already dangerous situation that von Arnim had hitherto declined to exploit.

But von Arnim made no attempt to follow up on his crushing success at Sidi Bou Zid. Instead, he committed a blunder that proved to be a turning point in the Tunisian campaign. On 16 February he had sent the 10th Panzer Division north toward Fondouk but refused to dispatch 21st Panzer to Rommel at Gafsa. The Desert Fox had delayed the start of his attack by twenty-four hours on the assumption that he would face far stiffer American resistance than was actually encountered by Kampf-gruppe DAK, whose thrust to Gafsa was unopposed because Fredendall had ordered the area abandoned at the news of the attack at Faid Pass.

Not only was von Arnim uncooperative with Rommel, but he made no attempt to use all his forces. Neither panzer division was employed in a major offensive role, and the remnants of the Allied force in the Sidi Bou Zid sector were permitted to withdraw when they ought to have been annihilated. Von Arnim's dithering would soon prove to be the most telling of the Axis mistakes in Tunisia.

Rommel made several fruitless attempts to convince von Arnim to release 21st Panzer and to press his advantage and continue the attack toward Sbeitla, imploring von Arnim that "tactical successes must be ruthlessly exploited." His plea fell on deaf ears, and a frustrated Rommel was left to mount his attack on Kasserine Pass with an inferior force.

Unfortunately for the Axis, Kesselring was absent in Germany at this critical moment. Upon learning of the situation on 15 February, he immediately placed Rommel in command of Army Group Afrika, the senior Axis command in Tunisia. Even so, without von Arnim's cooperation Rommel lacked the strength to carry out his plan. To complicate matters, the command arrangements between Italy and Germany required Kesselring's order to be approved by the Commando Supremo in Rome, and that ponderous headquarters was not geared to make expeditious decisions. Approval did not come until 19 February, and by then it was already too late. The 10th Panzer Division had been diverted far to the north at Fondouk, and although both this division and 21st Panzer were to have been turned over to Rommel, von Arnim deliberately withheld part of 10th Panzer and the newly arrived Tiger tanks.

The German objective was now Le Kef, and Rommel ordered Kampfgruppe DAK to attack via Kasserine Pass and Thala while 21st Panzer thrust to Le Kef via Sbiba. Kasserine was the gateway to the southern approaches to the Western Dorsal, and it was here that the DAK force began their attack in a driving rain on 19 February. Their immediate opposition was Task Force Stark, a provisional force of combat engineers, artillery, and an infantry battalion of the 26th Regimental Combat Team (RCT) of the 1st Division, whose commander, Colonel Alexander N. Stark, had been ordered by Fredendall to defend Kasserine.

With the 10th Panzer on the way, Rommel believed Kampfgruppe DAK could take and possess Kasserine by dawn on 20 February. However, the DAK commander, Major General Karl Buelowius, had difficulty displacing Stark's force, which occupied the high ground along both sides of the pass. The DAK force lacked both the combat power and the aggressiveness of the two veteran panzer forces that von Arnim had withheld. In fact, Kampfgruppe DAK was a rather motley and understrength collection of German and Italian armored and motorized infantry forces whose commanders were unable to match the aggressiveness of the officers who had served Rommel so well throughout the long desert campaign. British historian Kenneth Macksey has accurately described DAK force as "the rump of a tired desert army."

Their task was not made easier by the Allies. For once, reinforcements were on the way. The British 6th Armoured Division's 26th Armoured Brigade sent Lieutenant-Colonel A. C. Gore's 10th Battalion, the Rifle Brigade, and they fought a brilliant delaying action along the road to Thala to cover the withdrawal of Task Force Stark. To the northeast the 21st Panzer Division was turned back at the Sbiba gap by elements of General Charles Ryder's U.S. 34th Division.

Even though Kasserine fell to Rommel before 20 February was over, Stark's troops had held the pass long enough to affect the outcome of the Axis offensive. The failure of the Germans to take Kasserine the day before was merely one of a string of costly Axis mistakes. The Rommel–

von Arnim rivalry, Kesselring's untimely absence at the decisive moment, and Commando Supremo's dithering all contributed to Rommel's failure to achieve his grand design.

To be sure, the Germans won a tactical victory at Kasserine, but strategically they had gained little of consequence. With his lines of communication now dangerously lengthened and his flanks vulnerable to Allied counterattack, Rommel had to contend with the reality that it would not be long before Eighth Army attacked the Mareth Line to the east. Unable to turn the Kasserine offensive into a deep exploitation that might cause the collapse of the Tunisian front, and similarly thwarted at Thala where the advance of 10th Panzer was stopped cold by Nickforce, a British-American-French task force, Rommel called off the offensive on 22 February, and the Germans began withdrawing to their previous positions along the Eastern Dorsal. In their wake they left the Allies in a state of shock.

TWO

The Battle for Tunisia

THE ROMMEL WHO FOUGHT THE BATTLE OF Kasserine Pass bore scant resemblance to the commander who had masterminded the brilliant successes of the Afrika Korps in Libya. The exploits of the Desert Fox had captivated even Churchill, who lauded him as "a great general," and in the eyes of the British populace Rommel had attained larger-than-life status. By 1943, however, his glory days were a thing of the past, and Rommel was now engaged in a grim fight for survival against a conservative but implacable enemy.

There is no clearer evidence of Rommel's decline than his final battle in early March at Médenine, in which he launched an ill-conceived spoiling attack by the Panzerarmee Afrika intended to disrupt the forthcoming Eighth Army attack against Mareth. Montgomery, while continuing massive preparations to assault the Mareth Line, had established powerful defensive positions between Medenine and Mareth into which the unsuspecting Afrika Korps plunged.

Montgomery's positions took full advantage of the defensive strength of the terrain and were even stronger than those at Alam Halfa. A powerful armored reserve and the massed artillery of Eighth Army were ready for battle. Had Rommel attacked immediately after withdrawing from Kasserine, he might well have succeeded, but by early March it was too late. The Rommel of old would not have sent his tanks into the teeth of the British defenses across open terrain, but at Medenine he launched the 15th and 21st Panzer divisions out of a heavy mist straight into a killing ground. The Axis commanders displayed an astonishing degree of disorder, and Rommel showed his weariness by a near-total lack of involvement in the battle.

The battle was swift and bloody, and over fifty panzers were left burning on the battlefield. Medenine was the nadir of Rommel's illustrious career. He had left Africa the day before the battle, disheartened and ill from his two grueling years in the desert. In Berlin several days later he was severely rebuked by Hitler, who steadfastly spurned his plea that "for the Army Group to remain in Africa was now plain suicide."

Rommel's star had been on the wane ever since Alam Halfa. He was out of favor with Hitler; his standing with Kesselring, who resented his high-handedness at Alamein, was scarcely better; and in von Arnim he had an implacable rival. North Africa, which has been called "the grave-yard of generals," had claimed its most famous victim. Now von Arnim assumed command of Army Group Afrika in his stead.

FAID, SIDI BOU ZID, AND KASSERINE were humiliating defeats for the U.S. Army, which had results far beyond the battlefield.* Not only were American tactics and dispositions unsound, but some troops under attack had abandoned their positions and equipment and fled to the rear in panic. Equally disturbing was the fact that American armor and artillery were simply no match for the superior German armament.

As the news from the front grew worse by the hour, Eisenhower began a painful reassessment of what had gone wrong. His naval aide, Commander Harry Butcher, wrote in his diary that "the proud and cocky Americans today stand humiliated by one of the greatest defeats in our history. . . . The casualty lists . . . and the loss of equipment are having a sobering effect upon the wishful thinkers at home who have had us practically storming Rome, and some even Berlin, by now." To Marshall, Eisenhower wrote, "Our people, from the very highest to the very lowest have learned that this is not a child's game."

Included in the ULTRA intercepts of German message traffic were scornful comments about American fighting ability which so infuriated Eisenhower's Chief of Staff, Major General Walter Bedell Smith, that he said it made his hair stand on end. The only Axis commander not deceived by the poor American performance was Erwin Rommel himself. He saw that the tactical conduct of the American defense at Kasserine had been first class, and he was certain they would quickly correct their leadership deficiencies. Rommel also instinctively understood that America's industrial capacity would soon provide new weapons equal to those of the Wehrmacht.

---

*American losses were nearly 6,000, including more than 300 killed and 3,000 captured or missing in action.

Kasserine dismayed the Allied high command, and as the bad news continued to flow from the battlefield, it was evident that unless there was an immediate improvement in leadership and training, the long-term effects could be disastrous. The most visible impact of Kasserine was in the attitude of the British, who regarded the battle as clear evidence that American fighting ability was mostly bravado.

The American leadership failures had begun at the top with Eisenhower, who exhibited the uncertainties and inexperience of high command. In the early days of the campaign this was discernible by his tendency to interfere in the tactical dispositions of small units on the battlefield and by his hesitation to redress the obvious problems festering within II Corps. His biographer, Stephen E. Ambrose, notes that even though he had lost confidence in Fredendall, he remained unwilling to remove a protégé of Marshall's.

Within days, however, unmistakable evidence began to appear that the lessons of Kasserine had imbued the top American leadership with the necessary determination to reclaim their lost honor. Considerable credit for this was due to Major General Ernest Harmon, the barrel-chested veteran cavalry officer whom Eisenhower had summoned from his 2d Armored Division in Morocco when he learned of the German offensive. Finally accepting the fact that Fredendall had lost control of II Corps, Eisenhower sent the outspoken Harmon to the front to help reverse the situation through any means necessary.

Although highly regarded by Marshall and at first by Eisenhower as well, Fredendall had proved to be a shockingly inept commander. Loud, profane, and bitterly anti-British, the fifty-eight-year-old Fredendall pictured himself as a hard-boiled tough character. He was flagrantly opinionated, and the objects of his wrath included those both above and below him in the Allied chain of command. Fredendall was utterly out of touch with his command, stonewalled any attempt at cooperation with Anderson, feuded constantly with his subordinate commanders, and generally broke every known principle of leadership in the employment of his corps. At the time of Kasserine, II Corps headquarters was located some sixty-five miles behind the front lines in an enormous underground bunker that two hundred combat engineers had labored for weeks to construct when their skills were urgently needed elsewhere. Eisenhower was among the visitors who came away genuinely embarrassed by what he saw there. Although he undoubtedly recognized that Fredendall's appointment was a dreadful mistake, he nevertheless failed to act at that time—on the dubious premise that the moment was not right for a change. His admonition that Fredendall visit his troops fell on deaf ears.

When Harmon arrived at II Corps at 0200 hours on the morning of 23 February, he found Fredendall in a nervous state, more concerned about the fate of his headquarters than of his corps. He asked Harmon if the corps headquarters ought to be moved. Harmon thought it an inane question to ask someone arriving in the dead of night with no idea whatsoever of the situation. But his reply was typical Harmon: "*Hell no!!*" Apparently satisfied, Fredendall turned over the running of the battle to Harmon, and as if to prove that he had entirely washed his hands of all responsibility, disappeared to bed for the next twenty-four hours. Fredendall's performance in Tunisia was a shameful example of poor leadership at a moment of the war that demanded a commander with courage and nerve.

Fortunately for the U.S. Army, that leader had arrived. The aggressive Harmon had brought common sense and firm leadership to the rapidly deteriorating front when it was most needed, and II Corps responded with alacrity to his presence. One of the first places Harmon had visited was Thala, where "Nickforce," under the command of Brigadier Cameron Nicolson (the second in command of the 6th Armoured Division), was defending against the advance of 10th Panzer. What the weary Harmon found there was a feisty "Gunner"* who told him, "We gave them a —— bloody nose yesterday and we'll do it again this morning!" On his own initiative Harmon immediately countermanded an order from Anderson to withdraw a U.S. artillery brigade to the rear. "I figured that if I won the battle I would be forgiven. If I lost, the hell with it anyway," he wrote later. The brilliant performance of "Nickforce" was undoubtedly a major factor in Rommel's decision to call off the German offensive.

After helping to restore order in the II Corps sector, Harmon sent a scathing after-action report to Eisenhower that bluntly condemned Fredendall as unfit for command. Several days later he told Patton that he considered Fredendall a moral and physical coward. Eisenhower offered the command of II Corps to Harmon, who refused, stating he could not accept the appointment after recommending the relief of its commander. "My recommendation," he told Eisenhower, "would be to bring Patton

---

*The British term for a Royal artilleryman. Nicholson had been sent by General Anderson on 20 February to take command of all Allied troops fighting northwest of Kasserine and to improvise a task force in an attempt to stem the German advance.

here from Morocco. . . . Let me go back to my Second Armored. That's the best way out of this mess."

Fredendall was dismissed by Eisenhower, and George Patton was hastily summoned from I Armored Corps, then training in Morocco, as the II Corps commander. Partly from fear of adding to the embarrassment of American failure in the first ground combat of the war against the Axis, Fredendall's relief was made to appear as if he was returning home because of his ability to train troops.* Although other general officers were relieved later in the war for relatively minor transgressions, Fredendall, who had sullied American leadership in North Africa, returned home to a hero's welcome, the command of a training army, and a promotion to lieutenant general.

AS THE GERMANS BEGAN WITHDRAWING to the Eastern Dorsal through Kasserine Pass in what the II Corps G-2 described as "one of the greatest tent-folding acts of all time," they were harassed by the Allied tactical air forces, now headed by Air Marshal Arthur Coningham, the veteran former commander of the Desert Air Force. One of British Air Chief Marshal Sir Arthur Tedder's first acts when he became the Allied Air Commander-in-Chief after the Casablanca Conference was to reorganize his tactical air into the Northwest African Tactical Air Force under Coningham. Although there were still many obstacles to overcome before air and ground elements would begin working together with the same kind of harmony Eighth Army had experienced with the Desert Air Force, the signs of progress were encouraging.

When he arrived to assume command of II Corps on 6 March 1943, Patton encountered Major General Omar N. Bradley, a recent arrival in North Africa who had been sent to the front by Eisenhower as an observer. Although neither officer had previously served with the other, Patton took an immediate liking to Bradley, but he refused to countenance what he termed "one of Ike's goddamn spies" in his command and quickly orchestrated the assignment of Bradley as his deputy. Despite their vast differences in outlook and temperament, the pairing of Patton and Bradley began one of the most unusual and effective relationships in military history: the mercurial Patton, who might curse one moment and the next get down on his knees to ask for God's help, and the un-

---

*Eisenhower was far too generous in his official judgment of Fredendall in *Crusade in Europe*, and while that general was not entirely to blame for the setbacks in Tunisia, later, in Northwest Europe, Eisenhower would instantly relieve any officer he saw hesitate or fail.

flappable, pragmatic Bradley, who despised theatrics and profanity of any sort.

ALTHOUGH THE AMERICANS' RECOVERY FROM Kasserine was rapid and significant, it made virtually no impression on General Sir Harold Alexander when he arrived to assume command of Allied ground forces on 19 February 1943. Alexander's inspection of his new command left him dissatisfied with Anderson, dismayed by Fredendall, and exceedingly pessimistic about American fighting ability. To Brooke he sent a gloomy assessment of the American soldier and his leaders: "They have excellent equipment and weapons but they simply do not know their jobs as soldiers . . . from the highest to the lowest, from general to private soldier. . . . They are soft, green and quite untrained. Is it surprising then that they lack the will to fight . . . and show no eagerness to get in and kill [their enemy]?"

Alexander warned Brooke that the problem was "very serious indeed," and "unless we can do something about it, the American Army in the European theatre of operations will be quite useless. . . . I have only the American 2d Corps. . . . If this handful of Divisions here are their best, the value of the remainder may be imagined."

His report to Eisenhower was far more diplomatic. When they overcame their inexperience, he said, the U.S. Army would be the equal of any fighting soldiers in the world. For now, Alexander acted at once to implement a plan that included an end to the "penny-packet" employment of II Corps, a step which Eisenhower eagerly accepted and Patton on his own initiative had already begun to implement.

What Alexander brought to the campaign was a stability it had badly lacked under the temporary battlefield command of Anderson. A veteran of many campaigns and a fearless commander who was widely respected by Americans and British alike, Alexander began restoring cohesion by streamlining the messy and inefficient command structure. Units parceled out across the front were sent back to their divisions. Anderson's 120,000-man First Army was left in the north; French forces, which now numbered 50,000, remained in the center; and for the first time II Corps was united in the south as a force of over 90,000 troops, consisting of the 1st Armored Division and the 1st, 9th, and 34th Infantry divisions.

The second phase of Alexander's plan was to unite his ground forces with Eighth Army, which was scheduled to drive through the Gabes Gap, a narrow passage between the sea and the salt lakes of the Chott el

Fedjadj, and breach the Mareth Line situated fifteen miles farther east at Wadi Akarit. The 18th Army Group, as the combined forces were designated, would then strangle Axis forces in northern Tunisia, while the air force and navy prevented the arrival of reinforcements and sealed off any escape by sea.

Alexander's emphasis on unity of command, his insistence that henceforth there would be no further withdrawal, and his creation of an army group reserve were all welcome steps. He also established battle schools run by British officers and instituted an intensive training program to harden his troops, raise their fighting spirit, and gradually expose them to battle experience. In short, Alexander left no doubt that he had come to command, with the implication that the British professionals had taken over from American amateurs. Henceforth, the campaign in Tunisia would be run the British way. Although he was never relieved of the command of First Army, Anderson's responsibilities were limited.

Unfortunately, Alexander's campaign plan clearly favored the employment of British forces at the expense of II Corps, whose operations were to be limited to anchoring the southern flank, and did nothing to enhance Eisenhower's attempt to forge a genuine Allied force that would operate with equal responsibility. Eisenhower's problem was that Kasserine had left him with no alternative except to give his new ground Commander-in-Chief a free hand.

Although the American commanders in Tunisia had the highest personal regard for Alexander, they bitterly resented what they perceived as a patronizing attitude on the part of the British. A private letter from Montgomery to Alexander on 8 March typified the prevailing British attitude toward II Corps: "Don't let them be too ambitious and ruin the show."

One of Alexander's intiatives that quickly became extremely unpopular was the employment of British liaison officers to advise and assist the U.S. commanders. In early April, when Harmon took over the 1st Armored Division from Orlando Ward and held his first staff meeting, it was a *British* officer who rose to provide the situation report. When Harmon brusquely asked him who he was, the officer replied he was the liaison officer from 18th Army Group. Harmon summarily expelled the officer, who was told not to return unless personally invited. Harmon had been told by Eisenhower that the British considered the 1st Armored Division "noncombat-worthy." "I just don't believe that," Harmon informed his officers. "This battlefield no longer is going to be the grave-yard of the First Armored; it's going to be the symbol of its resurrection."

The problem facing American commanders was clear-cut: to improve the performance of U.S. troops, and in the process to convince their skeptical British ally that the fighting qualities of the American soldier were the equal of any in the world. The leadership that would accomplish that was now on the scene. In Patton, Bradley, Harmon, Ryder, Allen, and Manton S. Eddy of the 9th Infantry Division, the commanders were now in place who could avenge Kasserine and restore American pride in the process.

MAJOR GENERAL GEORGE S. PATTON, JR., had only ten days to make his presence felt before II Corps was to conduct a diversionary attack ordered by Alexander. His arrival brought about a dramatic transformation in the corps. Using shock tactics to cajole, bully, and exhort his men into believing that they were capable of defeating the Germans, Patton seemed to be everywhere at once, employing every leadership technique learned during his thirty-three-year military career. The men of II Corps were forcibly reminded that Kasserine was behind them and that "a tough new era had begun."

Patton was determined to begin the reversal of American fortunes by taking to the offensive. Alexander, who was anxious to divert as many German units as possible from Mareth, ordered him to confine his actions to the mountains of the Eastern Dorsal. Patton had other ideas and devised an ambitious two-phase plan. As the main elements of the 9th and 34th divisions demonstrated toward Faid and Fondouk, the 1st Armored and an infantry regiment of the 9th Division were to recapture the area southeast of Kasserine, drive through the Maknassy Pass, and threaten to break out into the coastal plains on the other side. The 1st Infantry Division would then capture Gafsa and drive toward Gabes via El Guettar. If successful, the threat to the German-Italian Army would be considerable. In Patton, II Corps had a warrior, like Rommel, who had come to fight. The night before the start of the offensive Patton told the corps staff: "Gentlemen, tomorrow we attack. If we are not victorious, let no one come back alive."

Alexander's prescription was far more conservative: II Corps was to regain the ground lost the previous month. This included airfields for Tedder's airmen and the capture of Gafsa, which was to become a logistical base for Eighth Army when it broke the Mareth Line. By *threatening* to break out toward Gabes, Alexander believed he could convince von Arnim to commit his reserve at Gafsa rather than at Mareth when Montgomery launched his breakthrough attempt.

Despite heavy rains, the operation opened auspiciously the night of 16–17 March as the 1st Infantry Division seized Gafsa and moved reconnaissance elements toward El Guettar. Von Arnim took the bait and overreacted to the threat posed by the II Corps offensive, perceiving it to be part of a coordinated Allied plan to envelop his rear, trap the Italian First Army, and—if successful in driving to the coast—the Afrika Korps as well. He committed 10th Panzer to the II Corps sector to reinforce the Italian Centauro Division defending El Guettar and the Maknassy Pass, which was the key to his defense of the Eastern Dorsal.

On 22 March, 10th Panzer arrived at the very moment when the 1st Armored Division was attempting to breach the hitherto-undefended Maknassy Pass. Aware of the limited American role dictated by Alexander, and perhaps overly concerned by the Luftwaffe's ability to attack from nearby bases, Orlando Ward had elected to regroup and renew his attack the following day. This unfortunate decision resulted in another stinging setback for 1st Armored, and it infuriated Patton, who had counted on the success of this operation as a basis for an expanded corps offensive that considerably exceeded Alexander's directive. Patton decided it was time for a change of commanders in the 1st Armored Division, and he installed Harmon in place of Ward.*

Patton's fortunes improved when an armored battle group of the 10th Panzer Division, supported by infantry, assault guns, artillery, and Stuka dive-bombers, was encountered the morning of 23 March on the open plain along the Gabes-Gafsa highway east of El Guettar. The 1st Infantry Division, backed by massed artillery and tank destroyers, was disposed in the hills overlooking the highway. The battle raged throughout the day, and the ambushed 10th Panzer lost thirty-two tanks and suffered heavy infantry losses before withdrawing in disarray. Patton's elation was tempered by his disgust over the poor German tactics. "They're murdering good infantry," he complained. "What a helluva way to waste good infantry."

By the standards of World War II the battle of El Guettar was a minor engagement, but for the United States Army it was a significant victory.

---

*Although relief from command was generally career-ending, there was considerable compassion for Ward, who returned to the United States to command the Tank Destroyer Center at Camp Hood, Texas. In 1945 he was given command of another armored division in Northwest Europe.

Patton's corps had successfully carried out an important mission and had begun the process of redemption for Kasserine. The lesson for von Arnim and his commanders was equally clear: The U.S. Army was no longer an adversary to be taken lightly.

Patton was disappointed to learn that Rommel had already left Africa but consoled himself with the knowledge that he had bested the Germans in battle. He would have preferred another solution: "Let me meet Rommel [face-to-face] in a tank and I'll shoot it out with the son-of-a-bitch."

MONTGOMERY'S OFFENSIVE AGAINST THE Mareth Line began on 19 March to coincide with Patton's thrusts along the Eastern Dorsal. His plan was to maneuver Lieutenant-General Bernard Freyberg's New Zealand Corps* on a lengthy two-hundred-mile left hook to the west of the Mareth defenses. Once in position, Freyberg was to attack the Axis rear through the Tebega Gap toward El Hamma, while Lieutenant-General Sir Oliver Leese's 30th Corps assaulted the Mareth defenses at Wadi Zigzaou.

The winter weather favored the Axis defenders of Wadi Zigzaou. Heavy rains had turned the normally dry terrain into an impassable swamp that swallowed tanks and vehicles. Those Valentine tanks of 30th Corps which managed to cross the wadi were left at the mercy of a powerful counterattack by the 15th Panzer Division, which took a fearsome toll of British tanks and supporting infantry. The 30th Corps was never permitted to gain the initiative, and despite exhortations from Montgomery it soon became painfully clear that the attack at Wadi Zigzaou could not succeed. After twenty-four hours the Eighth Army commander acknowledged failure and called off the attack. The battlefield had become a slaughterhouse; it was a stunning reminder that the Tunisian campaign was far from over.

To add to Montgomery's problems, the Germans had not been deceived by Freyberg's end run. Von Arnim replied at once to the New Zealand threat by sending the 21st Panzer and 164th Light divisions to Tebega to oppose Freyberg, while 15th Panzer went to plug the defenses along the Wadi Zigzaou, where their counterattack on 22 March helped to convince Montgomery that he must now pin his hopes for breaking the

*The New Zealand Corps consisted only of Freyberg's own 2d New Zealand Division and the British 8th Armoured Brigade, augmented by additional artillery, armored cars, and General Jacques LeClerc's L Force. Its total strength was approximately 25,000 men, 151 tanks, 112 field guns, and 172 antitank guns.

Mareth defenses on the left hook. Freyberg's advance across the desert sands and the many treacherous wadis of the Matmata Hills swiftly turned into a nightmare journey.

In an attempt to regain the initiative Montgomery attached the commander of 10th Corps, Lieutenant-General Brian Horrocks, to the British 1st Armoured Division and ordered him to follow Freyberg's path and reinforce the attack on the Tebega Gap. At the same time, Major-General Francis Tuker's 4th Indian Division was ordered to execute a shorter version of the left hook and attack along the sector formerly occupied by the 164th Light Division.

After being initially rebuffed at Tebega, the newly reinforced New Zealand Corps, backed by a furious aerial bombardment from the Desert Air Force, at last broke through toward El Hamma. It had taken Eighth Army nine of the most difficult days it had yet fought in North Africa to break the Mareth Line.

The final battle in Tripolitania occurred in early April at Wadi Akarit, where 30th Corps fought a murderous battle which cost 1,300 British casualties. It failed to bag the main Italian and German forces, which escaped to Enfidaville and thus avoided the trap that an Allied breakthrough at Maknassy would have produced.

With the escape of Panzerarmee Afrika and the arrival of Eighth Army, both the German and Allied army groups were at top strength. Ahead lay the climactic battle of the Tunisian campaign.

AS THE DESIGNATED AMERICAN INVASION commander for Sicily, George Patton knew that his tenure as II Corps commander was temporary. In mid-April Eisenhower ordered him back to Morocco to hasten the planning for Operation HUSKY. Patton urged Eisenhower to promote Bradley as his replacement and to replace Major General Ernest J. Dawley's VI Corps—then slated for the invasion of Sicily—with II Corps. Eisenhower agreed, and VI Corps was transferred to Mark Clark's newly formed Fifth Army and Bradley was given his first corps command.

Omar Bradley was another of the midwesterners who rose to prominence during World War II. Too poor to afford college, he had given no thought to a military career until learning that he could obtain a free education if he qualified for West Point. He entered the academy in 1911 and graduated in Eisenhower's class of 1915, which later became known as "the class the stars fell on." Although he missed combat duty in World War I, Bradley's career was enhanced during the interwar period while on Marshall's staff at Fort Benning. There he successfully passed the

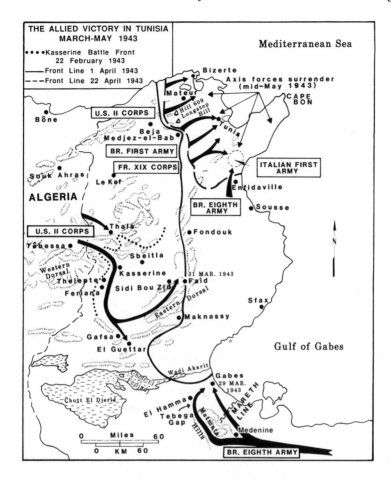

scrutiny of Marshall, whose famous black notebook began to fill with the names of future commanders.

During the early years of the war Bradley rose quickly from lieutenant colonel to major general. After he had commanded the 82d Division and a National Guard division, Marshall decided not to appoint him to a corps command in the United States, as might have been expected. Instead, he sent him to North Africa, where Eisenhower badly needed high-quality officers. With no small boost from Patton, Bradley had convincingly demonstrated the wisdom of Marshall's decision. Bradley found that his first battles were not with the enemy but with the Allied high command. The improved American performance had done little to restore British faith in her ally.

One of the major complaints about the inexperience of the U.S. Army was a British allegation that the 34th Division had performed badly during the battle of Fondouk in early April. While Patton created yet another diversion in the southeast, Alexander had ordered a provisional British corps commanded by Lieutenant-General John T. Crocker to attack the Eastern Dorsal at Fondouk and cut off the impending retreat of the Italian First Army by capturing Sousse. The U.S. 34th Division, under Major General Charles Ryder, was given the task of forcing the pass at Fondouk by a frontal attack. Ryder had planned an encirclement operation but had been firmly overruled by Crocker, who refused to alter his decision. The unhappy result was that the 34th failed to dislodge the German force guarding the pass and suffered heavy casualties.

Crocker was severely critical of Ryder and the 34th Division and pinned full responsibility for the failure on them, claiming their leadership was timid, inexperienced, and excessively cautious. Bradley knew his West Point classmate Ryder to be a sound tactician whose judgment was reliable, and he sensed that the British criticism would humiliate a division whose only shortcoming was the need for an opportunity to develop self-confidence. Before his departure Patton had supported Bradley's challenge to a proposal by 18th Army Group to withdraw the 34th Division to the rear for retraining. Both officers believed this would shatter the morale of the division and ruin Ryder's career. Alexander reluctantly gave in, but the incident only served to harden American resentment. The onus was now upon Bradley and II Corps to prove the British wrong.

Ever since Kasserine, the senior American commanders in Tunisia had been seething with frustration over what they considered unfair criticism, the British officers' loose talk to war correspondents, and Eisenhower's order that Americans were not to criticize the British. Even Bradley began to question the wisdom of Eisenhower's reluctance to restrain his ally.

Throughout Tunisia the growing pains of the new alliance abounded and were by no means confined to national rivalries. The veterans of Eighth Army were as contemptuous of their British comrades in First Army as they were of the American II Corps. The unhappy result was a poisoning of the atmosphere that extended across service lines and was typified by an unpleasant incident involving Patton and Coningham over close air support.

Patton had become incensed at what he believed was the exceptionally poor close air support of II Corps, and soon after taking command made his displeasure known at the highest level. Coningham, in turn, sent an intemperate signal to every Allied HQ in Tunisia which, in effect, called Patton a liar and suggested that II Corps was not battleworthy. At the instigation of Air Chief Marshal Tedder, Eisenhower moved quickly to defuse an explosive situation by sending Coningham to apologize personally to Patton.

Although the ultimate fate of the Axis forces in Tunisia was now clear, the campaign was far from over. Arrayed against von Arnim was a massive Allied force consisting of the British First and Eighth armies, the French corps, and U.S. II Corps. Yet those who had battle experience, like Montgomery, were well aware that even in their present desperate circumstances the Axis forces would never surrender without a bitter fight.

Alexander's continued mistrust of American fighting ability was made crystal clear in his plan for Operation STRIKE, the decisive battle of the campaign. The II Corps was again relegated to the minor role of protecting the Allied left flank, while the British would make the main effort— a partridge drive to corner Army Group Afrika in the Cape Bon peninsula.

The insignificance of the U.S. role did not escape the attention of Marshall, who believed that Eisenhower had yielded too much to the British. What most disturbed the Chief of Staff was the implication in the American press that the 34th Division had spoiled British chances of trapping the Italians and the Afrika Korps, and that U.S. troops were being given menial tasks on the battlefield. Marshall cabled his feelings to Eisenhower, questioning the diminished American role, which he rightly viewed as a matter of national pride and prestige. Marshall's message was a polite but unmistakable directive to act at once.

Bradley was equally dissatisfied, and several weeks earlier had visited Algiers to complain personally to Eisenhower about the slight to his corps, insisting that American troops had won the right to a share of the final Allied victory in Tunisia. He proposed that II Corps be employed as a unit in an independent drive to Bizerte to block an Axis escape to the west. While Bradley undoubtedly impressed on Eisenhower the need for the United States to show the flag more, it was Marshall's prodding that finally resulted in Eisenhower's insistence to Alexander that II Corps be given a meaningful role in STRIKE. Bradley's plan was accepted, and Bizerte was assigned as the II Corps objective.

Bradley and his corps proved equal to the challenge. The key to a successful thrust to Bizerte was to neutralize the German defenses along the Sidi Nsir–Mateur road, which was dominated by the well-defended Hill 609. The task of capturing this critically important strongpoint was deliberately assigned to Ryder's 34th Division. "Get me that hill," said Bradley, "and no one will ever again doubt the toughness of your division." What ensued was one of the most savage battles fought in Tunisia, as Ryder's men battled for five days to capture a series of nearby hills. When they finally seized Hill 609 by a combined tank-infantry assault, the 34th Division found that their ordeal was only beginning. Next they successfully fought off a series of desperate German counterattacks.

Under Harmon's aggressive leadership the 1st Armoured Division also regained its lost honor. After the 34th Division captured Hill 609, Harmon's armor spearheaded a drive through the German defenses along the sector known as "the Mousetrap," on the road to Mateur. The attack broke the back of the Axis defense of Bizerte and was instrumental in the great success of the II Corps offensive. At its conclusion Bradley modestly signaled Eisenhower: "Mission accomplished."

The final Allied offensive had commenced on 19 April as the 18th Army Group pincers crushed Army Group Afrika in a vise from which there could be no escape. As II Corps closed the jaws of the trap by capturing Bizerte and cutting off von Arnim's only escape route, British and French forces completed the operation by forcing Army Group Afrika onto the plain of Tunis, where it was compelled to surrender.

The fate that befell the Axis army in Tunisia was a bitter pill for von Arnim, who found that Hitler had ruthlessly and needlessly left his army to wither and die in the Allied trap. His appeals for food, fuel, and ammunition were ignored by Berlin. Although starved for resupply, the troops of Army Group Afrika gamely resisted Alexander's relentless onslaught to an honorable end. The plight of some of the best formations of the Wehrmacht was epitomized by the commander of the Afrika Korps, whose final defiant signal read: "Ammunition shot off. Arms and equipment destroyed . . . D.A.K. has fought itself to the condition where it can fight no more. The German Afrika Korps must rise again— Cramer, General Commanding."

On 12 May von Arnim surrendered, and the 250,000 survivors of Army Group Afrika became Allied prisoners of war. The following day Alexander cabled Churchill: "Sir, it is my duty to report that the Tunisian campaign is over. All enemy resistance has ceased. We are masters of the North African shores."

Allied inexperience and miscalculations in North Africa had been more than offset by the inconsistency of their adversary. The Germans had squandered a golden opportunity at Sidi Bou Zid and Kasserine to strike a killing blow that might well have changed the outcome of the campaign. In North Africa the cost was staggering: an entire army group of about 240,000 men.* The Germans could ill afford to lose nearly a quarter million crack troops to a hopeless venture when German troops were being annihilated on the Eastern Front with shocking rapidity.

For the Allies the Tunisian venture was a proving ground. As Bradley later noted, "In Africa we learned to crawl, to walk, then run." The price of this experience for the fledgling U.S. Army was not cheap. American losses were 18,221, including 2,715 killed. Overall Allied losses between 12 November 1942 and 13 May 1943 were 70,341: French—16,180, British First Army—23,545, and British Eighth Army—12,395.

That Tunisia was a battlefield laboratory was all too evident from the experience of Kasserine, which for all its bitter aspects became a lesson that American commanders were doggedly determined never to repeat. It also marked the emergence of a new generation of American generals who were to make their mark throughout the remainder of the war. The performance of these men was to provide powerful evidence that these lessons were never forgotten.

Unfortunately, as events in Sicily would prove, the redemption was not recognized by Alexander and other senior British officers. An incident between Anderson and Harmon prior to Mateur is illustrative. "I was at work in my tent when Anderson arrived," recalled Harmon. "He looked me over in a rather supercilious manner and inquired what I planned to do with an armored division in that terrain. Pointing out the positions on the map, I explained the plan Bradley and I had worked out for the armored rush on Mateur. Anderson waved his swagger stick vaguely and commented, 'Just a childish fantasy, just a childish fantasy.' With that he stalked out of the tent . . . under my breath I muttered to myself, 'I'll make that son-of-a-bitch eat those words.'" The operation was indeed a great success.

With the Allies in complete control of North Africa, a turning point in the war had come. They, and not Hitler, would henceforth dictate the time and place of future engagements. Although the German Führer refused to acknowledge that the Axis effort in North Africa was anything more than a sideshow, the defeat of Army Group Afrika was the second disastrous German setback of 1943.

---

*The exact number of Axis losses has long been in dispute. Alexander's dispatch claimed the capture of 250,000 German and Italian troops, while the British official history records a total of 238,243, and the U.S. official history about 275,000.

THREE

Operation HUSKY

THE DEFEAT OF AXIS FORCES IN NORTH AFRICA left the German and Italian high commands certain that the Allies would soon employ their massive sea, air, and ground forces elsewhere in the Mediterranean. Hitler was never in any doubt that Allied intentions included an invasion to gain a foothold into southern Europe. Among the possible sites were the lightly defended Aegean, mainland Italy, and, most obvious of all, the islands of Sardinia and Sicily.

What the Axis leadership did not suspect was that the Allies were seriously divided over future strategy in the Mediterranean. Some of the most contentious disagreements of the war were to occur in the process of agreeing on a common strategy. Although Allied planners had for some time been developing a number of possible options for future action after the campaign in Tunisia ended, there had been no firm agreement between the top leaders of Britain and the United States. Although Churchill and the British Chiefs of Staff were committed to a strategy which would exert pressure on the Axis and support Russia by drawing German forces away from the Eastern Front, where the Red Army was still on the defensive despite the crushing victory at Stalingrad, the British were still not prepared to support, in more than token form, the American desire for a cross-Channel invasion of Northwest Europe in 1943. Although Churchill accepted the eventual necessity of the cross-Channel invasion, and indeed insisted that he had been the first to proclaim that the decisive campaign would have to be fought in Europe, he sought to buy time for its planning and preparation by nibbling away at what he termed "the soft underbelly" of Germany. Also, the Prime Minister saw any action to restore the balance in the Far East as clearly out of the question for the foreseeable future. Only in the Mediterranean was there any immediate possibility of continuing the momentum that had begun in North Africa.

The architect of American strategy and spokesman for the U.S. Chiefs of Staff was George Marshall, who disagreed with Churchill and argued forcefully for the invasion of Europe in 1943. As one British officer noted in his diary, "The U.S. regarded the Mediterranean as a kind of dark hole, into which one entered at one's peril."

An Anglo-American clash was inevitable when the Allied leadership met at Casablanca in January 1943 to resolve their future strategy. Churchill and Roosevelt remained aloof and left the resolution of their differences to the Combined Chiefs of Staff,* who wrangled with one another for nearly ten days during some of the most arduous negotiations ever to occur between the two allies. Brooke, the chief British strategist and head of their Chiefs of Staff, came to Casablanca fully committed to an invasion of Sicily to follow the Tunisian campaign.

Eventually, thanks largely to the mediation of Field-Marshal Sir John Dill, the senior British representative in Washington, the two sides reached a compromise. Although it did not please Marshall, it was the best the United States could attain. In return for further Allied operations in the Mediterranean, the British agreed to renew planning for the cross-Channel invasion, Operation OVERLORD.† In the meantime the Allies would exploit their growing strength in the Mediterranean by invading the island of Sicily, which would not only signal their return to Europe but eventually enable them to carry their effort into mainland Italy. Command of the invasion forces of Operation HUSKY was given to the current Allied commander in the Mediterranean, Dwight Eisenhower.

THE PLANNING FOR HUSKY BEGAN ON a sour note in early February 1943, as the invasion commanders found themselves preoccupied with the faltering campaign in Tunisia. The command structure for HUSKY was one

*The term Combined Chiefs of Staff (CCOS) was given to the U.S. and British Chiefs of Staff operating together to formulate strategic policy and command guidance for the Allied commanders in the field.

†The Casablanca Conference was a masterpiece of the art of compromise. In return for HUSKY, the British committed themselves to ROUNDUP (a large buildup of U.S. forces in the United Kingdom as the first vital step on the road to a cross-Channel invasion), but without a specific date for OVERLORD, they had merely acknowledged the inevitable. The questions of when and where to mount OVERLORD would not be resolved until the Quebec Conference in August 1943.

of the British triumphs at Casablanca. Brooke was chary of Eisenhower's lack of high-level command experience and less than impressed with the state of affairs in Tunisia. To compensate for Eisenhower's inexperience, and with Churchill's blessing, he orchestrated the appointment of Alexander as the ground Commander-in-Chief for HUSKY, as he was in Tunisia.

Command of Allied naval and air forces also went to British officers: Admiral Sir Andrew Browne Cunningham and Air Chief Marshal Sir Arthur Tedder. The practical effect of this organization made Eisenhower little more than a figurehead with little control over the actions of his British subordinates. Not only did they all have to agree on the invasion plan, but if Eisenhower disagreed with their actions, he had to either persuade them to change a decision or resign. He had no authority to replace them.

From the outset Eisenhower realized that he had been manipulated by the British. Imposing his will on the operation would require much of his energy. Moreover, at that time his own position was none too secure, leaving no real latitude for a protest to the Combined Chiefs of Staff for a change.

Thus, from its inception as a strategic compromise at Casablanca, the planning of Operation HUSKY was plagued by interminable problems of organization and command. The Combined Chiefs had directed Eisenhower to create a separate headquarters to plan HUSKY, and by late January 1943 an inter-Allied, interservice planning group was formed in Algiers which became known as Task Force 141, so named for the room in the St. George's Hotel where the first meeting took place. Until the end of the Tunisian campaign it remained a part of the AFHQ Operations section (G-3), after which it came under Alexander.*

Force 141 was always less than effective because Alexander paid scant attention to the planning of HUSKY. His preoccupation with the Tunisian campaign was to become a serious point of contention during the planning for the invasion of Sicily. Both of the designated invasion commanders (Montgomery, whose Eighth Army would form the ground element of the [British] Eastern Task Force, and Patton, whose I Armored Corps[+] would form the [U.S.] Western Task Force), were equally com-

---

*After Tunisia the 18th Army Group was deactivated but in fact merely changed its designation to Force 141, the title it retained until D-Day, when it was officially activated as 15th Army Group.

[+] On D-Day it was redesignated U.S. Seventh Army, to give it equal status with Montgomery's Eighth Army.

mitted to their respective affairs in Tunisia. Patton had no early involvement in HUSKY and was thrust into the command of II Corps after Kasserine. Only Montgomery took an active interest in the planning, and what he saw filled him with gloom.

Inasmuch as the majority of British forces for Sicily were to be drawn from those already in the Mediterranean and launched from there, Montgomery's Eastern Task Force headquarters was established in Cairo under the designation Force 545. Lieutenant-General Miles Dempsey, the 13th Corps commander, was chief of staff until mid-April, when Montgomery sent his own chief of staff, Major-General Francis de Guingand, to assume this role. Patton's Western Task Force headquarters was initially located at Rabat, Morocco, as Force 343.

The Canadian 1st Division and the U.S. 45th Infantry Division were to be staged directly from Britain and the United States, respectively. London and Washington thus became two of *five* separate planning operations in five widely scattered locations. The inevitable result was considerable confusion, which was compounded by the inclusion of the three British commanders, Middle East, each of whom was required to play a role in the forthcoming campaign. To add to the confusion, Cunningham, Tedder, and Alexander each established their operational headquarters in different locations, despite pleas to the contrary from the British Chiefs of Staff.*

The first weeks of planning were extremely critical and urgently required someone to provide guidance at the highest level so that the various planning staffs would understand the direction their effort was expected to take. In theory, the planning of a joint amphibious operation should center on the requirements of the ground forces and their mission. In practice, many factors combined to ensure that logic was lost in a morass of confusion, disorganization, and disharmony. As the ground force commander this responsibility was Alexander's. However, he found himself too involved with his command problems in Tunisia. Eisenhower was too far removed from the planning, and too deeply absorbed in his

---

*The cumbersome Allied command structure in the Mediterranean was further complicated by the fact that the British maintained three separate commands: Middle East Forces, under Commander-in-Chief General Sir Henry Maitland Wilson; naval forces under the Commander-in-Chief, Mediterranean, Admiral Cunningham; and the Middle East Air Command under Air Chief Marshal Sir William Sholto Douglas. In the words of the British official history, "The system of command of a great inter-Allied force drawn from the sea, land and air services of two nations cannot be simple."

own problems in Tunisia, to give HUSKY anything more than token attention. By default it fell to the staff of Force 141 to solve questions that required the guidance of a commander. They were unsuccessful and unable to maintain the June timetable decreed by Churchill and Roosevelt at Casablanca. The British official history later noted that five months seemed a sufficiently wide margin, "but brute facts were to show that it was narrow."

SICILY HAD LONG BEEN AN OUTPOST of Mussolini's modern-day Roman empire. Even though an integral part of Italy, the island's inhabitants never viewed themselves as Italian. Fiercely independent, the Sicilians had known war and occupation from the dawn of civilization in what had become one of the most varied racial melting pots on earth. Repeatedly conquered by various tribes and nations over the centuries, tormented by the Mafia and the ravages of poverty across a harsh land, the Sicilians had welcomed neither the Italian Army nor its German ally.

Theoretically the island was a military fortress garrisoned by an Italian army of over 300,000 men, backed by a small German contingent that until June 1943 never consisted of more than the equivalent of a division. Moreover, until 1943 the Axis powers gave it only token attention as a possible Allied target. When the new Axis commander, General Alfredo Guzzoni, arrived in May, he found Sicily's naval defenses virtually nonexistent, its air defenses inadequate, and the ground forces poorly trained and their equipment archaic.

Numerous problems confronted the Allied planners. Throughout Sicily the road net was sparse, and except for the coastal strips in the invasion sector the island was dominated by mountains and rugged hills, which would severely limit the maneuverability of Allied armor and wheeled vehicles. The only exception was the plain of Catania, a broad, marshy lowland which drained a huge watershed from the nearby mountains. Immediately to the north of it was Mount Etna, one of the world's largest and most active volcanos. The enormous area covered by Mount Etna was totally unsuitable for cross-country movement of motor vehicles, and any advance toward Messina would have to proceed along a narrow coastal shelf. Situated at the northeast extremity of Sicily, Messina lay just across the strait that divided Sicily from the mainland and was the primary Axis logistical lifeline to Italy. Its capture was the ultimate objective of the Allied armies. If there were to be landings in southeastern Sicily, the invading force would have to gain control of the terrain immediately south of the key port city of Catania, where the coastal road (Route 14) crossed the Simeto River at an obscure place called Primosole Bridge.

The initial invasion plan produced by Force 141 called for a series of amphibious landings by task forces of varying sizes from D-Day to D plus five along the six-hundred-mile coast of Sicily. When he first learned of the proposed plan, Montgomery was horrified by this return to penny-packet warfare. Calling the plan "a dog's breakfast," Montgomery denounced the entire HUSKY planning effort as "a hopeless mess."

For the next three months he repeatedly warned his superiors in typically blunt language that unless a sensible plan were soon developed, the Allies would be in serious trouble. To Brooke he sent numerous back-channel cables and letters complaining of the stalled planning. And to Alexander went exhortations to take a firm grip over Force 141 now, while there was still time. Montgomery argued pragmatically that "if we do HUSKY, it must succeed." Privately he confided to Brooke that it was easier to fight the Germans than it was to restore sanity to the Sicily planning. Brooke, however, was powerless to interfere, since to do so would have been a vote of no-confidence in Eisenhower.

Eisenhower's worst fears soon became reality as the committee system exacerbated the ever-widening divisions between the force commanders. Tedder was insistent on the prompt acquisition of airfields in southeastern Sicily for his tactical aircraft, while Cunningham demanded maximum security for his ships, hence his backing of the multiple invasion plan, which dispersed the Allied fleet. Montgomery, acting in the absence of Alexander, contended that the only acceptable plan which would guarantee the success of the invasion was to concentrate all the ground forces in the southeastern corner of Sicily.

For three months the debates raged within the Allied high command, with no visible result. A number of invasion plans were proposed, considered, and then scrapped because none satisfied the full committee. Even worse, there was mounting evidence of Allied conservatism. In April, Churchill reacted with cold fury when presented with a pessimistic signal from Eisenhower stating that the HUSKY planners feared failure if more than two German divisions were encountered by the invaders. The Prime Minister's scathing reply to "these pusillanimous and defeatist doctrines" which would "make us the laughingstock of the world" struck a nerve at AFHQ.* Marshall's suggestion that AFHQ consider a sur-

---

*Churchill also observed, "What Stalin would think of this when he has 185 German divisions on his front, I cannot imagine."

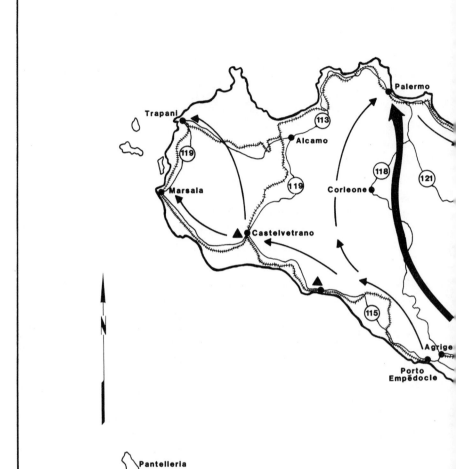

THE INVASION OF SICILY:
OPERATION "HUSKY"
10 JULY–16 AUGUST 1943

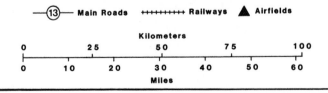

—⑬— Main Roads ++++++++++ Railways ▲ Airfields

Kilometers

| 0 | 25 | 50 | 75 | 100 |

| 0 | 10 | 20 | 30 | 40 | 50 | 60 |

Miles

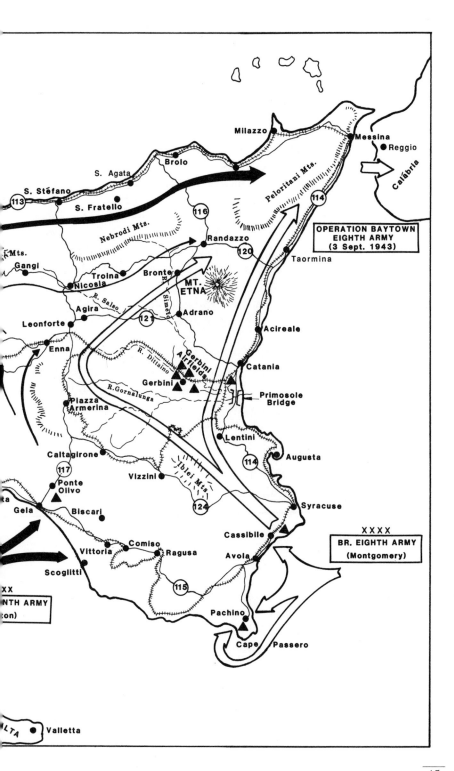

OPERATION BAYTOWN
EIGHTH ARMY
(3 Sept. 1943)

XXXX
BR. EIGHTH ARMY
(Montgomery)

XX
NTH ARMY
on)

Messina
Reggio
Calàbria
Milazzo
Brolo
S. Agata
Peloritani Mts.
S. Stéfano
113
S. Fratello
114
Nebrodi Mts.
116
Randazzo
120
Taormina
Mts.
Gangi
Troina
Bronte
Nicosia
MT.
ETNA
R. Salso
Agira
121
Adrano
Acireale
Leonforte
R. Dittaino
Gerbini
Airfield
Enna
Catania
R. Simèta
Gerbini
Piazza
Armerina
R. Gornalunga
Primosole
Bridge
Lentini
Caltagirone
Augusta
117
114
Vizzini
Ponte
Olivo
Iblei Mts
124
Gela
Biscari
Syracuse
Comiso
Ragusa
Cassibile
Vittoria
Ragusa
Avola
Scoglitti
115
Pachino
Cape Passero

LTA   Valletta

prise landing by a small force against the weak defenses of Sicily *before* the inevitable buildup which would follow victory in Tunisia was never seriously considered.

A calculated act of insubordination by Montgomery finally forced the planners to decide on a compromise plan. In late April, frustrated by the inaction and deeply worried that the planning stalemate might never be broken in time for the invasion, Montgomery—at considerable risk to his reputation—deliberately precipitated a crisis by signaling Alexander that he intended to employ the entire Eighth Army in southeastern Sicily. The result was outrage within the counsels of the Allied high command, further dampening the prospects for a solution to the impasse.

A stormy meeting on 29 April not only failed to resolve Allied differences but also further exacerbated the bad feelings toward the Eighth Army commander. On 2 May a frustrated Montgomery arrived in Algiers and allegedly cornered Bedell Smith in the lavatory of AFHQ. There he outlined his proposed plan and insisted it be presented at once to Eisenhower.

Montgomery's lavatory discussion with Bedell Smith broke the logjam at last. The HUSKY debates had been entirely a British internecine quarrel, and although Eisenhower's claim that he was not fully aware of the extent of the rift was implausible, he did exercise his authority by insisting it be settled at once. HUSKY thus became the only major operation of war where one of the key decisions was orchestrated in an Algerian privy!

Montgomery's plan was quickly approved by the Allied leadership, and although it did nothing to endear him to his associates, there was general relief all around that at long last HUSKY was back on track. Tedder was assured of the highest priority for the capture of Axis airfields in the Gela sector, but Cunningham was never comfortable with the plan, which he believed exposed the Allied fleet to unnecessary risk of enemy retaliation.

Although it has been incorrectly portrayed as an attempted power grab, Montgomery's compromise plan, conservative as it was, was the soundest of the five plans the Allies had considered. In an address to his fellow commanders on 2 May Montgomery candidly admitted he could be a "tiresome person," but few would quarrel with his logic. "I have seen so many mistakes made in this war, and so many disasters happen, that I am desperately anxious to try and see that we have no more. . . . If we have a disaster in Sicily it would be dreadful."

The approved invasion plan called for Eighth Army to land four divisions and one independent infantry brigade along a fifty-mile front in southeast Sicily, from Syracuse to the Pachino peninsula. At the same time, along the south coast Patton's forces would make their primary landings at Gela and Scoglitti, respectively, with the 1st and 45th Infantry divisions of Bradley's II Corps, while to the west at Licata, Major General Lucian K. Truscott's heavily reinforced 3d Infantry Division would land to protect the Seventh Army's left flank. The object of the two assault landings was to seize a firm Allied bridgehead in southeastern Sicily and, in the process, capture the key ports of Syracuse and Licata and the airfields near Gela, from which Tedder's airmen would operate in support of the advancing ground forces.

D-Day was designated as the early morning hours of 10 July, during the full moon. No one hoped that the Allies could achieve strategic surprise, but in an attempt to secure tactical surprise there was to be no pre-landing bombardment by the navy.

The landings were to be preceded by U.S. airborne and British glider landings to seize key targets around Gela and Syracuse. Colonel James M. Gavin's reinforced 505th Regimental Combat Team (82d Airborne Division) and the British 1st Airlanding Brigade (1st Airborne Division) were the spearhead forces of a bold night operation, the first of its kind ever attempted.

Once ashore, Eighth Army's mission was to capture first the ports of Syracuse and Augusta and then the plain of Catania. Most of Sicily is covered by mountains and rugged hills except for the plain of Catania, an eighteen-mile-long and twelve-mile-wide lowland located directly south of Mount Etna. On the northern edge of the plain the Italians had constructed an airfield complex around Gerbini that the Allied air command required to support operations in northeastern Sicily. Eventually the British were to drive north to capture the port city of Messina. An enemy force controlling the plain of Catania could dictate the ability of an attacker to capture Messina.

Other than the capture of the Gela airfields, Montgomery's plan left Patton's U.S. Seventh Army with only the distinctly secondary mission of protecting the Eighth Army's left flank. Although disappointed and disgusted at playing second fiddle to Montgomery and the British, Patton was uncharacteristically reticent. Urged by other senior Allied commanders to protest his diminished role, Patton emphatically refused with the comment: "No, goddammit, I've been in this Army thirty years and when my superior gives me an order I say, 'Yes, Sir!' and then do my god-damndest to carry it out."

The odd man out in the Allied hierarchy was Alexander, who played no meaningful role in the HUSKY planning, and who had conspicuously failed to develop his own strategic or tactical plan for the capture of Sicily. During the planning the respected Alexander was regarded even by his admirers, who included both Patton and Bradley, as weak and vacillating.

Although the invasion plan was limited to the capture of the island of Sicily, how this objective was to be carried out was left deliberately vague. Montgomery and Patton, however, always assessed the aim as the capture of Messina and the resultant isolation of all Axis forces remaining in Sicily. Messina was, in fact, the *only* strategic target in Sicily. Nevertheless, Alexander elected to allow the land battle to develop before committing his two armies to a course of action. As a result, Montgomery and Patton, without specific guidance from Alexander, developed problems that became the source of the well-publicized inter-Allied quarrels in Northwest Europe in 1944 and 1945.

THE PROBLEM FACING THE ALLIES WAS HOW to draw Axis attention away from Sicily when, as Churchill observed, "anybody but a bloody fool would *know* it [the target] is Sicily." Hitler and the German high command were hoaxed by a clever series of large-scale deception operations masterminded by the British. The best known of these operations turned out to be as simple and as old as the Trojan horse: the notorious "man who never was."

In April the corpse of a Royal Marine officer, Major William Martin, washed ashore in southern Spain near Huelva, where an Abwehr agent was known to be operating. Chained to his wrist was a briefcase containing highly sensitive documents destined for Alexander which revealed that Sicily was merely a ruse to deflect Axis forces from the real Allied target, the Balkans. The corpse and its authentic documents were clever plants designed to hoodwink the Germans into believing that the British *wanted* the Germans to believe the target in the Mediterranean was Sicily.

After the war, evidence revealed that Operation MINCEMEAT had been successful. Photographs of the contents of Major Martin's briefcase were soon in Berlin, where the Germans fell for the false information hook, line, and sinker. Other ongoing deception measures in the Mediterranean amplified the believability of the lie. In early June OKW ordered

the 1st Panzer Division to be shifted a thousand miles away from southern France on a wild goose chase to the Peloponnesus. Intelligence ap-
preciations flowing from Berlin reinforced the German conviction that
the next attack would definitely come in the Balkans. When it had become certain that the Germans had taken the bait, Churchill (then in
Washington for the Trident Conference) received a cryptic message
from London which read simply: "MINCEMEAT swallowed whole."

Only Alfredo Guzzoni among the senior Axis commanders was not
deceived by Operation MINCEMEAT. On the contrary, he was convinced
that the Allies intended to invade southeastern Sicily. Guzzoni's problem
was that the Italian Sixth Army was badly positioned to repel an enemy
invasion, and its units were unfit for combat; in some units officers did
not even know how to operate their own guns. Italian morale was dreadful, and the pragmatic Guzzoni knew there was too little time to alter the
deeply rooted inferiority complex that had pervaded the Italian Army
since the beginning of the war.

Guzzoni's dire warnings of the sorry state of Sicily's defenses went un-
heeded in Rome, where Mussolini had fallen victim to his own fantasies
about the invincibility of the Italian Army. Il Duce's response was to
boast that any invader would be smashed "at the water's edge."

After the debacle in Tunisia, Hitler seemed less inclined to sacrifice
German troops so casually in lost causes, and in response to Italian re-
quests for assistance agreed only to send the newly recreated Hermann
Göring Division to augment the also recently formed 15th Panzer Grenadier Division.* He also sent General Fridolin von Senger und Etterlin
to Sicily as the German liaison officer to Guzzoni and ordered a corps
headquarters positioned in southern Calabria to take over tactical command of all German forces if an invasion came. Its commander was General der Panzertruppen Hans Valentin Hube, a one-armed tank officer
with a brilliant combat record. When von Senger arrived, he too was appalled by the inadequacy of Sicily's defenses and was quick to perceive
that the woeful state of the Italian Army was a reflection of the deteriorating relations between Berlin and Rome.

---

*The original Hermann Göring Division was lost in Tunisia. A Luftwaffe unit
directly under the control of its namesake, the Hermann Göring was commanded by
the aggressive former commander of Göring's personal bodyguard, Lieutenant General Paul Conrath, who impressed Kesselring with his fervor to engage the enemy.
The 15th Panzer Grenadier Division was formed from disparate independent units
based on the island and the remnants of the 15th Panzer Grenadier Division who had
managed to escape from Tunisia.

By early July the two German divisions were in position to assist in repelling an invasion. The problem was that Kesselring and Guzzoni disagreed over the defense of the island. Recognizing that he could not protect the entire Sicilian coastline, Guzzoni wanted to form a powerful counterattack force, utilizing as its core the armor of the two German divisions. These mobile forces would be positioned in the eastern half of Sicily, safely out of range of naval gunfire and poised to deliver a crushing blow while the invaders were still vulnerable.*

Although he too believed the Allies were likely to target southeastern Sicily, Kesselring felt obliged to cover a possible invasion of western Sicily with a portion of the 15th Panzer Grenadier. In the back of his mind was the dispersion of German forces in the all-too-likely event that the Italian Army in Sicily defected to the Allies. Thus the 15th Panzer Grenadier Division was split into three kampfgruppen and placed in several positions across the breadth of Sicily. One of the kampfgruppen was sent to eastern Sicily to augment a battle group of the Hermann Göring Division, which had arrived minus nearly a third of its combat strength.

IN EARLY JUNE THE ISLANDS OF PANTELLERIA and Lampedusa, midway between Sicily and Tunisia, were heavily bombed for a week prior to being seized by the British 1st Division, whose sole casualty was a soldier bitten by a mule. Pantelleria's excellent airfield was quickly turned into an important Allied tactical air support base.

The HUSKY plan called for the Allied air forces to conduct around-the-clock bombing of targets in Sicily, Sardinia, Italy, and elsewhere in the Mediterranean, with the object of neutralizing the Axis air capability. The effort was an exceptional success: both Axis air forces were left a shambles, with the Italian force all but extinct as a fighting unit and the Luftwaffe severely crippled from the terrible hammering by Tedder's air forces.

By late June feverish activities to prepare for HUSKY at bases all over the Mediterranean began winding down, and final preparations were completed for D-Day. The invasion forces all staged from the Middle East and North Africa, with the exception of the U.S. 45th Infantry and 1st Canadian divisions, which sailed directly from the United States and Scotland to form part of the vast battle armada of nearly 2,600 naval vessels that participated in HUSKY. Under the command of Vice Admiral H.

---

*The same strategy Rommel attempted to employ in the defense of Normandy.

Kent Hewitt and Admiral Sir Bertram Ramsay, eight naval task forces were formed for the invasion on 10 July. To keep the Axis guessing for as long as possible, the convoys in the western Mediterranean began heading east toward the Aegean before sweeping north toward Sicily at the last possible moment.

THE INVASION OF SICILY BEGAN TRAGICALLY when the British glider force that was to land on the island ahead of the seaborne forces encountered dangerously high winds, smoke from the island, and heavy flak both from enemy guns and, unexpectedly, from friendly naval vessels which mistakenly fired on the aerial armada. Extremely poor coordination and cooperation between the air forces and the naval and ground forces had for some time been the object of serious contention, and the air plan was vague about specific support to the invasion troops, aerial routes, and other important details. To make matters worse, the aircrews had very little training in the tricky business of airborne operations and the discipline of convoy flying. Moreover, the navigational devices in use at this early stage of the war were crude, and it was specifically as a result of the several fiascos in Sicily that more sophisticated equipment was later developed.

Patton became so concerned about the lack of cooperation from the airmen that he pleaded with Hewitt for U.S. Navy carrier support. "You can get your Navy planes to do anything you want, but we can't get the Air Force to do a goddam thing," he declared. Hewitt was in no position to oblige, and both invasion forces sailed from North Africa without the slightest idea of what air support they would have on D-Day, what the aerial routes for the airborne and glider forces would be, or even if there would be any support forthcoming at all.

The combination of wind and mishaps left the British formations in complete disarray. Many were thrown off course, and most of the gliders were released too soon and thus forced to ditch into the heavy seas or land far short of their assigned landing zones. The few Red Devils* who did make it to Sicily that night were forced to land in terrain never meant for glider landings. Some were shot down, still others exploded on impact. Stone walls that dotted the landscape took a further toll. Of the 147 gliders involved, nearly half crash-landed in the sea, drowning 252 Red Devils. As the dawn rose over Syracuse Bay, the incredible sight of doz-

---

*The nickname given the 1st Airborne Division by the Germans in North Africa.

ens of gliders dotting the water with men standing silently on their wings came into view. Inexperience, wind, and enemy flak were a fatal combination that turned the operation into a first-class disaster.

The fifty-nine gliders that actually made landfall were scattered over a twenty-five mile area of southeastern Sicily. A mere twelve landed on their assigned landing zones near the brigade objective, the Ponte Grande Bridge outside Syracuse. Instead of a force of over 2,000 men to seize Ponte Grande Bridge by a coup de main, a tiny platoon-sized ad hoc force of infantry, engineers, and glidermen managed to seize the bridge from its Italian defenders. Reinforced to eighty-seven men by dawn on D-Day, the small unit fought off Italian attacks for seven hours. Finally the surviving fifteen men were forced to surrender. Within the hour they were freed by a patrol from the 5th Division, and the bridge was retaken a half hour later. As one participant recalled, "The Italians, to judge by the numbers of their dead who littered the bridge . . . had paid a very high price for their half hour or so of triumph."

The U.S. 82d Airborne fared little better when the winds and flak, both enemy and friendly, dissolved the neat V-formations into a confused jumble over a large area of southeastern Sicily. More than 3,000 paratroopers were scheduled to land in four drop zones northeast of Gela to establish an airhead to protect the 1st Division from an expected enemy counterattack from the north. Instead, the men of the 505th were scattered over a thousand-square-mile area, including some who landed in the Eighth Army sector.

Among the missing was the regimental commander, Colonel Gavin, who landed some twenty-five miles east of Gela. Rounding up a small band of eight other paratroopers, Gavin heeded one of the first lessons taught him at West Point: he began marching toward the sound of the guns. Their ordeal as they attempted to reach the Gela battlefield included an intense firefight with a large Italian patrol. The last man to cover the withdrawal of the American force was Gavin, who was heard to state, "This is a hell of a place for a regimental commander to be."

Although isolated from his men, frustrated, and uncertain of the situation he faced, Gavin would have been somewhat less apprehensive if he had known of the panic his men were creating. The paratroopers quickly discovered that by assuming a guerrilla role they could raise havoc all over southeastern Sicily. Enemy patrols were ambushed, telephone lines cut, and weapons captured and turned on the enemy, leaving most convinced they were being attacked by a massive force that was all around them. Reports began filtering in to Guzzoni's Sixth Army headquarters in Enna of parachute and glider troops all over southern Sicily. According to the reports, "thousands" of parachutists were roaming the hills and valleys. Italian estimates ran to as many as 20,000 to 30,000 paratroopers. Soon the German high command in Berlin was warning that measures would have to be developed to counter the effects of parachutists such as this American force, which had "made themselves known in a particularly unpleasant manner."

UNLIKE THE AIRBORNE AND GLIDER OPERATIONS, the amphibious invasion of Sicily that began a few hours later was a great success. The first units began landing in the Eighth Army sector shortly after midnight. Although considerable confusion prevailed on the 5th Division beaches, the remainder of the landings went smoothly. Special Air Service, Commando, and Royal Marine units slipped ashore and silenced key targets. British casualties were exceptionally light, and by dawn the landing was so successful that a jubilant Montgomery at once exhorted the commander of 30th Corps to move inland, while the 13th Corps was urged up the coast toward Catania without delay.

The first of the Seventh Army landings took place at Licata at 0330 hours, and Truscott's 3d Division, meeting little resistance, was soon in control of the city. Soon after the landings began the telephone in a beach bunker rang and was answered by war correspondent Michael Chinigo of the International News Service, who happened to be passing by. In fluent Italian he assured the anxious Italian general on the other end that rumors of an Allied invasion were entirely false.

Major General Troy H. Middleton's 45th Infantry Division encountered serious problems in landing one of its three regimental combat teams near Scoglitti. The 157th Regimental Combat Team not only went ashore too far to the west and in complete disarray, but some landing craft came to grief on the rocks, drowning twenty-seven men, while others became mired in sandbars offshore. Enemy resistance was mixed: in some places it was stubborn, in others the Italian defenders surrendered quickly. By dark on D-Day the 45th Division had managed to push nearly seven miles inland.

The most important and difficult of the three American landings took place at Gela, where a Ranger force under Lieutenant Colonel William O. Darby created a powerful diversion by attacking the town while the principal 1st Division landings were made along the beaches of the plain of Gela to the east. By mid-morning, after a short but vicious battle with the Italian Livorno Division, Darby's Rangers had cleared Gela, as the

1st Division began linking up with scattered elements of the 82d Airborne that were beginning to make their presence felt.

The U.S. landings brought an immediate response from the Hermann Göring Division, which formed into two task forces and launched its expected counterattack against the 1st Division from the hills overlooking Gela. General Conrath had hoped to launch his attacks before the American force could establish a beachhead, but the deployment of both forces was severely delayed because of Allied air harassment and a monumental traffic jam on the narrow, winding roads, and it was not until many hours later that these forces went into action. Conrath split his forces into two kampfgruppen: a tank-heavy force that would attack from the north and an infantry-heavy second force that would thrust from the northeast. They would converge at the junction of Route 115 and the road to Niscemi. Known as Piano Lupo, this key road junction was guarded by heavily fortified bunkers whose original Italian defenders had been ousted by a small force of Gavin's paratroopers and 1st Division infantry who had banded together into an improvised ad hoc force. Now under American control, Piano Lupo became an ideal blocking position from which to repel an enemy counterattack.

The tank-heavy kampfgruppe moving south from Niscemi was devastated by heavy and extremely accurate naval gunfire from U.S. warships in the Bay of Gela and harassed by the U.S. infantry and paratroop force. Within minutes of attacking, the Germans were forced to withdraw in chaos back toward Niscemi, where Conrath would develop fresh plans for a second counterattack the following morning. A 1st Division officer gleefully radioed his superior, "Tanks are withdrawing; it seems we are too much for them."

A similar attack by an Italian armored force, Mobile Group E, was also smashed, while to the east, from Biscari, the infantry-heavy task force of the Hermann Göring Division had little success against the 45th Division. Its commander was so ineffective and cooperation between tanks and infantry so poor that he was summarily relieved by General Conrath that night after abandoning his troops. The supporting Tiger tanks found themselves unable to maneuver effectively away from the narrow Sicilian roads and sustained heavy losses.

During the morning of D-Day a force of the Italian Livorno Division attacked at Gela with an antiquated World War I tank force from the north and an infantry force from the northwest. Some of the Renault tanks penetrated into Gela, where a heated battle took place before the survivors were driven back into the hills. The infantry, marching in nineteenth-century parade-ground formation, were slaughtered on the plain northwest of the city. For a unit rated one of the best in Sicily, the Livorno commanders' tactics were a sad illustration of the ineptitude of the Italian Army.

Inside Gela the Italian tanks tangled with Darby's Rangers in a lethal game of hide-and-seek. Using the buildings as cover, the Rangers, now in the role of defenders, employed hand grenades and rocket launchers against the tanks. Some Rangers worked from the rooftops, throwing stick grenades at the Italians. Two of them ran out of grenades, lugged fifteen-pound blocks of TNT to the top of the building, and dropped them on the tanks. During this engagement Darby won the Distinguished Service Cross for personally destroying an Italian tank. Several days later Patton offered Darby a regiment in the 45th Division and a promotion to full colonel. Darby declined, saying he preferred to remain with his beloved Rangers. An amazed Patton wrote in his diary that this was the first time he had ever seen a man turn down a promotion. "Darby is a really great soldier."

After their first attack was rebuffed by the 1st Battalion, 180th Infantry Regiment, the Germans regrouped and attacked a second time. This time they were on the verge of exploiting a dangerous gap between the 1st and 45th divisions that could easily have placed the Big Red One beaches east of Gela in grave jeopardy. Once again, German leadership was found seriously wanting, as the Germans panicked and fled to the rear. Thus the one German opportunity to have seriously interfered with the Gela and Scoglitti landings on D-Day was badly bungled.

Gela had been envisioned as the most important and difficult of the three American landing sites, and it was not chance that had led Patton to select Terry Allen's 1st Division for the Gela landings.* Early in the HUSKY planning it had been intended to use the green 36th Infantry Division (a Texas National Guard unit) as one of the U.S. invasion forces. Patton already had a similar unit in the 45th Division, and did not want two-thirds of his invasion force consisting of untested divisions. Patton pleaded to Eisenhower that "I want those [1st Division] sons-of-bitches.

---

*Patton was no stranger to either Allen or the 1st Division. Both had come under his command in Tunisia. The stormy friendship between Patton and Allen dated back to early in the interwar years when both were still cavalrymen, and led to Allen's division being given the toughest job in Sicily. Omar Bradley, by contrast, had little use for Allen and held him responsible for the 1st Division's notorious lack of discipline in North Africa. "He was possibly the most difficult commander I had to handle throughout the war," Bradley later wrote.

I won't go on without them!" Eisenhower acceded and the 1st Division quickly demonstrated the astuteness of Patton's decision.

BY THE END OF D-DAY THE BRITISH HAD YET to make serious contact with German forces, and the only major engagement had come at Gela, where the Hermann Göring Division and the Italians had failed miserably to drive the 1st Division back into the sea.

So ended the first unsuccessful attempts by Axis forces in Sicily to crush the invasion, and while there was indeed cause for elation at the success of the Allied landings, it was equally evident the counterattacks at Gela had been badly bungled. Even though the Allied foothold across a broad front had already left Guzzoni's strategy for the defense of Sicily a useless vestige of wishful thinking, the real test was yet to come.

FOUR

The Battle for Sicily

DURING THE FIRST TWO DAYS OF OPERATION HUSKY 80,000 men, 7,000 vehicles, and 900 guns came across the beaches. Men and equipment streamed ashore in seemingly endless waves. The exception was at Gela, where mines, sandbars, and occasional but furious Axis air attacks slowed the landing of artillery and armor.

The Allied glider landings did not surprise Guzzoni, whose first orders were to counterattack the expected landings at Gela and to reinforce the threatened naval bases at Syracuse and Augusta. He considered it a hopeless waste of time to attempt to react to each of the many Allied landings. The best he could hope to accomplish was to commit his reserves to the most critical sectors. While Syracuse represented the most serious weakness, Guzzoni believed that the forces already in place— Group Schmalz (the kampfgruppe positioned in the Catania sector, consisting of panzer and panzer grenadier units of the Hermann Göring and 15th Panzer Grenadier divisions) and the Napoli Division—could prevent a successful British thrust into the plain of Catania. He therefore ordered Paul Conrath's Hermann Göring Division to launch the main counterattack against the Gela landings.

Guzzoni was dismayed, however, to find that by early on 12 July the defenses protecting the Syracuse fortress area had ignominiously collapsed and that the breakdown was rapidly spreading in the direction of Augusta. The British, spearheaded by the 5th Division, were everywhere consolidating their grip and thrusting to the north. The 30th Corps quickly cleared the Pachino peninsula of what little resistance remained, while the 23d Armoured Brigade, under the control of the 51st (Highland) Division, was outside the mountain city of Vizzini by dusk on 12 July. On the same day the Canadians made contact with the U.S. 45th

Division at Ragusa.* The port of Syracuse was captured undamaged, and with the most important logistic base safely in his hands, Montgomery could concentrate on exploiting his success by launching a drive up the east coast toward Messina before the Axis defenders could react.

The crucial day was D plus one, when the Hermann Göring Division unleashed a furious armored thrust designed to drive the U.S. 1st Division back into the sea and roll up the 45th Division flank. Its attack began in conjunction with yet another attack against Gela by the Italian Livorno Division. The axis of advance was the same as D-Day: the infantry-heavy eastern task force, supported by a Tiger tank company, again attacked the 45th Division, while the armor-heavy thrust from Niscemi was spearheaded by medium Mark IV panzers, aided by Axis aircraft which pounded the fleet and beach areas.

Terry Allen had only four infantry battalions in reserve at Gela, and the landing of the supporting armor and artillery was delayed. This time the Germans penetrated the thinly held front in several places. At the 1st Division command post Allen began receiving reports of panzers overrunning his positions across the Gela front. The Italians were halted outside Gela by heavy artillery and mortar fire. Tanks of the Hermann Göring and Livorno divisions launched parallel attacks down both sides of the road to Ponte Olivo airfield. Patton witnessed the action and demanded of a young naval liaison officer, "If you can connect me with your goddam Navy, tell them for God's sake to drop some shell fire on the road." Guns from the cruiser U.S.S. *Boise* began doing just that.

Conrath's panzers managed to debouch onto the open plain of Gela and headed straight for the beaches. A dangerous gap had been found, and the 1st Division was now in mortal danger unless the panzers' thrust could be contained. The embattled Americans now became defenders as the most important of the battles raged along Route 115. The last line of defense became a small tank element of Combat Command B, 2d Armored Division, plus an artillery unit whose tubes were fully depressed to provide direct fire. As other tanks came ashore, an officer reported to the Combat Command B commander, Colonel I. D. White, and asked what the plans and orders were. White brusquely replied, "Plans hell! This may be Custer's last stand." In the end, it was the valiant stand of this small force, supported by naval gunfire, that defeated the Hermann Göring Division only a few hundred yards from the Gela beaches.

---

*While awaiting the arrival of the Canadians, several members of the 45th Division amused themselves by manning the town switchboard and responding to anxious calls from Italian garrisons asking for information about the invasion.

Ultimately, no German tank penetrated beyond the Gela highway. The fighting was so close and so intense that the naval guns were temporarily silenced for fear of hitting friendly forces. The German commanders found their attack had run its course. Unable to counter the relentless hail of fire, they began slowly to pull back toward the foothills to the north. As they did so the U.S. Navy supplied the coup de grace by harrassing them with naval gunfire. On the battlefield the Germans left behind the burning wreckage of sixteen panzers, whose oily black smoke served as mute evidence of the fierce battle. The official naval historian later wrote that Gela was the first time the U.S. Navy had provided close support to a land battle in what he called "a shining example of Army-Navy coöperation."

Similar battles raged into the following day around Piano Lupo and along the Niscemi road before the Germans withdrew. Gavin later praised the "remarkable performance" of the airborne as a small band of paratroopers helped to accomplish the mission of the entire regimental combat team.

To the east near Biscari, Colonel Gavin and a small paratroop force had arrived in time to establish defensive positions on Biazza Ridge overlooking the Biscari road and the Biscari-Gela road junction. There they found themselves by chance the only Allied force between the Germans and their unhindered exploitation of the exposed left flank of the 1st Division. Against Gavin was the entire eastern kampfgruppe of the Hermann Göring Division: over seven hundred infantry, the Tiger tank company, and a supporting artillery battalion.

The eastern kampfgruppe had failed to resolve their leadership problems, and although they exerted considerable pressure on the airborne, the German advance was not aggressive, thus enabling Gavin's tiny force to hold out throughout the day despite steadily mounting casualties. Gavin knew the odds were against him but refused to budge, telling his men: "We're staying on this goddamned ridge—no matter what happens."

The airborne had acquired two pack 75-mm howitzers, both of which were employed as direct-fire antitank weapons. Nevertheless, by evening the situation had become very grim. Sudden relief arrived in the form of six Sherman tanks sent by Bradley, which appeared to the accompaniment of loud cheers from the weary paratroopers. Throughout the day stray paratroopers had materialized to join the fray, and at dusk Gavin decided the time had come to strike back. With the Shermans in support, he audaciously counterattacked the Germans. A Tiger tank was captured intact, as were twelve 120-mm mortars. Although the Germans had not been inclined to be aggressive, their location still posed a grave threat to the right flank of the 1st Division.

Neither side knew it, but a decision to break off the counterattack had already been made and the Hermann Göring Division ordered to withdraw inland, where they would later man new defensive positions along what came to be known as the Etna Line. Syracuse had fallen easily to the British, and Guzzoni had quickly recognized that the gravest peril was now in the east, where the Axis defenders were under increasing pressure to prevent a breakthrough to the plain of Catania. Unless the Etna Line was manned soon, the road to Messina would be undefended if, as was increasingly evident, Group Schmalz and the Napoli Division were unable to contain the British advance north of Syracuse.

Meanwhile, the action at Gela had been a near-run thing, and had it not been for the countless instances of American bravery and initiative in the early stages, the German counterattacks would have succeeded. Conrath had lost his only opportunity to strike a killing blow, and the next day he delivered a stinging rebuke to the men of the Hermann Göring Division, threatening to impose death sentences in serious cases of cowardice or ineptitude.

The American triumph at Gela was marred, however, when an aerial convoy bearing the 504th Regimental Combat Team, which was to parachute into the Gela bridgehead, arrived at night, immediately after heavy Axis air attacks on the fleet. It was shot to pieces by friendly naval and ground fire despite warnings of its arrival. One hundred and forty-one paratroopers and aircrewmen were killed, twenty-three aircraft were lost, and thirty-seven others were severely damaged. The incident cast a pall over the future of Allied airborne operations.

The Gela battles were the key to the Axis defense of Sicily. Slim as it was, the Germans' only hope of defeating the invasion lay in a decisive counterattack on the beaches. If the Seventh Army could be severely disrupted or even defeated, the Eighth Army's left flank would have been unprotected and the Allied air forces would have been denied the three important Gela airfields. The stern defense of the Gela beachhead by the 1st and 45th Infantry divisions, supported by Gavin's airborne regiment, doomed the Axis to eventual defeat. The superior forces of the Allied armies were free to continue pouring men and matériel ashore.

The abortive counterattacks at Gela were witnessed by General von Senger, who, as historian Charles B. McDonald has written, "saw the panzers crumble before the American fire and looked beyond them to the spectacle of hundreds of ships lining the horizon . . . [and] acknowledged to himself that Sicily was lost."

HITLER QUICKLY ACCEPTED THE FACT THAT the Allied invasion of Sicily was a fait accompli which Axis forces had no hope of reversing. In the early days of the campaign the leadership of the Hermann Göring Division, with the possible exception of Conrath, had not even begun to live up to the forceful reputation the division had acquired in North Africa. The shining exception was Colonel Wilhelm Schmalz, who had turned out to be the star of the division. His superlative leadership was the principal reason why Dempsey's 13th Corps was slow in driving north of Syracuse to the plain of Catania. Indeed, Schmalz's beleaguered kampfgruppe had become the *only* battle-worthy Axis force between Eighth Army and Messina, as the Italians had collapsed. However, the Germans had no intention of ceding Sicily without a fight, and Hans Valentin Hube's XIV Panzer Corps headquarters was ordered to the island, as were elements of the elite 1st Parachute Division, which was alerted to drop into the plain of Catania to reinforce Group Schmalz.

BY D PLUS TWO THE ALLIES WERE POISED to exploit the absence of a coordinated Axis defense of the island. Both Army commanders, however, still found themselves without either a firm plan of action or even guidance from Alexander, who preferred to await further developments before asserting himself. (After the war Alexander indicated that he never had any intention of doing so until Seventh Army had seized the Gela airfields and Eighth Army had control of the ports of Syracuse and Augusta and the plain of Catania.)

Alexander was powerfully influenced by the conviction that American fighting ability was still inferior to that of the British army. He refused to acknowledge that the U.S. Army now fighting in Sicily bore scant resemblance to the army that had been humiliated at Kasserine five months earlier. The 15th Army Group commander entered the Sicily campaign believing firmly that the troops of Eighth Army were more experienced and reliable than any in Patton's Seventh Army.

What passed for strategy was Alexander's idée fixe that Patton would act as the shield in his left hand while Eighth Army served as the sword in his right. One of Montgomery's senior staff officers has written that "the two armies were left largely to develop their operations in the manner which seemed most propitious in the prevailing circumstances." The crux of the matter was that Alexander was simply not prepared to entrust Seventh Army with anything more than a secondary role in the campaign.

Bradley's later recollection of the strategy of the campaign was that the first objective was to push inland, take the high ground, protect the beaches, and get the airfields. Once securely established, the Allies were to cut Sicily in half, face east, and roll up all Axis forces trapped between them and Mount Etna and the eastern coast. How this was to occur was left unanswered. Beyond this generalized purpose lay an assumption that the overall Allied objective was Messina. During the pre-invasion planning AFHQ called Messina the key to the island, even though Alexander never saw fit prior to D-Day to provide even the vaguest guidance; nor did he anticipate the speed with which the two armies would push inland from the bridgeheads. In short, Alexander did nothing to prepare either himself or his two army commanders to fight the campaign in Sicily. The inevitable result was that his two strong-willed subordinates began to act independently of Alexander and each other.

On 12 July Montgomery proposed what Alexander had envisioned all along: that Eighth Army make the main effort to cut Sicily in two; and he found ready acceptance from the Allied ground Commander-in-Chief. However, Montgomery's proposed route of advance crossed the inter-army boundary and interfered with the route of advance of the U.S. 45th Division. Montgomery signaled Alexander that he wanted the troublesome boundary line moved farther to the west. Neither Alexander nor Montgomery recognized that the 45th Division was not only better prepared but in a much better position to carry out this task.

Alexander therefore ordered Patton to hand over the Vizzini-Caltagirone highway to Eighth Army. As a result, Bradley was forced to move the entire 45th Division back to the Gela beaches and then north to new positions on the left flank of the 1st Division.

In cutting the 45th Division out of the action, neither Alexander nor Montgomery ever acknowledged that 30th Corps had yet to capture Vizzini, which the Hermann Göring Division successfully defended until the morning of 15 July. Although the order disgusted Patton, he complied without protest. Bradley was thunderstruck. "My God," he told Patton, "you can't let him do that." Bradley believed this was an instance where Patton, as the Seventh Army commander, ought to have resisted Alexander's order, and perhaps he should have. But the root of the problem was neither Monty's impetuousness nor Patton's apathy but Alexander's unwillingness to take control of the ground campaign at its most crucial moment.

So ludicrous was the situation that once the orders were issued transferring the disputed boundary and Route 124 to Montgomery, the Canadians encountered stiff resistance while the 45th Division stood help-
lessly by, unable to come to their aid even though their artillery was
within one mile of the highway. What the better-positioned American
infantry, with the advantage of close artillery support, could have accomplished with relative ease became an ordeal for the Canadians, who
lacked not only artillery but tanks and transport. (One of the least known
but most crucial factors throughout the campaign was the chronic shortage of motor transport within Eighth Army, which forced the British infantry to advance on foot in the boiling sun of the Sicilian summer where
temperatures exceeding one hundred degrees were the norm.*)

Memories of this frustrating incident haunted Bradley for the remainder of his life. In his autobiography, *A General's Life,* he recalled
often wondering, "If I received such orders now, would I really obey
them?" Undoubtedly Bradley would have agreed with Montgomery's remark to Patton during the campaign. In a direct reference to Alexander,
whom he esteemed as a friend but disdained as a commander-in-chief,
he said, "George, let me give you some advice. If you get an order from
Army Group that you don't like, why, ignore it. That's what I do."

Alexander's decision effectively reduced the American role to that of a
protective shield on the left, while Eighth Army was charged with carrying out the conquest of Sicily. In so doing, Montgomery split his army
instead of concentrating on a decisive drive to Messina via the plain of
Catania. In the rugged mountains of Sicily there was no possibility of
mutual support between Oliver Leese's 30th Corps, operating inland,
and Miles Dempsey's 13th Corps, whose mission was to attack up the
east coast. As the U.S. Army official historians would later write, "No
enemy force of any size opposed either the 1st or 45th Divisions. . . .
General Bradley . . . was ready and willing to take Route 124 and Enna,
thus encircling the German defenders facing Eighth Army. In North Africa the remainder of the 82d Airborne and 2d Armored Divisions lay
ready to sail for Sicily to reinforce the American effort." Instead, when

---

*Malaria was also rampant in Sicily and claimed more casualties (11,500 in Eighth
Army and 9,800 in Seventh Army) than the enemy. The majority of the British transport vehicles did not land in Sicily until after D plus five. The situation might have
been alleviated had there been animal transport. The original Eighth Army order of
battle called for seven companies of pack mules, but a staff officer made the foolish
decision to cancel the requirement. By contrast, former cavalry officer Truscott made
very effective use of improvised animal transport in the 3d Division.

Alexander upheld Montgomery's unilateral decision, "for all practical purposes, Seventh Army could have stayed on the beaches; its brilliant assault achievements were completely nullified by the new British plan."

This was the first of several squandered opportunities that would have altered the course of the battle and ended the campaign sooner. Bold leadership was needed but not forthcoming, with the unhappy result that Montgomery was permitted to dictate Allied strategy because it came close to Alexander's own imprecise, ill-defined ideas.

NOT ONLY WAS THE GREAT BOUNDARY LINE dispute opened on 13 July, but on the same day Montgomery initiated a bold plan to deliver an unstoppable British thrust to Messina. Aware of Schmalz's thinly held defenses, he ordered the 1st Parachute Brigade of the 1st Airborne Division to seize the strategically important Primosole Bridge by coup de main the night of 13–14 July. The bridge was situated some five miles south of the port city of Catania, where Route 114 crossed the Simeto River. Once the British gained control of the bridge, there were no enemy forces to the north to impede a rapid advance to Messina.

While the airborne held the bridge, the British 50th Division, reinforced by the 4th Armoured Brigade, was to spearhead a drive north along Route 114 and link up with them by nightfall on 14 July. This powerful airborne-infantry-armored task force would then establish a bridgehead north of the river and complete the operation by seizing Catania the following day. The 50th Division offensive was to be supported by No. 3 Commando, which was to seize another important bridge north of Lentini.

Once again, a major night Allied airborne operation failed disastrously. The problems were all too familiar: fire from friendly antiaircraft guns, flak, inexperienced aircrews, and poor navigational devices. Of 145 aircraft employed in the operation, a mere 30 managed to release their troops on the correct drop zone. The remainder who made it to Sicily were wide of the mark by anything from one-half to twenty miles. Only 4 of the 19 gliders found their landing zone. Thus, instead of a formidable force of over 1,800 paratroops at Primosole Bridge, only 300 ever saw action there. Their equipment met with a similar fate and became a prime resupply source for the German airborne.

The British did not learn until the following morning that the bridge was not held lightly by the Italians, as supposed, but by tough German paratroopers of the 1st Parachute Division. The first German element had arrived the evening of 12 July when a regiment landed west of the bridge and immediately reinforced Group Schmalz outside Lentini. The timing was perfect for the hard-pressed defenders. Schmalz now possessed the strength to seriously delay the advance of the 50th Division and upset the timetable for the relief of the British at Primosole Bridge.

Also unknown to Allied intelligence, only hours before the British airborne operation a German parachute machine-gun battalion had arrived and established positions south of Primosole Bridge, along the exact route to be taken by the troop carriers. Both friendly and enemy flak helped turn the landings into a chaotic scene that one trooper described as "Dante's Inferno." Flak and artillery and machine-gun fire filled the northern plain with a Fourth of July atmosphere. Particularly vulnerable were the large Horsa gliders, which became sitting ducks for the German gunners emplaced south of the bridge. One glider crash-landed adjacent to the bridge, and the pilot and copilot were thrown through the broken Perspex windows of the cockpit. They were found mangled and bleeding on the grass. A paratroop lieutenant thanked God he had gone into battle by parachute, and not by glider.

Despite the chaos, a small force of British airborne troops managed to capture Primosole Bridge during the early morning hours of 14 July. The confusion during the remaining hours of darkness left the British unaware of the German paratroopers nearby. These were the only calm moments before what would later that day become one of the few encounters of World War II between opposing airborne forces. The outcome of Montgomery's gamble to seize Catania and end the campaign quickly hinged on seizure of the bridge and timely relief by the tank-infantry driving up Route 114 from Lentini.

Throughout the morning of 14 July Lieutenant-Colonel John D. Frost's 2d Parachute Battalion was completely out of contact with the British force at the bridge and was able to beat off a series of attacks by the German machine gunners. At noon the Germans struck back at the bridge. They were well aware of the vital importance of Primosole Bridge, and throughout the afternoon they initiated one counterattack after another to dislodge the British airborne. Again and again these attacks were beaten off, each time with decreasing success. As time ran out, there was no sign of the relief force. The beleaguered airborne did not know that the 50th Division had encountered stiff resistance from the newly reinforced Group Schmalz, which tenaciously delayed their advance in the rocky hills around Lentini.

By dusk the airborne at Primosole Bridge had long since lost radio contact with Eighth Army; as their ammunition ran out, the brigade commander, Brigadier Gerald Lathbury, was obliged to order the bridge abandoned.* He had held the bridge for longer than expected with only a fraction of his brigade. No more could be asked of them, and surrender was a senseless alternative. The survivors were ordered to infiltrate enemy lines in an attempt to join the remnants of Frost's battalion, which had managed to hold the high ground south of the river.

About 1930 hours the first tanks of the 4th Armoured Brigade rumbled into the woods south of the bridge, followed several hours later by a dirty and exhausted company of infantrymen of the 6th Battalion, the Durham Light Infantry Regiment. The next day the Durhams† launched the first of a series of costly attacks to retake the bridge from the German airborne, who used the vineyards along the north bank of the river to great advantage. Further reinforcements soon brought their numbers to some one thousand, and although the Durhams managed to recapture the bridge early on 16 July, they could not advance north to Catania. The entire Eighth Army advance had been reduced to what at times was a one- or two-battalion front, and such attacks were insufficient to dislodge the Germans. The vineyards became a landscape of death as the combat became so close and intense that it was often hand-to-hand, with bayonets, knives, and sometimes fists.

For five grim days the British failed time and time again to advance more than a token distance toward Catania. Even so, there was still time to have achieved Montgomery's objectives. Catania's handful of German defenders had long since been stripped away to reinforce Primosole Bridge, and the city was virtually undefended from a seaborne assault. With Montgomery's blessing, Dempsey planned to mount an amphibious end run into Catania with a reinforced brigade of the 5th Division, which certainly would have succeeded in trapping the Germans and opening the road to Messina. Inexplicably, the operation never took place. By 18 July Montgomery conceded that the plans to send the 13th Corps directly to Messina had failed, and he switched his main effort to the northwest, where 30th Corps was ordered to break the German defenses along the newly formed Etna Line and sweep around the northern edge

---

*After heavy losses No. 3 Commando was also forced to abandon the bridge north of Lentini, which the Germans did not have time to destroy during their retreat.

†The 151st Infantry Brigade of the 50th (Northumbrian) Division consisted of the 6th, 8th, and 9th battalions of the Durham Light Infantry, all veterans of the campaigns in North Africa. The 151st was usually referred to as the Durham Light Infantry Brigade.

of Mount Etna to the coast below Messina.* However, by shifting his main effort to the west, Montgomery had hopelessly split Eighth Army and unwittingly presented the Germans with an opportunity to delay the 30th Corps advance long enough to establish the Etna Line and thus deny the British any hope of cutting off Messina.

In spite of its lopsided superiority, Eighth Army was unable to capture Catania—a stunning and unnecessary failure. Catania was the key to the strategic prize of Messina, but an insignificant effort was made to employ close air support or naval gunfire from the numerous supporting warships offshore. Instead the British commanders elected to fight a stolid, one-dimensional battle that left them unable to dislodge the German paratroopers, who fought magnificently. Thus the Germans' brilliant defense thwarted the second favorable Allied opportunity to achieve a rapid and decisive victory in Sicily. First, there had been the boundary-line dispute at Vizzini, and now, a second opportunity was lost at Catania. Nearly forty years later John Frost justifiably recalled this forgotten battle as "bitterly disappointing."

INEVITABLY, PATTON WEARIED OF HIS ARMY playing second fiddle to Montgomery and the British. Stung by Eisenhower's criticism of his role in the airborne tragedy the night of 11 July and frustrated by Alexander's clear bias in favor of Eighth Army, Patton decided the time had come to take matters into his own hands. On 17 July he arrived unexpectedly at Alexander's headquarters in North Africa to make a personal plea for a greater American role.

Patton shrewdly recognized that the British had a bear by the tail on the plain of Catania and that geography and Montgomery's influence made it fruitless to attempt to alter the role of Eighth Army. However, he most certainly could gain control of his own destiny by getting a green light from Alexander and letting the mobility of his army do the rest. Alexander was clearly caught off guard and was hardly in a position to refuse Patton after giving a free rein to Montgomery. He agreed to Patton's plan to use II Corps for a drive to the north coast, near Términi, to cut the island in two, while the remainder of Seventh Army was detached for a secondary (and largely useless) offensive to clear western Sicily.

---

*Unfortunately, very little has been written about the Sicily campaign—including the British official history, which is woefully inadequate—and while they were alive no one ever asked either Montgomery or Dempsey about the decision to abandon the end run to Catania.

Patton did not bother telling Alexander that this included the capture of Palermo, the capital of Sicily. In reality, the drive to the north coast was a clever ploy by Patton to maneuver Seventh Army into a position to capture Messina.

At that moment Patton's army was in an ideal position to break through the Etna Line and encircle the Germans, who were now giving the British 30th Corps the same bloody nose they had administered on the plain of Catania to 13th Corps. In the rough, mountainous terrain of central Sicily, where the road net was poor and vehicular mobility severely limited, the Germans were able to mount an effective defense, giving ground when necessary and then forcing their attackers to start all over again. Every advance became an expensive proposition.

The Etna Line defenses, however, were incomplete and were weakest precisely where Alexander might have used II Corps to break them and thus tighten a noose from which the only escape was retreat or surrender. For the second time during the campaign Alexander had an opportunity to strike a killing blow with Seventh Army, but again he failed to act, letting his prejudice overrule common sense.

For his drive into western Sicily Patton formed a Provisional Corps consisting of the 82d Airborne, 2d Armored, and the 3d Infantry divisions under the command of his trusted deputy, Major General Geoffrey Keyes. This force rapidly crushed all Italian resistance in its path. The 3d Division, whose troops had undergone exceptionally rigorous pre-invasion training, accomplished the amazing feat of marching over one hundred miles through formidable mountainous terrain in a little over seventy-two hours.* Palermo fell on 21 July, and the GIs entering the capital city were greeted by thousands of flag-waving, cheering Sicilians.

The capture of Palermo was of no strategic importance; its real significance was its headline value in the world's press. Bradley viewed it as a vain and useless exercise that merely delayed a drive on Messina, but Patton shrewdly saw Palermo as a means of restoring the confidence of American troops in themselves and in the process calling attention to their exploits in Sicily—publicity which, up to then, had been largely reserved for Montgomery and the British.

While the press focused on Palermo and the sweep into western Sicily, II Corps, with little fanfare, was thrusting toward the northern coast of

---

*Major General Lucian K. Truscott, the division's tough commander, insisted that his infantry learn to increase their marching ability from three to five miles per hour. The successful result was called the "Truscott trot."

the island. On 23 July the 45th Division completed its mission of cutting Sicily in two, while on their right, Terry Allen's 1st Division captured Enna and Petralia. Patton lost no time ordering II Corps to begin a new offensive along the north coast. When they began to encounter stiff resistance from the newly arrived 29th Panzer Grenadier Division, Patton sensed that the 45th Division needed a rest and replaced them with the 3d Division. To the south Allen's 1st Division also turned east and began a similar offensive along Route 120, one of only two east-west interior roads in northern Sicily.

To Patton's amazement, Montgomery proposed at a meeting of the Allied ground commanders on 25 July at Syracuse that Seventh Army rather than Eighth Army capture Messina.* Although outwardly delighted, Patton reacted to Mongomery's plan with deep suspicion, believing there was undoubtedly some ulterior motive he was unable to fathom. The truth was that Montgomery had by then accepted the likelihood that the British would never be properly positioned to capture Messina and had decided that by implementing a coordinated Anglo-American offensive Patton could do so and end the campaign. In the years since the war, in both books and films, much has been made of the alleged intense rivalry between the two commanders for the bragging rights to Messina. The truth is that the rivalry was largely a myth. The only rivalry that existed was in the mind of Patton, who simply never accepted that Montgomery would willingly grant an American army the prize of Messina.†

Certainly Patton's distrust was by no means unfounded. Ever since the D-Day landings Montgomery had behaved as if the campaign were a British war, with the Americans there solely for his support. His tactics at Vizzini, where he imperiously usurped Bradley's boundary (earning him the everlasting enmity of the soft-spoken American), and his manipulation of a pliant Alexander, who granted his every wish, was an arrogant assertion that only the British could win the important battles in Sicily. What Patton in his frustration never grasped was that by 25 July this was no longer the same cocksure Montgomery who had only days

---

*On 13 July Alexander had given Eighth Army the exclusive use of the four roads leading to Messina, which effectively banned Seventh Army from any participation in its capture.

†Especially misleading is the film *Patton*, which depicts an angry Montgomery encountering a smirking Patton in a square in Messina and being forced to watch in humiliation as Patton is greeted as the conquering hero by the populace. The incident is complete fantasy.

earlier envisioned a quick and cheap victory, and that the farthest thing from his mind was to claim Messina for the British.

For all his outward arrogance, which infuriated most Americans, Montgomery was first and foremost an honorable man and a professional soldier. He had learned in the trenches of France during World War I to abhor the senseless waste of men so casually practiced by the British leadership. In Sicily he demonstrated that he would not jeopardize the Allied effort for the sake of personal glory.

Even if he had wanted to act otherwise, Montgomery's strategy of fighting separate battles with each of his corps was on the verge of bankruptcy after the calamitous failure to break through to Catania. Thus what appeared to the Americans to be a sweeping change of heart was in reality nothing less than a sobering awareness that this campaign was not going to be won by a spectacular unilateral British advance to Messina. To the contrary, without strong American pressure against the northern end of the Etna Line, Montgomery's left hook around Mount Etna would have left 30th Corps vulnerable to a counterattack from the northwest.

Not only was Montgomery fighting separate corps battles, but because of the large frontages and the harshness of the terrain, each of the divisions was also fighting its own independent battle. Instead of "hustling" the Germans, as he had predicted to Alexander, the four divisional offensives all developed unfavorably as the Germans savagely resisted all attempts to crack their defenses along the northern edge of the plain of Catania.

BY THE THIRD WEEK OF THE CAMPAIGN the Germans had skillfully carried out a succession of delaying actions by using the mountain terrain to maximum advantage. Hube had managed to tighten his defenses to a point where the Etna Line now ran from Catania to Adrano, northwest to Troina, and then to the north coast west of St. Ágata where it was called the San Fratello Line. The twin keys to collapsing the German defenses were at Adrano in the Eighth Army sector and Troina in the American sector. Both were mountain towns from which ran the only roads toward Messina. The sudden loss of either would have left the Germans open to encirclement—and certain defeat.

The Hermann Göring Division was defending the largest frontage, from Catania to a point several miles southeast of Troina, an area that normally would have been defended by an entire corps. That division continued to respond to the attempted advances of the British 5th and 51st divisions by resisting fiercely. Around the Gerbini airfields south-

The Allied invasion fleet en route to the French Moroccan coast, November 1942.
U.S. Army Signal Corps; George C. Marshall Library

U.S. tank destroyers moving through Kasserine Pass, 1942.
U.S. Army Signal Corps; George C. Marshall Library

General Dwight D. Eisenhower eating lunch in field, Tunisia, 1943.
U.S. Army Signal Corps; George C. Marshall Library

British and American leaders conferring in North Africa, 1943. *Top row, left to right:* Frank McCarthy, Thomas Handy, Arthur Tedder, Andrew Cunningham, Harold Alexander, Bernard Montgomery; *seated, left to right:* Anthony Eden, Alan Brooke, Winston Churchill, George Marshall, Dwight Eisenhower.
U.S. Army Signal Corps; George C. Marshall Library

Generals Sir Harold R. L. G. Alexander and Sir Bernard L.
Montgomery, 1942.
U.S. Army Signal Corps; George C. Marshall Library

German mechanized light field howitzer moving up in North Africa.
U.S. Army Military History Institute

Sergeant Nathan Praitt, *third from left,* greets Lieutenant General
George S. Patton, Jr., *pointing,* as he lands at Gela, Sicily, July
1943. The sergeant had been Patton's stable boy at Fort Riley,
Kansas, years before. Brigadier General Hobart R. Gay is stand-
ing next to Patton.
U.S. Army Signal Corps; George C. Marshall Library

American troops going ashore near Licata, Sicily, 1943.
U.S. Army Signal Corps; George C. Marshall Library

Sergeant Norwood Dorman of Benson, North Carolina, and memorial statue to Italian soldiers of World War I, Brolo, Sicily, 1943.
U.S. Army Signal Corps; George C. Marshall Library

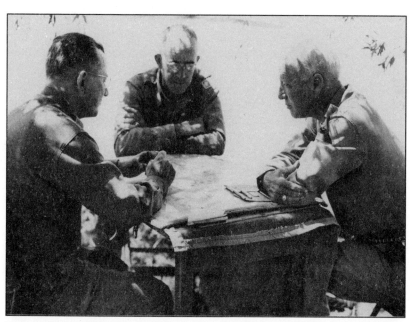

Major General Troy H. Middleton, Commanding General, U.S. 45th Infantry Division; Lieutenant General Omar N. Bradley; and Lieutenant General George S. Patton, Jr., confer in an olive grove near the front in Sicily, 1943.
U.S. Army Signal Corps; George C. Marshall Library

U.S. self-propelled artillery in action in Sicily, 1943.
National Archives

Canadian troops roll ashore in DUKW vehicles near Reggio, Italy, after crossing the Strait of Messina from Sicily, September 1943.
British Army Film Unit; U.S. Army Military History Institute

Burning Allied ships in the harbor of Bari, Italy, following a German air raid, 1943. Among the sixteen vessels destroyed were two munitions ships.
U.S. Army Signal Corps; George C. Marshall Library

A British soldier kicks open the door of a house at Colle, Italy, while another covers him with a captured German automatic pistol, 1943.
U.S. Army Military History Institute

Axis leaders. *Top, left to right:* German Field Marshal Albert Kesselring and General Enno von Rintelin with Crown Prince Umberto of Italy. *Bottom left:* German Generals Jürgen von Arnim, *foreground,* and Hans Cramer. *Bottom right:* German General Heinrich von Vietinghoff.

west of Etna the veteran Highlanders of the 51st Division suffered heavy losses as they tried and failed repeatedly to sustain the initiative. After a week of heavy fighting Montgomery again tossed in the towel and ordered the 51st Division to call off its attacks. Farther to the west the Canadians, who had entered the campaign as an untested force, were rapidly becoming veterans during equally ferocious infantry battles around Assoro and Leonforte.

The narrow front in the central highlands was held by Major General Eberhard Rodt's 15th Panzer Grenadier Division, while the 29th Panzer Grenadier Division ably defended the San Fratello Line. Although the Italian forces were now out of the fighting for good, Hube no longer needed them. He now had full control of the defense of Sicily, which OKW had secretly intended all along.

THE FALL OF MUSSOLINI IN LATE JULY MADE virtually no impact on German operations in Sicily. Guzzoni immediately appeared at Hube's headquarters to pledge his continued support. As the Axis commander-in-chief in Sicily, technically he was still in control, though at no time did the Italians ever issue a single directive to Hube or attempt in any way to influence his conduct of operations.

Hube's most vulnerable point was the boundary between Rodt and Conrath southeast of Troina, a hole which the Germans had again and again managed to keep plugged by concentrating their defenses along key terrain and obvious routes of approach.

Not only did the Germans have to contend with unending harassment from the air, where Tedder's air forces now exercised total dominance, but they were rapidly feeling the effects of a growing shortage of supplies, ammunition, and fuel—not from any interruption of their efficient ferry service across the Strait of Messina, but rather from Allied air interdiction of the road and rail net in central and southern Italy. Hube's chief of staff later recalled that the German supply situation "little by little became critical . . . from the end of July we lived from hand to mouth."

Hube also knew that time was rapidly running out and that he would soon be obliged to order the evacuation of Sicily. There was to be no repeat of Tunisia. Plans were already well under way for a mass evacuation across the strait, although there was pessimism about how well it would succeed. Hube's staff also began to refine the details of how they would conduct a series of delaying actions to Messina. The key was Rodt's panzer grenadiers, and they performed brilliantly by repeatedly slowing the U.S. 1st Division's advance along Route 120. They defended every successive hill mass, counterattacked frequently, and generally made American progress a painful and costly experience.*

It was expected that the Germans would again merely delay at the mountain city of Troina, but here Rodt elected to stand and fight. For nearly a week one attack after another by the 1st Division was beaten off in what Bradley described as "the most bitterly fought battle of the campaign." The barren, rocky terrain favored the defenders, and although the Germans suffered 1,600 killed—nearly 40 percent of the divisional strength—they bought sufficient time for Hube to complete his plans for the evacuation. On 6 August Troina finally fell, not because of an American victory but because their weary enemy had decided it was time to give ground voluntarily. Both sides were spent after the battle, and the exhausted 1st Division was replaced during the climactic advance on Messina by Major General Manton S. Eddy's newly arrived 9th Infantry Division.

RELATIONS BETWEEN PATTON AND BRADLEY reached a low point at about this time. As individuals the two commanders had almost nothing in common, and Bradley had been growing more and more resentful over what he believed was his superior's unwarranted interference in the conduct of his corps's battle. Patton's profanity and theatrics irked Bradley, who believed Palermo, and now the fixation with Messina, were thinly disguised ploys for headlines and personal glory at the expense of his troops.

Angered by what he considered the slow progress of the 3d Division against the tough 29th Panzer Grenadiers, Patton ordered what turned into a bitterly controversial amphibious end run at Brolo to trap the Germans from the rear. An earlier operation had helped to finally break the German grip on the San Fratello Line. But this time Bradley and Truscott both requested a twenty-four-hour postponement, and an enraged Patton stormed into the 3d Division command post and threatened to relieve Truscott if the operation was not executed at once.

A reinforced infantry battalion of the U.S. 3d Division under the command of Lieutenant Colonel Lyle Bernard managed to land without incident, but its presence was soon detected and the operation nearly turned into a disaster when the Americans came under heavy siege. Task Force

---

*The new eastward offensive by II Corps was across such harsh and mountainous terrain that the 1st and 3d divisions were required to fight completely separate battles with no possibility whatever of mutual support.

Bernard escaped annihilation thanks only to timely naval gunfire as the remainder of the division fought doggedly to relieve them against tenacious German resistance. At one point the situation became so desperate that Bernard radioed Truscott, "Enemy counterattacking fiercely. Do something." The Navy arrived—literally in the nick of time—and began delivering welcome supporting fire. The GIs ashore began to cheer. One said, "The goddam navy. The good old navy. Jesus, there ain't nothin' like navy guns." Two more times the navy left, only to be recalled to help break up German counterattacks.

Bernard's 650-man force suffered heavy casualties as a result of the swift and violent German reaction to this dire threat to their rear.* Task Force Bernard lost 171 men and most of its supporting tanks and artillery. The operation accomplished little other than to force the German commander to abandon his positions a day early. A larger force of regimental combat team size would undoubtedly have succeeded in trapping the 29th Panzer Grenadier Division at Brolo, thus collapsing the northern anchor of Hube's defenses. The effects on other German units would have been equally calamitous, particularly to Rodt's 15th Panzer Grenadier Division, whose escape route to Messina would have been severed, and the unsatisfactory ending to the Sicily campaign might have been averted.

There was considerable bitterness against Patton throughout II Corps. Bradley was furious and later wrote that Patton's decision had left him "more exasperated than I have ever been," but "as a subordinate commander of Patton's I had no alternative but to comply with his orders." Equally unimpressed with the Brolo operation were the Germans, one of whom said he could not "understand why the Allies with their overwhelming sea power had not done this sort of thing earlier, more often and on a bigger scale."

The battles in the incredible summer heat, in terrain unfit for anything but a mule, and with constant casualties from mines, snipers, artillery, and mortars left even the elite 3d Division battle weary. The lasting memory of one battalion commander was "how damn tired we got just going day after day."

FOR BRADLEY THE LAST STRAW WAS THE TWO well-known slapping incidents that occurred in evacuation hospitals, when Patton believed he had

---

*Although no reason has ever been given for not mounting a larger operation, General Truscott probably believed that a force of regimental size would have been too cumbersome to carry out these raids into the German rear.

encountered malingerers. In both instances Patton had flown into a rage and cursed and slapped a soldier, one of whom later turned out to have malaria and diarrhea. The incident became a cause célèbre within Seventh Army and left Patton's popularity with his troops at an all-time low. It so angered a group of correspondents that they took the matter to Eisenhower in an attempt to have Patton removed from his command. Eisenhower was horrified that Patton's foolishness might cost him a valuable commander he could not afford to lose. "I simply cannot let that happen. Patton is *indispensable* to the war effort—one of the guarantors of our victory," he declared.

Patton was severely reprimanded and ordered to apologize personally to his two victims and to every soldier and unit in Seventh Army. The correspondents honored Eisenhower's plea to avoid publicizing the incidents. Several months later, Drew Pearson sensationalized the story on his weekly radio show, where it created a storm of controversy across America. However, Eisenhower, Marshall, and Secretary of War Stimson refused to sacrifice Patton on the altar of public opinion, and l'affaire Patton faded away in time.

WHEN THE GERMANS BEGAN THEIR FLIGHT from Sicily they fully expected catastrophic losses. A preliminary evacuation began in early August, and by the time the final evacuation commenced the night of 11 August they had already withdrawn over 13,000 troops and considerable equipment. Ferry traffic in the Strait of Messina was efficiently organized and performed flawlessly under the cover of heavy antiaircraft support.

Although the Allied air forces made a halfhearted and largely futile effort to interdict the evacuation, they not only failed to attack the correct targets but deliberately avoided employing the one weapon which could have made a difference: their B-17 strategic bomber force. The result was that instead of enormous losses the Germans pulled off a stunningly successful strategic withdrawal. By the time it ended on the morning of 17 August they had extricated nearly 55,000 troops, 9,789 vehicles, 51 tanks, and 163 guns, mostly by daylight.*

By the time the 3d Division entered the smoking ruins of Messina that same morning, the last German had long since departed. The German naval commander who had masterminded the evacuation was Captain

---

*Virtually unknown is the fact that the Italians staged their own successful evacuation that transported about 70,000 troops to the mainland.

(Baron) von Liebenstein, and he had every right to exult: "We have not given up a single German soldier, weapon or vehicle into enemy hands."*

The last days of the battle for Sicily were a dismal conclusion to a campaign that had been beset from the start by controversy and indecision. For thirty-eight days the Allies fought some of the most difficult battles of the war, in terrain every bit as harsh as they would find ahead of them in Italy. Yet their enemy had defied them to the end and had added the final insult by accomplishing one of the most successful strategic withdrawals in military history. At Dunkirk British ingenuity and grit had saved the soldiers of the British Expeditionary Force but not their precious equipment. In Sicily the Germans had not only saved themselves but virtually everything capable of being ferried to the mainland. Only the dead were left behind. Defiant to the end, the Germans justifiably emerged from the campaign believing they had given as good as they got. There was an understandable pride in having fought well against an overwhelmingly superior force. The result was that a German army corps which never exceeded 60,000 men and which was devoid of air and naval support managed to thwart and then delay the might of two Allied armies whose combined strength of 467,000 was nearly eight times greater.

FROM THE TIME OF ALEXANDER'S DECISION to force Seventh Army into a secondary role and Montgomery's errant decision to switch his main effort from the plain of Catania to the highlands, the Germans, not the Allies, had been in control of the timetable for the Sicilian campaign. After uncertain beginnings at Gela where the Hermann Göring Division had performed poorly, Group Schmalz delayed the British advance just long enough to permit the reinforcement of Primosole Bridge by the tenacious paratroopers of the 1st Parachute Division, who held their ground against nearly impossible odds. In the defense of Troina and the San Fratello Line the German army in Sicily performed admirably against superior air, sea, and ground forces. At the end they added the final insult by the brilliant planning and execution of their great escape.

The Allies had squandered one opportunity after another to end the Sicily campaign with a stunning victory. Instead, by any objective assess-

---

*After he took over in May 1943 von Liebenstein turned a ragged and grossly inefficient ferry service in the Strait of Messina into a model operation, including what was likely the first roll-on/roll-off truck operation ever undertaken.

ment they gathered a harvest of bitter fruit. One historian has aptly described Sicily as "an Allied physical victory, a German moral victory." Others have been less charitable. In Whitehall a War Office after-action report derided the campaign as "a strategic and tactical failure" and "a chaotic and deplorable example of everything that planning should not be."

There was ample blame for all elements of the Allied high command, including the failure of the commanders to establish a joint command and control headquarters in North Africa or Malta, despite warnings from the British Chiefs of Staff that to do otherwise violated "one of the most important precepts of Combined operations." The Allies needlessly prolonged the reduction of Sicily by ponderous and largely ineffective tactics. The reasons were varied: Eisenhower's lack of direct involvement, Alexander's inept leadership and unjustified mistrust of American fighting ability, Montgomery's unfortunate changes of strategy, the failure of the air forces to make more than a token effort* to impede the German evacuation, and the navy's failure to block the Strait of Messina. On the positive side, the campaign did lead directly to the fall of Mussolini, and the U.S. Army finally came of age in Sicily under the leadership of Patton and Bradley. The brilliant and audacious effort to mask the objectives of Operation HUSKY had also succeeded beyond the wildest dreams of its British architects.

The German commanders were scornful of Allied tactics. Kesselring believed that Calabria should have been at least a secondary target, while another senior general called the failure to seize the Strait of Messina incomprehensible. From the outset the Allies had taken the safe, conservative path. The invasion plan was Montgomery's version, which opted for safety in numbers, and was in no small part the result of the misjudgment of the Allied planners, who overestimated the resistance the Italians would offer. The original plan for multiple landings, while bold in conception, was flawed, and Montgomery's compromise plan tried to use only the Eighth Army to seize Messina, relegating Patton's Seventh Army to a minor role.

Nevertheless, as the campaign unfolded, opportunities to win a decisive victory were squandered, and the Allied ground forces were left to fight a needless frontal battle of attrition. What ought to have been a

---

*Only 18 percent of the Allied fighter and fighter-bomber force was committed to operation in the Strait of Messina, and a mere 5.5 percent of the heavy bomber forces.

brief and decisive victory lasted thirty-eight days at no small cost. German losses are believed to have totaled nearly 29,000 (4,325 killed, 6,663 captured, and an estimated 17,944 wounded), while the Allied armies lost 11,843 British and 8,731 American killed, wounded, missing, and captured.

Secondary landings elsewhere along the Sicily coast were never seriously considered, even though by D-Day the Allies controlled both the air and the sea. Not only was Allied strategy overly conservative, in some instances it was downright foolish. Air attacks on Sicilian towns and cities, which were "blotted out by bombing from the air on a scale unprecedented in the history of war," failed miserably when the Germans made a point of not defending urban areas. British historian J. F. C. Fuller, in *The Second World War, 1939–45*, has called "this insensate [saturation] bombing of villages . . . asinine."

The key to Sicily was not in the air but on the sea. HUSKY was an enormous improvement over TORCH, and it provided valuable lessons in the development of airborne and amphibious warfare that would be put to good use the following summer in Normandy. The Axis evacuation of Sicily, however, could have been halted only by an integrated joint air-naval effort, which was never forthcoming, thus realizing the worst fears of Brooke and the British Chiefs of Staff.

Sea power was the greatest weapon the Allies possessed, and it was never pressed anywhere near its full capability. Too often, in fact, it was treated as a commodity too precious to be employed in any operation involving risk. Admiral Andrew Cunningham was a naval commander known for his aggressiveness and dash. In Tunisia he had anticipated an Axis Dunkirk, and his edict to "SINK, BURN, DESTROY. Let Nothing Pass" was ruthlessly and effectively enforced by the Allied naval forces. Yet he exhibited an uncharacteristic conservatism when it came to operations in and around the Strait of Messina. Some believed vivid memories of the disastrous British venture into the Dardanelles in 1915 had dissuaded Cunningham.

Fuller wrote the epitaph for the Sicilian campaign when he noted that "in coastal operations he who commands the sea can nearly always find an open flank leading to the enemy's rear—the decisive point in every battle. This was *the* lesson of the Sicilian campaign and it was not learnt."

FIVE

Planning the Invasion of Italy

THE INVASION OF SICILY HASTENED THE downfall of Benito Mussolini and his fascist government, both of which were deposed in late July 1943. There were wild celebrations in Rome, and King Victor Emmanuel III immediately appointed Field Marshal Pietro Badoglio to head the Italian government. Although Badoglio proclaimed that the war would go on as before, within weeks he began secretly negotiating an armistice with the Allies. In September Italy seceded from the Rome-Berlin Axis.

The fall of Mussolini came as a shock to the German leaders. Despite the initial assurances of Italian loyalty from Badoglio, Hitler jeered derisively, "They say they'll fight but that's treachery! We must be quite clear: it's pure treachery!" It was also "the biggest impudence in history. Does that man imagine that I will believe him?" Cooler heads dissuaded the enraged Führer from attempting a coup. Instead the Germans moved quickly to revive earlier contingency plans for a series of military actions to be taken in the event of an Italian collapse.

Rommel was hastily recalled from a special mission to Greece and given command of the newly formed Army Group B. For the time being the two countries avoided military clashes, but neither side for one moment trusted the pledges of the other. As Rommel made preparations to occupy Italy, the Germans began moving fresh troops in under the pretense of having to reinforce Kesselring in the event of an Allied invasion.

While the Germans pondered their survival and Italians their future, the Allies had at long last acted on Eisenhower's recommendation that an invasion of Italy follow the fall of Sicily. The Casablanca Conference had failed to formally ratify such a move, even though no one on either side held the slightest doubt that the Allied campaign would be carried into Italy. OVERLORD was not scheduled until May 1944, and the massive Allied force in the Mediterranean could not be left in Sicily and North Africa without a new mission.

Eisenhower was authorized to begin planning two operations to be directed against Italy at such time as Sicily should fall. A U.S. Fifth Army had been organized in the spring of 1943 to plan and execute operations in Italy, and for months Mark Clark's troops had been preparing for an amphibious invasion south of Naples at Salerno. And toward the end of operations in Sicily, Montgomery withdrew Miles Dempsey's 13th Corps to begin planning an invasion of Calabria, code named Operation BAYTOWN.

Considerable disagreement still remained within the Combined Chiefs of Staff both over future operations in Italy and the scope of Operation AVALANCHE, the Salerno operation. At the Quebec Conference in August, the U.S. and British military chiefs clashed over the scope of further moves in the Mediterranean. They did agree, however, that OVERLORD would take precedence and that Eisenhower would have to carry out operations in Italy with considerably reduced forces.*

Churchill's Mediterranean strategy envisioned continued Allied operations into Italy and, if possible, an offensive that would carry them into northern Italy. From there, he argued, Allied aircraft could be employed in a direct support role in OVERLORD operations. Marshall remained determined that nothing must be allowed to detract from OVERLORD. He therefore resisted any agreement beyond Operation ANVIL[†] and the capture of Rome.

What was lacking then and throughout the Italian campaign was a statement of Allied grand strategy. If the political goals were vague, the aims of the forthcoming military operations were even less clear. At Casablanca it was never resolved whether Sicily was to be the stepping-stone to a larger objective in Italy or merely an end in itself. The British continued to believe passionately in the necessity for a strong Allied presence in the Mediterranean as a vital ingredient to the defeat of Germany. At the same time the American leadership was left with the impression that neither Churchill nor Brooke was completely sold on the merits of the cross-Channel invasion.**

---

*Seven U.S. and British divisions were to be transferred to the United Kingdom to prepare for the cross-Channel attack.

[†]A major diversionary operation in southern France designed to coincide with the D-Day landings in Normandy.

**In recent years numerous British accounts and memoirs have stressed that Churchill and Brooke were indeed committed to Operation OVERLORD. An equal

The British had long feared that the United States would insist on halting further active military operations in the Mediterranean once Sicily was successfully conquered and Allied control of the region in the air and on the sea was supreme. This fear drew Churchill to North Africa in May 1943 to dissuade the American leadership from such a move. As Eisenhower later related, "He frankly said that he wanted to do his utmost to see that no such disaster—as he called it—would occur." The decision to continue operations into Italy after Sicily was as much of a compromise as HUSKY, and again hinged on British backing for cross-Channel operations.

DURING AUGUST THE ALLIES PURSUED secret negotiations with the new Badoglio government for the surrender of Italy. At Casablanca, the Allies insisted on unconditional surrender, and while the Italians were anxious to join them, their representatives soon learned they had virtually no bargaining position. As the negotiations dragged on, the Italians admitted that they had no other options, but, deeply concerned about what was certain to be a violent German reaction, they pleaded for the announcement of the Italian surrender to be withheld until the Allies could land and protect Rome. The Allies became convinced that surrender was feasible but that some concession was necessary in order to spur completion of the deal and enlist Italian aid against the Germans.

The Allied concession was dictated in part by the belief it was essential to remove the Italian Army from the battlefield before the invasion of Salerno. As Allies, the German and Italian armies made uncomfortable bedfellows; nevertheless, left united, the combined Axis forces in Italy would number approximately thirty-five divisions and pose a considerable threat to the Allies, whose numbers were far smaller. Nevertheless, the governing factor in the decision was the effective range of Allied tactical aircraft. Naples represented the maximum range of Tedder's Sicily-based squadrons. Even at this distance air cover would only amount to approximately twenty minutes over the battle front. Hence the Allied planners recommended that the Fifth Army invade Italy along the Gulf of Salerno approximately twenty miles south of Naples.

---

number of American participants were of the opposite view. In an unpublished memoir Eisenhower described how Brooke privately expressed deep misgivings about the cross-Channel venture and spoke favorably of a "thrust and peck" strategy of hammering Axis flanks to the benefit of the Red Army, whose responsibility, he said, should be the destruction of Hitler's land forces.

The Allied commanders were worried about control of the southern regions of Sicily and the vital shipping lanes of the Strait of Messina. They also decided that a force was necessary in southern Italy to draw valuable German reserves away from Salerno. No consideration seems to have been given to the fact that the Germans might simply refuse to do battle in southern Calabria.

The shortage of landing craft was a major headache throughout the war in the Mediterranean and Northwest Europe. There were never enough of them available, and with American priorities split between Europe and the Pacific, a constant struggle ensued to obtain adequate numbers to mount amphibious operations. Even worse for the Italian theater was the knowledge that by early 1944 most of the Mediterranean-based shipping would be shifted to the United Kingdom for OVERLORD. It also meant that BAYTOWN, the drive into southern Italy, must necessarily precede AVALANCHE, because there were not enough vessels for simultaneous landings. Once Montgomery gained a foothold in the toe of southern Calabria, the landing craft would be committed to the Salerno landings, which were scheduled for 9 September, a week after BAYTOWN.

Among those who considered BAYTOWN a wasteful and unnecessary operation was Montgomery, who believed that the same lack of coordination and strategic goals that had characterized operations in Sicily now threatened operations in Italy. The focus of his grievance was his friend Alexander, about whom he had few illusions when it came to masterminding a major operation of war. "The trouble is there is no higher-up grip on this campaign," he complained to Brooke. His uncompromising stand over HUSKY had all but worn out his welcome as an arbitrator of Allied policy, and consequently his complaints about the futility of BAYTOWN fell largely on deaf ears.

There was considerable merit to Montgomery's complaints. Years later he called BAYTOWN "a unique incident in the history of war," in which "I had been ordered to invade the mainland of Europe with the Eighth Army—but had been given no object." He cited a vague directive from Alexander charging Eighth Army to follow the enemy north and engage them, in order to assist AVALANCHE. Montgomery saw no reason to bother with a costly and laborious drive north through southern Italy in the first place. "If AVALANCHE is a success, then we should reinforce that front, for there is little point in laboriously fighting our way up Southern Italy. It is better to leave the enemy to decay there or let him have the trouble of moving himself up from the foot to where we are concentrated."

Montgomery attempted to persuade Eisenhower to cancel BAYTOWN and use the threat of landings in Calabria as a means of tying down forces which might otherwise imperil Clark's Fifth Army at Salerno. Montgomery was not against the concept of tying down the maximum number of German divisions in Italy, away from France and the Eastern Front, but he advocated a firm plan of action that would employ the combined strength of the two armies in the furtherance of a single stated goal. This recommendation was not well received at AFHQ and only served to enhance his reputation as a difficult subordinate.

The decisions made by the Allied high command during this period of the war in the Mediterranean reflected both a lack of strategic goals for the Italian campaign and an occasional and uncharacteristic rashness. An example of the latter was the serious consideration given to an operation code named GIANT II, an attempt to seize Rome using the 82d Airborne Division. Its most powerful advocate was AFHQ Chief of Staff Bedell Smith who sold both Alexander and Eisenhower on its merits.

The problem turned out to be that the assumptions upon which GIANT II were based were dangerously faulty. The plan was to drop the division outside Rome, where it would link up with approximately four divisions of Italian troops. Together they would seize Rome by coup de main, with assistance from the citizens of Rome, who, according to Smith, would "drop kettles, bricks, [and] hot water on the Germans in the streets of Rome." This, thought Smith, would force Kesselring to beat a retreat to the north. Militarily the Eternal City was of considerable importance as the key road and rail center for German forces operating in southern Italy. Psychologically the seizure of one of the two capital cities of the Rome-Berlin alliance would be of immense value to the Allies.

Among the opponents of GIANT II was Mark Clark, who at a stroke would lose his strategic reserve force for AVALANCHE if the plan were executed. He needed the 82d for employment in blocking positions along the Volturno River, to prevent panzer reserves from rushing to the aid of General Heinrich von Vietinghof's Tenth Army at Salerno. Clark was outraged and told Eisenhower "No! That's my division! . . . Taking away the Eighty-Second just as the fighting starts is like cutting off my left arm." Eisenhower, however, refused to budge, and Clark was left with a vague assurance that he would get the division back as soon as GIANT II was completed.

GIANT II also met strong opposition from the outspoken commander of the 82d Airborne, Major General Matthew B. Ridgway, who insisted that he would not send his division unless there was a better assurance of

THE INVASION OF ITALY AND THE ADVANCE TO THE GUSTAV LINE

SEPTEMBER–DECEMBER 1943

success than the word of AFHQ staff officers. At Ridgway's instigation, Eisenhower sent the 82d Division's artillery commander, Brigadier General Maxwell Taylor, on a secret mission to Rome to investigate, and he soon found that Smith's claims were absurd. Not only was the Italian will to fight dubious, but there were two veteran German divisions nearby in strategic reserve.

Only hours before the operation Taylor radioed Eisenhower that GIANT II must be called off. Not only did the situation bear no relation to the claims of its backers, but, as Taylor pointed out, there was sufficient airlift capability only to move the equivalent of a reinforced regiment to Rome. Taylor's urgent message barely arrived in time to cancel the operation. Some planes had already taken off but were recalled in time.

Although the idea of a quick capture of Rome made good sense, the participating elements of the 82d Airborne Division would have become the unwitting victims of a monumental military blunder. Even worse would have been the disastrous consequences for Allied forces at Salerno without the 82d Airborne.

THE ITALIAN CAMPAIGN OPENED DURING the early morning hours of 3 September 1943 when Allied guns began a massive barrage against suspected enemy positions on the Italian side of the Strait of Messina. More than four hundred tons of high explosive were hurled into Calabria in advance of three brigades of Canadian and British infantry, who landed only to find that there was no sign of their enemy. Anticipating the invasion, the Germans had prudently withdrawn several days earlier and were now in fresh positions in the rough, mountainous terrain of central Calabria at the neck of the Italian boot. The few Italian defenders left to guard the Strait of Messina offered scant resistance; they were happy to surrender to the Allies and end their involvement in a war they detested.

Within hours Dempsey's 13th Corps, the spearhead force of Eighth Army, was rapidly advancing north, with little to impede them. The greatest menace came from mines and the thorough job of demolition performed along the sparse road net of southern Calabria by the German engineers, whose handiwork had to be undone by their British counterparts. During the first five days of the new campaign Eighth Army advanced some one hundred miles to the point where the leg of southern Italy meets the Italian boot. As the Allies were soon to discover, these five days would be the only period of the Italian campaign that could be labeled easy going.

The same day that Montgomery halted Eighth Army to regroup, Mark

Clark's Fifth Army was poised to invade the beaches along the Gulf of Salerno. Here the campaign would begin in earnest, and in the black days that followed, the Allies would fight to avert a military disaster.

The Sicily campaign had been over for only three weeks, and already the Allies were about to pay dearly for permitting the German forces to escape capture.

SIX

The Salerno Landings

OPERATION AVALANCHE, THE INVASION OF Salerno, was designed by its architects to take advantage of the imminent collapse of Italy as Hitler's ally and to gain an Allied foothold on the Italian mainland. Salerno was selected mainly because of its proximity to Naples, which the Allies wanted for its excellent port facilities, rather than its suitability for an amphibious landing. The basic concept of the plan was simple. Once ashore and in control of a bridgehead, Mark Clark's Fifth Army would link up with Montgomery's Eighth Army driving north from Calabria. Together the two armies would continue offensive operations toward Rome under the command of Alexander, whose 15th Army Group would control all Allied ground operations in Italy.

As it would throughout the war in the Mediterranean, a shortage of landing craft exerted an enormous influence on the AVALANCHE invasion plan, reducing the scope of the landings to three divisions (two British and one American), Darby's Rangers, and a British Commando force.*

The Salerno landings were to be carried out by two corps. On the left was the British 10th Corps, under the command of an outspoken and colorful former cavalry officer and Alexander's former chief of staff in the Middle East, Lieutenant-General Richard McCreery. On the right was Major General Ernest J. Dawley's U.S. VI Corps, the unit originally scheduled to carry out the Gela landings in Sicily.† In reality, however,

---

* This highly trained force consisted of three battalions of U.S. Rangers under the command of Lieutenant Colonel William O. Darby and two battalions of British Commandos led by Brigadier Robert Laycock.

† It will be recalled that in April 1943 Patton had persuaded Eisenhower to shift VI Corps to Fifth Army and substitute Bradley's II Corps for the Gela landings. Patton

AVALANCHE in its initial stage was to be little more than a corps-sized invasion.

The 10th Corps consisted of two infantry divisions that had fought in North Africa: the 46th under Major-General J. T. L. Hawkesworth and the 56th under Major-General D. A. H. Graham. The VI Corps consisted of a single assault division, Major General Fred L. Walker's 36th (Texas National Guard) Division. In floating reserve were two regimental combat teams of the 45th Infantry Division.* Although the numbers looked impressive, the plan developed for AVALANCHE would shortly demonstrate how inadequate they really were.

The Gulf of Salerno, so named for the small port of Salerno tucked into its northern corner, is situated on the west coast of Italy fifty miles south of Naples. The landings were to take place along a narrow plain between Salerno and the ancient city of Paestum thirty miles to the southeast. Although there were excellent beach gradients and ample exits, the sector chosen for the landings was dominated by rugged mountains from which there were only two exits leading to Naples. The most serious drawbacks to the Salerno sector were that the Germans would dominate the heights surrounding the landing beaches, and the thirty-five-mile-long invasion sector was far too large for the size of the AVALANCHE force. Another problem was the Sele River and its tributary, the Calore. The Sele formed a natural physical barrier between the British and U.S. forces, and its steep banks would require bridging if there was to be any semblance of mutual support between the two forces.

The plan called for the Rangers and Commandos to land west of Salerno: Laycock's force at Vietri and Darby's farther west at Maiori. Their objective was to seize key high ground leading from Salerno to Naples and establish blocking positions against German reinforcements attempting to reach the Salerno bridgehead via Route 18 or along the coastal road. Their mission was of vital importance, for without control of the corridors leading from the beachhead, Fifth Army would be in serious trouble.

With the 46th Division on the left flank and the 56th Division on the

---

knew little of Dawley and preferred a commander and corps he had confidence in to carry out the invasion of Sicily.

*The shortage of landing craft was never more evident than in the limitation imposed on the VI Corps reserve. There were sufficient craft to employ less than two-thirds of the 45th Division: a full regimental combat team of three rifle battalions and a second with only two battalions of infantry.

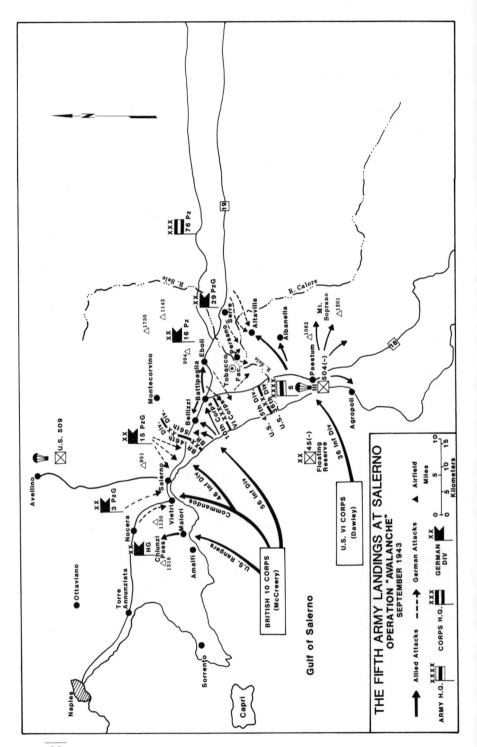

THE FIFTH ARMY LANDINGS AT SALERNO
OPERATION "AVALANCHE"
SEPTEMBER 1943

Gulf of Salerno

Capri

BRITISH 10 CORPS
(McCreery)

U.S. VI CORPS
(Dawley)

Allied Attacks   XXXX ARMY H.Q.
German Attacks   XXX CORPS H.Q.
Airfield   XX GERMAN DIV

Miles   0   5   10   15
Kilometers   0   5   10   15

76 Pz

29 PzG

16 Pz

15 PzG

3 PzG

HG

△1730
△1142
△994
△951
△1130
△1316

△1082   Mt. Soprano   △1201

R. Sele
R. Calore
R. Sele

Tobacco
Factory
FaC.
Persano
Serre

Altavilla
Albanella
Paestum
504(-)
Agropoli

Eboli
Battipaglia
Bellizzi
Montecorvino

Salerno
Vietri
Maiori
Amalfi
Sorrento

Nocera
Chiunzi
Pass
Torre
Annunziata
Ottaviano
Avellino

Naples

U.S. 509

Commandos
46 Inf Div
56 Inf Div
U.S. Rangers

BR 46th DIV
BR 56th DIV
10th XXX
VI Corps
U.S. 45th DIV
U.S. 36th DIV

5

36 Inf Div
45(-)
Floating
Reserve

88

right, McCreery's corps had the mission of assaulting between the Sele River and the city of Salerno. While Graham captured the vital Montecorvino airfield and the high ground to its immediate north, Hawkesworth's division was to wheel left, seize Salerno, link up with Darby and Laycock, and reinforce the vital mountain passes. In the American sector, Walker's Texans, supported by tanks, were to land south of the Sele River at Paestum to anchor the Fifth Army's right flank.

In all, Clark's invasion force would by nightfall on D-Day consist of 27 infantry battalions, 150 supporting Sherman tanks, and a large number of antitank guns, with the backing of nearly 400 guns and assorted self-propelled artillery along with the guns of Vice Admiral Hewitt's Western Naval Task Force and Rear Admiral Sir Philip Vian's Support Carrier Force consisting of Royal Navy carriers, battleships, cruisers, and destroyers. On D plus one the reserve force of Major General Troy Middleton's two 45th Division regimental combat teams would land and assist the 36th Division.

IN NORTH AFRICA, ALBERT KESSELRING had exercised command through two independent-minded subordinates, von Arnim and Rommel. His imprint on the battle for Tunisia had been minimal, but as the fighting was about to shift to Italy, all that changed. More so than any other German campaign of the war, the battles fought in Italy were a product of Kesselring's genius for defensive operations. Throughout the campaign it was Kesselring who dictated German strategy—by the firm exercise of command and by his skill at maneuvering his forces shrewdly against the Allies during the longest and bloodiest campaign fought by the Anglo-American Alliance in all of World War II.

Nevertheless Kesselring was rarely free from orders and guidance emanating from OKW or Hitler, and there were occasions when he found that his most serious problems were with Berlin rather than the Allies. Although he had escaped censure from Hitler for ordering the evacuation of Sicily before obtaining the Führer's official permission, he had to fight constant battles with OKW and the twin nemeses of all German commanders in the field, General Alfred Jodl and Field Marshal Wilhelm Keitel.*

---

*Keitel headed OKW and was universally regarded as a vassal of Hitler and an officer whose main attribute was a willingness to carry out without question the orders of his Führer. Behind his back Keitel was sneeringly referred to as *Der Lakaitel* (lackey). Jodl was Keitel's deputy and the real power within OKW; he either

Kesselring's quarrels with OKW revolved around how the Germans ought to conduct the defense of Italy. Some in Berlin favored a strong defense in the northern Apennines, which Kesselring opposed. With considerable difficulty he finally convinced Hitler that German strategy should be to defend south of Rome along Italy's narrowest point—from the vicinity of Pescara on the Adriatic, across the peninsula, and through the Liri Valley to the Gulf of Gaeta, north of Naples, the area which later came to be known as the Gustav Line.

Such a defense offered the advantages of denying the Allies air bases in central and northern Italy and discouraging any attempt to invade the Balkans and threaten the crucial sources of raw materials used to feed the German war machine. Kesselring realized he could not hold southern Italy indefinitely, but he far preferred defending there than in the Apennines and the Po River valley in the north. To his credit, Kesselring overcame the intrigues of Rommel, Hitler's displeasure, and the second-guessers at OKW, and he was able to conduct the Italian campaign according to his own conception and strategy.

Contrary to the expectations of some of the Allied commanders, including Clark, there was really no mystery as to where in Italy the Allies would invade; the only major question was *when.* Of all the decisions about AVALANCHE, easily the most controversial was Clark's election to forgo a preliminary bombardment by the navy in an effort to achieve tactical surprise. His decision was opposed by Admiral Hewitt, who argued forcefully that "any officer with a pair of dividers could figure out that the Gulf of Salerno was the northernmost practicable landing place for the Allies; reconnaissance planes would snoop the convoys; in short, that it was fantastic to assume we could obtain tactical surprise." Implicit in Clark's refusal was the misguided assumption that naval gunfire would unnecessarily attract German reinforcements to Salerno.

Defending the Salerno sector was Major General Rudolf Sieckenius's 16th Panzer Division, which Kesselring had ordered there only two days earlier, on 6 September. On 7 September the division was alerted that an Allied invasion fleet was heading toward the Naples area, and the day before the landings the warnings were upgraded: an invasion was imminent.

The 16th Panzer Division lost no time in preparing defenses to counter

---

made or carried out most of the important policy decisions of the German armed forces.

an invasion. Mines were laid along the beach, and by the time the Allies began coming ashore two days later, some had been emplaced in the bay. Strongholds were begun for the emplacement of machine guns, quad-mounted 20-mm antiaircraft cannons, and the numerous other weapons in the German arsenal. The guns and emplacements of an Italian coastal division were seized, and the commander was shot for resisting.

Previously stationed in France for refitting after surviving Stalingrad, the majority of 16th Panzer's 15,000-man strength was composed of untried recruits. However, the division had a full complement of experienced officers and NCOs who quickly provided the necessary leadership to overcome this problem. Even though still short a battalion of heavy Mark V tanks and a 150-mm howitzer battalion, the 16th Panzer constituted formidable opposition.*

That same day—8 September—the BBC Overseas News broadcast the surrender of Marshal Badoglio's government to the Allies: "The Italian armed forces have accepted unconditional surrender." Over Radio Algiers Eisenhower told the world that the war with Italy had terminated. Communications to Kesselring's headquarters had been knocked out during an Allied bombing raid, and he suffered the embarrassment of learning of the surrender from Jodl. Badoglio had lost his battle with the Allies to withhold the announcement of Italy's capitulation until after the invasion of Salerno. Most members of the war-weary Italian Army greeted the news with a sense of relief. There were few true Fascists left and no desire to continue fighting as an ally of Nazi Germany.

Despite warnings by the invasion commanders not to take the capitulation of Italy as a sign that Salerno would be a walkover, many of the units did. The announcement of Italy's surrender made over the troop ships' public address systems was, as the official naval historian notes, necessary but "singularly ill-timed with reference to [the] embarked troops." The calmness of the bright and starry night as the Allied fleet steamed toward the Gulf of Salerno seemed almost mystical to some. Their illusions were to be rudely shattered the following morning, not only by the violent German resistance to the invasion but by the taunts in English over loudspeakers to "come on in and give up."

The surrender announcement was not unexpected in Berlin, and OKW immediately ordered Kesselring to implement a contingency plan that

---

*The division had more than 100 tanks, 176 other armored vehicles, 55 assault guns, a 105-mm howitzer regiment of 36 guns, and numerous antitank guns and deadly dual-purpose 88-mm guns.

would ensure German control of northern Italy, the evacuation of Sardinia,* and the seizure of the Italian government, which, as Kesselring's message to the troops of Tenth Army noted, had "committed the basest treachery by concluding an armistice with the enemy behind our backs. . . . We Germans must continue to fight . . . for the salvation of Europe and Italy. No mercy must be shown to traitors. *Heil Hitler!*"

WHILE THE GERMAN HIGH COMMAND WERE reacting to the loss of their onetime ally, events were rapidly unfolding at Salerno. In the early morning hours of 9 September a German signals officer manning an outpost overlooking the gulf observed the most awesome sight of his young life. In the blackness of the night the roar of heavy naval gunfire began erupting to the south from unseen ships as the Allied fleet began pouring a hail of shells along the beaches. What the officer did not know was that this was not the preliminary bombardment sought by Hewitt but only defensive fires aimed at keeping the German defenders at bay while the assault landings were taking place. Dawn revealed the presence of literally hundreds of ships, ranging from heavy cruisers and destroyers to the landing craft moving back and forth from the beaches.

The first of the Allied assault landings began on schedule. Unlike Sicily, however, where there was only scattered opposition on D-Day, the Allied invasion of Salerno was bitterly resisted by the 16th Panzer Division with every weapon in its arsenal. As the landing craft ferrying the troops of the three assault divisions began the long run (which averaged ten miles) from their transports to the beaches, they were greeted by seemingly endless volumes of tracer fire from machine guns emplaced along the beachfront, mortars, antiaircraft guns, antitank guns, and tanks farther inland, and, worst of all, from the dreaded 88-mm guns of the German artillery.

Men began to die. Many never made it to the beaches. The assault was particularly perilous in the 36th Division sector, where the first waves of Texans were pinned down by the gunfire. An infantry battalion commander saw panic and indecision begin to take control, and he spurred his men to push inland, their only escape from certain death. "Get up, you bastards!" he raged. "Get up and go!"

Some landing craft were hit by shellfire and blew up; others exploded

*Von Liebenstein, who masterminded the ferry operations in the Strait of Messina, repeated his feat in Sardinia, where the German garrison was successfully evacuated to mainland Italy.

after hitting mines emplaced in the bay or were hit by marauding Luftwaffe fighters, which bombed and strafed the invaders in the heaviest aerial resistance of the entire Mediterranean campaign. In the confusion others refused to challenge the hail of fire awaiting them, and the landings quickly turned into chaos as the correct beaches were missed and the timetable disintegrated. The result was a series of sporadic landings as troops, vehicles, and supplies came ashore haphazardly. Units that were supposed to assault certain objectives never appeared. Even so, however, the naval performance at Salerno had improved dramatically after Sicily. The majority of the assault forces were landed on time under exceptionally difficult circumstances.

The lead elements of Hawkesworth's 46th Division went ashore about 0330 hours, after the beaches had been subjected to heavy rocket fire. A battalion of the Hampshire Regiment was landed in confusion too far to the south, on a 56th Division beach. As they attempted to cross the Asa River to regain their correct sector they were savaged by panzers which, in the words of one survivor, created a scene of "terrible carnage."

These were the first shots the men of the U.S. 36th Division had ever heard fired in anger. By contrast, both British divisions had seen combat in North Africa, although as Graham and Bidwell note, they were of varied experience and uneven value. The 46th Division had fought in Tunisia but was "very slow, at times tactically careless and unenterprising in the attack."

The Ranger and Commando forces were all combat veterans, and their landings went smoothly west of Salerno. They quickly disposed of the slight resistance and began infiltrating into the hills. Darby's Rangers moved into the steep hills above Salerno toward their objective, the vital Chiunzi Pass through which Fifth Army was scheduled to move in its drive to Naples. At daylight Darby radioed to Clark, aboard Hewitt's command ship, that his Rangers were in possession and there to stay "until hell freezes over."

Although he was to be plagued throughout the battle by inadequate communications with his front-line commanders, the German Tenth Army commander, General Heinrich von Vietinghof, lost no time in reacting to the Allied landings, which he at once recognized as a major assault, not a diversionary feint. In southern Calabria, where it was fighting a delaying action against Eighth Army, the 26th Panzer Division was ordered to disengage at once and hurry north to reinforce the Salerno front. Other units in the Rome area were alerted for movement to Salerno. The first of the divisions ordered to Salerno was the Hermann Göring, which, after withdrawal from Sicily, had been refitting at Naples.

THE DECISION TO INVADE ITALY AT SALERNO had been viewed with varying degrees of optimism within the Allied high command. Although Clark was generally optimistic about the chances of Allied success, others were less enthusiastic, among them Alexander, who on 30 August called the shoestring operation "a dangerous gamble." Despite his misgivings about Salerno, however, Alexander saw no reason why the Allies should not capture Rome by mid-October at the latest. Nor had Eisenhower's previous experience with amphibious operations engendered any great optimism within his breast. Although he had absolute faith in his protégé, Mark Clark, he had learned from personal experience to mistrust the optimism of/his planners. Clark himself was not satisfied with Salerno as the invasion site, preferring that the landings be made north of Naples in the Bay of Gaeta, which was devoid of mountainous terrain advantageous to a defender. The deciding factor had been the limitations of air support.

As D-Day progressed, the AVALANCHE commanders, without a clear picture of what was taking place ashore, were growing increasingly frustrated. Sporadic reports indicated that all was not well, particularly in the 36th Division sector where Walker's men were receiving a horrendous baptism of fire. Panzers created havoc against the lightly armed American infantry while enemy machine guns and mortars added to the carnage of what one officer recorded as "just plain unadulterated hell." Attempts to attack the German tanks met with repeated failure. Badly needed supporting artillery and troops were unable to land under the heavy fire being directed their way, which turned the beaches into death traps. Offshore were the burning hulks of LCTs and LSTs hit by the German gunners.* Especially telling were the German defenses along the beaches, which might have been knocked out had Hewitt's advice been taken and the navy permitted to mount a powerful artillery bombardment before the assault landings. Clark had not been alone in reject-

---

*In the Mediterranean, the Allies introduced a series of new landing craft that was to play a vital role. First employed in Sicily, the series included the Landing Ship Tank (LST), Landing Craft Tank (LCT), Landing Craft Infantry (LCI), and Landing Craft Vehicle/Personnel (LCVP). These ingeniously designed vessels were solutions to the most pressing problems of amphibious warfare: the need to shift troops and material rapidly from ship to shore or from shore to shore.

ing Hewitt; Walker too had seen no useful purpose in "killing a lot of peaceful Italians and destroying their homes. The 16th Panzer is in the area but will not be strong in any one sector, especially along the beaches."

The relentless defense of the Salerno beachhead by the German army was typical of what the Allies had encountered in their battles in the Mediterranean. When they could, the Germans fought tenaciously to retain their positions; when that was impossible, they fought delaying actions until they could establish new defenses elsewhere. In Sicily they had been outnumbered, outgunned, outmaneuvered, and unable to meet the Allied invaders on the beaches. At Salerno, however, despite the large area of responsibility, the 16th Panzer Division was able to mount an effective defense from the outset, and had every intention of driving the Allies back into the sea. And, as the U.S. official naval historian points out, "unfortunately for us, the Germans were almost as well prepared to contest landings at Salerno as the Japanese would be at Tarawa two months later."

The principal threat to the 36th Division was the German Mark IV tanks that marauded near the beaches throughout the morning of D-Day. Few American tanks had yet been brought ashore, and air attacks and naval gunfire were required to beat off the German armored attacks. The most serious threat occurred shortly after 1000 hours, when thirteen panzers were spotted moving down Route 18 toward Paestum. It took combined air and naval gunfire to drive off the Germans, who lost five tanks before withdrawing.

Walker and his staff landed at 0730 hours and established a command post, but they had little idea of the overall situation. Their transport was lost during the landing, and as they made their way inland east of Paestum, German gunners in the hills above amused themselves by firing salvos at them. Walker witnessed the counterattack and was thankful that the German tanks had attacked in small groups and had failed to employ supporting infantry. These "could have caused us a lot of trouble if they had attacked in mass formation at an early hour."

With the aid of the air forces and the navy, the 36th Division somehow survived on D-Day despite the confusion and the vicious German resistance across the entire front at Paestum. Although the invasion did not go according to plan, the Division succeeded in making several impressive gains by the end of the day, including the town of Capaccio and several important pieces of contested high ground.

Walker's Texans earned the praise of Clark, who wrote that "no soldiers ever fought more bravely than the men of the 36th Division." Examples of gallantry and leadership came in many forms. One private collected a group of fifty men and led them in an attack that destroyed several machine-gun nests that had been tormenting the Texans. Another private single-handedly wiped out a Spandau machine-gun nest, while a sergeant braved intense fire to knock out an 88-mm gun position. The crew of a howitzer that came under tank attack set up and began direct firing without benefit of cover or concealment. And so it went as Walker's men acquitted themselves with distinction. The Texans not only absorbed the full fury of virtually everything the Germans could hurl at them and survived, but despite the numerous problems actually made significant gains. It was no small achievement for a green division in its first combat and yet to receive reinforcements. Although there were to be difficult days ahead, the Texans had surmounted their most formidable hurdle.

Considerable credit must go to the efforts of Brigadier General John W. ("Iron Mike") O'Daniel, a longtime friend of Clark sent by the Fifth Army commander to the 36th Division on special assignment to supervise the landing operations at Red and Green beaches. O'Daniel came ashore at 0430 hours and brought order out of the initial chaos. Acting as a sort of beachmaster extraordinaire, the tough, no-nonsense O'Daniel had not only taken a firm grip on the beach situation but in effect had become Clark's eyes and ears ashore during the early hours of the landings.

The 36th Division might not have survived its rough baptism of fire without the timely and valiant support of the Allied fleet. Time and time again destroyers and gunboats braved the intense German fire to maneuver close to the shore and deliver counterbattery fire or suppress a German counterattack against the invaders. Every ship in the Gulf of Salerno became a target, and even though Allied losses were less than anticipated, a considerable number of ships sustained varying degrees of damage.*

The gallantry displayed by the naval forces at Salerno was exemplified by Rear Admiral Richard L. Conolly, the officer who had commanded the JOSS invasion in HUSKY and who now was in command of an amphibi-

---

*Allied losses totaled three U.S. destroyers, one minesweeper, three Liberty ships, one tug, and six LCTs. Royal Navy losses were limited to five LCTs and the hospital ship *Newfoundland*, which was bombed by the Luftwaffe and sunk on 13 September. Despite their clear Red Cross markings, Allied hospital ships were repeatedly attacked by the Luftwaffe during the battle for Salerno.

ous task group of Commodore G. N. Oliver's Northern Attack Force off the 10th Corps beaches. Although senior in rank to his Royal Navy compatriot Oliver, Conolly unhesitatingly volunteered for his assignment. At Licata he had gained the nickname "Close-in Conolly," and on D-Day he reaffirmed it by his actions in responding to the fire of a battery of 88-mm guns in the hills overlooking Salerno. Unable to contact his supporting destroyers, Conolly used his own flagship, the U.S.S. *Biscayne*, to engage and destroy the guns. Few would dispute the fact that without the navy the situation would have been far more perilous. The division artillery commander may have said it best in a message to his navy comrades: "Thank God for the fire of the blue-belly Navy ships."

THE BRITISH IN THE 10TH CORPS SECTOR encountered varying degrees of resistance. The landings had been accomplished with comparative ease, but the remainder of D-Day was marked by numerous violent small-unit actions as German troops and tanks clashed with the invaders. Unlike the 36th Division sector, however, there were no dire threats to the survival ashore of either British division. As D-Day drew to a close, the German commander of the 16th Panzer, General Sieckenius, reckoned his front was relatively secure despite the various gains inland across the Salerno front. His greatest concern lay in the Eboli sector, where any Allied breakthrough into the plain beyond would pose the threat of dislodging the 16th Panzer Division. Sieckenius ordered all bridges over the River Sele blown and regrouped his defenses to meet any breakthrough attempt at Eboli. German Tenth Army commanding general Vietinghof also recognized the importance of holding firmly around Eboli, and he ordered the plain "held at all costs."

The Allies at Salerno now possessed a slender beachhead and a very uncertain future. The idyll that some had naïvely believed possible with the surrender of Italy had turned out to be a nightmare. Aboard Admiral Hewitt's command ship, *Ancon*, Clark as yet had no clear picture of conditions ashore. The Fifth Army commander's mood throughout that day had been somber, as snippets of information were relayed from the assault commanders.

The gravest threat to the Allies lay in the enormous seven-mile gap between 10th Corps and VI Corps, which Clark optimistically called "not too serious" but certainly would have to be corrected if the Allied force were to prevent the Germans from exploiting it. Eisenhower was not reassured, and as the situation deteriorated at Salerno in the week following D-Day, when it became increasingly uncertain whether the Allies could even retain their foothold, the Allied commander-in-chief was heard to entertain the possibility of disaster, in which case he would probably be "out." A cable to the Combined Chiefs of Staff noted that AVALANCHE "will be a matter of touch and go for the next few days . . . we are in for some very tough fighting."

SEVEN

A Near-Run Thing

GEORGE S. PATTON, JR., HAD BEEN APPOINTED reserve commander of Fifth Army in the event that Clark was killed or incapacitated. When he was briefed on AVALANCHE by the Fifth Army Chief of Staff, he at once identified the Sele River gap as a problem which the Germans could be counted upon to exploit. "I told him that just as sure as God lives, the Germans will attack down that river," he wrote in his diary that night.

Patton's astuteness and experience were not matched by Clark and his staff, who had no experience planning a major combat operation. The result was a deeply flawed invasion plan, in which the assault forces were dangerously overextended, particularly when they were matched against veteran panzer forces. With neither corps able to provide mutual support to the other, the Sele River and its several tributaries constituted a formidable obstacle to mutual reinforcement. The 36th Division was virtually a separate invasion force, and the 56th Division on the VI Corps left flank was ten miles away and itself obliged to cover a frontage of some fifteen miles.

The Ranger and Commando forces who went ashore west of Salerno were dependent on linking up with the British 46th Division, yet no consideration seems to have been given to what would happen if the division were unable to reach them within a reasonable time. Worst of all, the invasion force was to land directly into the line of fire of German gun emplacements in the hills overlooking the Gulf of Salerno. In addition, the forces allocated to a breakout from the bridgehead were inadequate. As Graham and Bidwell point out in their superb study of the Italian campaign, "The whole plan was an example of the Fifth Army staff's propensity to make plans on the map without any study of the ground or of possible enemy reaction. The result was that of the nine [infantry] brigades . . . available only two were allotted to the task of breaking out of the bridgehead; both infantry, marching on foot."

There was precious little time for the planning of AVALANCHE, and constant changes were being made to the loading plans up to the last moment. General Fred Walker was a hard-nosed Regular Army officer with a reputation for competence and an unwillingness to suffer fools gladly. The repeated demands to alter his loading plans, often to accommodate unnecessary equipment and supplies, infuriated Walker, who with good reason referred to the higher staffs as unreasonable, incompetent, and appallingly stupid. The important lessons of the Sicily campaign were, in fact, never assimilated by the Fifth Army planners, and this time "there was no Montgomery to argue the toss."

There was little the planners could do about the numbers of troops in the initial assault force, but their method of employing what they had available left much to be desired. It was correctly assumed that the Germans would concentrate their defenses to prevent the fall of Salerno and a subsequent Allied foothold in the passes leading to Naples. Nevertheless, of the three assault divisions, two were assigned defensive missions: the U.S. 36th, which was to guard the southern flank, and the British 56th, whose objectives of seizing and holding Montecorvino airfield were equally defensive. This left the British 46th Division with the principal offensive role, yet it was landed too far from its objective of Salerno to ensure the success of its mission. And, as the events on D-Day clearly demonstrated, AVALANCHE amounted to three separate invasion forces fighting entirely individual battles.

Unmistakable evidence of the German determination to hold Salerno came when the 26th Panzer Division began arriving from Calabria less than twenty-four hours after being notified of the situation to the north. Its advent, however, was delayed by a shortage of fuel, and instead of constituting a large combat-ready force from the outset, the 26th Panzer arrived piecemeal over a period of several days. The Germans thus missed a vital edge in their struggle to retain Salerno. Von Vietinghof was still worried about the possibility of yet another landing, and his overcaution left two panzer divisions in place outside Naples until 10 September. Their presence earlier, along with 26th Panzer, could have made Fifth Army's situation intolerable.

On 10 September (D plus one) badly needed American reinforcements began coming ashore, as the 157th and 179th regiments of the 45th Division Thunderbirds, in floating reserve offshore, joined the fray.

The 2d Battalion of the 179th Regiment, supported by B Battery of the 160th Field Artillery, was detached and sent inland to capture and hold the hills around Serre, some five miles east of Eboli. The main force's assignment was to plug the dangerous gap between VI and 10th corps along the Sele River salient. After an all-night march, it came under heavy German tank and infantry attack.

One of the 45th Division regiments, Colonel Charles Ankhorn's 157th Regimental Combat Team, was sent into the 10th Corps sector astride the left bank of the Sele River in order to capture the high ground around a tobacco factory near the village of Persano. The Americans found the Germans in control of this vital terrain, which had become a dagger pointed at the heart of the Allied gap. Attempts to drive the Germans out met with failure and the loss of seven Sherman tanks.

The uncertainty continued during the second day of fighting, as both sides continued to jockey for position and sought to muster reinforcements for the ultimate showdown. On D plus three the Germans struck back from the air, sinking thirteen craft, including a hospital ship. Two U.S. cruisers were also badly damaged as the Luftwaffe launched radio-controlled rocket and glider bombs of chilling accuracy.

On Sunday, 12 September, Kesselring visited the front to see the situation for himself, landing at Polla at the controls of a Ju-88, where he was greeted by von Vietinghof. Unlike the campaign in North Africa where there was so much distrust between the German commanders, at Salerno Kesselring and the veteran von Vietinghof were in accord. Kesselring approved the Tenth Army commander's plan to strike at the gap in the Allied lines but, aware of Eighth Army's eventual arrival, warned him of the menace of being outflanked by Montgomery. Fortunately for the Germans, Eighth Army was at that moment nearly 150 miles to the south and no immediate threat. To von Vietinghof's intense consternation, Kesselring insisted on piloting his Junker aircraft over the Salerno beachhead en route back to his headquarters in order to "feel the pulse of the battlefield."

Kesselring had provided Tenth Army with fresh units to augment the hard-pressed 16th Panzer. Attacking from the northeast were elements of three panzer and panzer grenadier divisions (26th Panzer, 29th Panzer Grenadier, and 16th Panzer) against VI Corps. Two other veteran divisions from Sicily, the Hermann Göring and 15th Panzer Grenadier, joined with the 3d Panzer Grenadier in launching counterattacks against McCreery's 10th Corps in the Montecorvino sector. Across the front the invaders were forced to cede terrain previously captured, including Battipaglia and Altavilla, the latter a particularly important bastion overlooking the VI Corps sector.

It is doubtful that von Vietinghof was aware of the Sele River gap when he met with Kesselring, but by the following morning the situation had clarified and the time had come for a major effort to exploit the Allies' weak point and destroy the invasion. To the north the Hermann Göring and 15th Panzer Grenadier divisions from Naples had already begun attacking the northern flank of the Allied bridgehead. In the VI Corps sector the 26th Panzer had now arrived in force. Clark had already committed his slender 45th Division reserves and had virtually nothing left with which to reinforce against a determined German counterattack.

The threat posed by German possession of the tobacco factory and the high ground in and around Persano was symptomatic of the worsening crisis across the Allied front. To the north of the tobacco factory British 56th Division troopers, already driven from the town of Battipaglia, were in danger of being overrun. General Graham exhorted his men not to "yield another inch. . . . I call upon every man to fight to the last round and the last breath!"

From the time he had come ashore on D plus one Clark had restlessly prowled the battlefield in an attempt to find solutions to his worsening situation. Wherever he could, Clark plugged gaps and exhorted his troops to hang tough, knowing that he had nothing immediately available to reinforce them. So dire had the situation become at Salerno that Clark was now contemplating the unthinkable: being driven back into the sea. He began making plans to embark VI Corps and re-land them in the British sector. The sorry situation at Salerno was summed up by Clark when he told his aide, "We're in a bad way. I don't know what the devil to do."

There was one slender thread of hope, and Clark seized on it. If he could hold on long enough for the 82d Airborne Division to arrive, there was still a chance to retain his grip on the VI Corps sector. He alerted Ridgway that it was imperative that reinforcements be parachuted into the Salerno bridgehead *that night.*

Clark's urgent request was delivered by a young P-38 fighter pilot who handcarried a letter to Ridgway. With Clark's admonition that the letter be personally given to Ridgway, "and no one else," the pilot handed the Fifth Army commander's message to the paratroop commander. "I want you to accept this letter as an order," wrote Clark. "I realize the time normally needed to prepare for a drop, but this is an exception. I want you to make a drop within our lines on the beachhead and I want you to make it tonight. This is a must." Ridgway thus had less than twelve hours to mount the most difficult of all airborne operations, a night drop under enemy observation and fire.

Ridgway understood how desperate matters had become at Salerno. There was no time for the niceties of a formal operations order or for working up an intelligence estimate. This was a situation that called for a "seat of the pants" performance that would test skill and experience to the fullest. Ridgway's response to Clark's plea was typical of one of the most confident and aggressive commanders produced by the United States in World War II: "Can do." Summoning his commanders and staff, Ridgway did not mince his words. It would be a tall order, but Fifth Army was in desperate straits and Clark needed the 82d Airborne right now. The briefings given the 82d paratroopers in the hectic moments leading up to the departure of the troop carriers had been reduced to simple, blunt GI language that, as one airborne historian has noted, "went something like this: 'The Krauts are kicking the shit out of our boys at Salerno and we're going to jump into the beachhead tonight and rescue them. Put on your parachutes and get on the plane. . . .'"

The hastily devised plan called for Colonel Tucker's 504th Parachute Infantry Regiment to jump along the beaches near Paestum that night (13 September) to help plug the Sele River gap. Pathfinders would precede the main drop to light up the drop zone, which would be momentarily illuminated just as the aircraft arrived overhead. It was an operation that demanded both perfect timing and coordination with the Allied gunners at sea and ashore, who must hold their fire—something they had been unable to do during the four previous glider and airborne operations in Sicily.

Even more daring was the second half of Clark's plan. The following night, 14 September, the troop carriers were to return, and Lieutenant Colonel Doyle Yardley's independent 509th Parachute Infantry Battalion, another battle-tested airborne unit that had fought with distinction in North Africa, was to drop twenty-five miles behind enemy lines at the village of Avellino, where they were to take the pressure off VI Corps by harassing the Germans in the hills overlooking Salerno.

WHILE THE 82D AIRBORNE PREPARED FOR its night drop into the Salerno bridgehead, the Germans struck with full fury on the afternoon of 13 September. As Clark had feared, their counterattack was centered around the tobacco factory and its adjacent high ground, where the Germans had established impenetrable positions, and in so doing had left the 45th Division in danger of being cut off and isolated. Backed by tanks, the Germans thrust down the Sele corridor and threatened the flanks of both American divisions. Neither Walker nor Middleton had been able to establish cohesive defensive positions. At best the American positions offered exposed flanks, with the Germans left in command of the key terrain and calling the shots. The result, on the afternoon of 13 September, was "absolute hell," as one GI later described the scene of smoking and burning vehicles, the whine of artillery and mortars, and the constant noise of German Spandaus as the enemy advanced down the corridor toward the sea. Unless something was done, and done quickly, there was a strong possibility of the Germans splitting the Allied line and turning Clark's flanks.

Across the battered American front came the order: "Hold at all costs." As the battle raged, U.S. losses began to mount with disturbing speed. Units were isolated from one another and chopped to pieces, communications were severed, and the battle became a struggle for survival. A mere sixty men were all that was left of one infantry battalion of the 36th Division at the end of the fight. "Desperate" became a frequently used but scarcely exaggerated word.

When Dawley reported the grim situation to Clark, the army commander replied, "What are you doing about it?" "Nothing," said Dawley, "I've no reserves. All I've got is a prayer." More candidly, a GI noted that "only God was protecting our left flank and HE was taking a ten-minute break."

As German tanks and infantry penetrated further into the Sele River gap, von Vietinghof became confident that Tenth Army would soon drive the Allies back into the Gulf of Salerno. In fact, he grew overly optimistic and prematurely signaled Kesselring and OKW that he had Fifth Army on the run: "Enemy resistance collapsing. Tenth Army pursuing enemy on wide front. . . . Maneuver in progress to cut off Paestum from retreating enemy."

Von Vietinghof mistakenly viewed the Allies' split forces—for which they were now paying a high price—as evidence that the battle was near an end. Sensing victory, he ordered his commanders not to let up but to "throw everything into the battle" in order to annihilate Fifth Army. It was a battle he believed would not last much longer.

ALTHOUGH CLARK HAD SET IN MOTION a partial remedy to the crisis, he elected to initiate plans for an evacuation of the VI Corps beachhead. To Admiral Hewitt came the bombshell message that he was strongly considering the urgent abandonment of the American sector and a reembarkation along the 10th Corps front, north of the Sele River. Hewitt was shocked by Clark's request, but his task was to support the ground forces, and like the dutiful commander he was, Hewitt proceeded with plans for the operation.

It was a measure of Clark's inexperience that he failed to take his corps and division commanders into his confidence. Walker, who was no great admirer of Mark Clark, and Middleton were particularly annoyed. The mild-mannered Middleton refused to take the scheme seriously. "Put food and ammunition behind the 45th," he informed Clark. "We are going to stay here." The Germans soon learned of the plan, too; in fact, they may have been aware of it even before the VI Corps commander. They lost no time exploiting their knowledge. The night of 13–14 September the infamous Axis Sally taunted the Americans: "They're bringing transports to take you off the beaches, boys. But this time you won't get away. . . . It's the end of the line for you."

Clark's contingency plans called for two possible maneuvers. One was for the evacuation of VI Corps; another was for a similar operation, but with McCreery's 10th Corps reembarking and moving to the U.S. sector. The British reaction to Clark's proposal was cold fury. Commodore Oliver thought any attempt to shorten the beachhead was suicidal, and when the outspoken McCreery learned what was afoot, he too was horrified. As word spread throughout the Allied command structure, there was little support for Clark's plan. What angered McCreery most was that Clark had failed to make any reference whatever to a reembarkation when they had met earlier on 13 September. His signal to the Fifth Army commander noted that inasmuch as there had been no such mention, there obviously could be no question of such an operation occurring.

Alexander, Cunningham, and Eisenhower were equally disturbed, and Alexander fully supported McCreery's position. Eisenhower wondered if his old friend Clark had lost his nerve, and his naval aide recorded that the commander-in-chief thought that "Clark should show the spirit of a naval captain. If necessary, he should go down with his ship." Nevertheless, Eisenhower was determined to move heaven and earth to save Fifth Army. Cunningham and Tedder cooperated fully by sending additional naval reinforcements to Salerno and by stepping up air support, which included the services of some B-17 strategic bombers to pound German positions.

With commendable understatement, Cunningham later wrote of the proposed evacuation that it "would have resulted in a reverse of the first magnitude—an Allied defeat which would have completely offset the

Italian surrender, and have been hailed by the Germans as a smashing victory." In retrospect it is clear that Alexander had no intention of letting Clark carry out a reembarkation operation at Salerno. Fortunately for the Allies, as the battle continued into its most critical stage, the Germans helped to ensure that there would be no need to carry out such an operation.

On the afternoon of 13 September the German panzer grenadier commander unwittingly let his enemy off the hook. The focus of the battle was in the area of the corridor where the Sele and Calore rivers converge, some two and a half miles south of the tobacco factory, where at first the Germans were successful. A large force of panzer grenadiers and twenty-one tanks had driven a battalion of the 157th Infantry Regiment from the tobacco factory, while another powerful force struck the 2d Battalion, 143d Infantry (36th Division), guarding the Ponte Sele road, forcing its retirement across the Calore River with enormous losses—508 casualties. The German panzers shot up everything in sight, and the veteran panzer grenadiers overwhelmed the Texans as much with the fierceness of their attack as they did with their heavy automatic weapons fire and grenades. Eventually the Texans would learn to counter such attacks, but on the afternoon of 13 September the German onslaught was too powerful to withstand. The way was now open for the Germans to strike toward the beaches at Paestum and drive a wedge between the two corps that would leave VI Corps outflanked.

In war, as in life, luck is frequently a factor as uncertain as a roll of the dice. The GIs who fought for their very survival would have scoffed at the notion they were getting a break, but a simple mistake by the German commander soon became the most important factor in the intense battles that ensued that grim afternoon of 13 September.

Supported by an infantry battalion, the main body of German tanks continued down the corridor between the two rivers, intending to cross the Calore River and continue to Paestum, five miles beyond. At this point the German attack came apart. The German force was part of the 29th Panzer Grenadier Division that had been rushed north from Calabria, and its commanders were unfamiliar with the terrain. The German commander's map failed to indicate that an all-important bridge had been destroyed, and the steep banks of the river made fording impossible. The result was a German attack leading to a dead end.

Across the river in the open fields was a hastily assembled American force that was determined to prevent any further German advance. It consisted primarily of two field artillery battalions of the 45th Division—

the 158th and 189th—augmented by several Sherman tanks and tank destroyers. The American commanders had rounded up every soldier they could lay hands on—cooks, administrative personnel, truck drivers, and even the Fifth Army band—and pressed them into service. This ad hoc force was the only element between the Germans and the sea.

In a scene reminiscent of the Gela counterattacks on 11 July, the American gunners, with some support from other nearby artillery units, poured nearly four thousand rounds into the German force. By nightfall the German commander had found no way around the obstacle he had stumbled into, and, unable to counter the hail of fire raining down on his column, admitted failure and pulled back up the corridor toward the tobacco factory. The crisis had passed. A determined band of gunners, bandsmen, and mixed troops had saved the day. Although Fifth Army was by no means out of the woods, the failure of the German counterattack on 13 September was a decisive factor in the battle for Salerno.

SO HASTY WERE THE FINAL PREPARATIONS for the drop of the 504th Parachute Infantry that the briefing for the troop carrier pilots took place by "the light of a few flashlights and maps held against the side of a plane" as the regiment was loaded. Ridgway's continuing nightmare was a repetition of the HUSKY airborne disasters. Would the naval and ground elements at Salerno be briefed in time and avoid firing on the defenseless troop carriers?

Fifty pathfinders with homing transmitters and radar devices landed with precision on the drop zone, which they marked with an enormous T lit by gasoline cans. Close behind came the 1,300 troops of Colonel Reuben H. Tucker's regiment. For the first time in the war an Allied airborne operation was carried out to near perfection. Despite a German air raid only moments before their arrival, the Fifth Army and Allied naval gunners followed orders not to fire after 9:00 P.M., no matter what. No one was more relieved than Tucker, whose regiment had been savaged by friendly fire the night of D plus one in Sicily.

It was a dramatic moment in the battle. When they saw the airborne arriving, the troops guarding the beach "stood in their trenches cheering themselves hoarse." Within minutes of landing, a confident Colonel Tucker reported to Clark that his regiment was ready for commitment. They were immediately sent to reinforce the hard-pressed 36th Division. When the Germans renewed their attempts to crush the Salerno beachhead on 14 September, they encountered not only Walker's infantry but the tough airborne troops of the 504th.

The success of the airborne drop encouraged Clark to order a second drop the following night, and the 2,200 men of Gavin's 505th Parachute Infantry Regiment duplicated the feat of the 504th. Within twenty-four hours Fifth Army had gained 3,500 valuable reinforcements and an additional barrier to von Vietinghof's plan to drive the Allies into the sea. For the first time VI Corps could establish a reserve and gain the flexibility of defending or attacking with a veteran infantry force.

Unfortunately, that same night Mark Clark pushed his luck too far. He had previously ordered a battalion-sized force to land at Avellino, an important road junction in the mountains twenty miles north of Salerno. The operation was carried out by Yardley's airborne battalion and was the first such operation to be launched in the rear of an active enemy front. The result was a fiasco.

Of the 640 paratroopers who departed Sicily, only 160 landed anywhere near Avellino. Everything that could go wrong did. The pathfinders were landed on the wrong drop zone and their radio equipment failed to alert the pilots ferrying the main body close behind, most of whom could locate neither the drop zone nor Avellino in the dark. The remainder were scattered over a wide area and were no factor in the brief battle that followed. Although some managed to carry out harassment and sabotage similar to that accomplished by the 505th in Sicily, the attack led by Yardley against Avellino failed. Many paratroopers were reported missing, though eventually most of the battalion returned to Allied control. It was an operation that should never have been attempted, and it was another opportunity for critics of the airborne to bolster their case.

THE ARRIVAL OF ALLIED REINFORCEMENTS and the gradual stabilization of their foothold at Salerno precipitated a critical decision by the German high command. Two panzer corps, the XIV and LXXVI, were in charge of the defense of the Salerno front, and coordination had not worked well. General Major Rudolf Sieckenius's 16th Panzer Division was operating in both corps sectors and had on more than one occasion been the recipient of conflicting orders. The inescapable fact was that despite the arrival of reinforcements from all over Italy, the numerous German counterattacks had failed to dislodge the Allies. The question was, what next?

All hope of a German strategic victory at Salerno was lost after the fighting of 13 September made it clear to the German corps commanders at the front that the Allies were not going to be pushed into the sea.

Urged on by Clark, who had restlessly patrolled the front offering encouragement and inspiration, the U.S. sector held. The Germans had enjoyed scant success against the British 46th Division, and despite von Vietinghof's unwarranted optimism, the two corps commanders realized there was little to be gained from another all-out attack.

German equipment losses had begun to mount, and fatigue was beginning to take its toll. The 16th Panzer Division, for example, was down to twenty-two tanks, and its men were exhausted from the virtually non-stop combat, the merciless artillery fire from both the sea and land, and increasingly heavy aerial attacks. Still, von Vietinghof was not prepared to give up Salerno without one last counterattack. Kesselring, who was briefed on the forthcoming attack by the Tenth Army commander the morning of 15 September, sanctioned the plan but warned against getting bogged down in "positional warfare."

On 16 September the attack was launched. The XIV Panzer Corps attempted to squeeze the British in a vise by simultaneous attacks on two sides of Battipaglia by the 26th Panzer Division, while the Hermann Göring and 15th Panzer Grenadier divisions attacked the 46th Division to the north, with the object of cutting off 10th Corps and rolling up its flanks.

The attack was quickly doomed to failure, not only by the timely presence the previous day of the Allied air forces but by devastating defensive fire which shattered the Germans even before they could launch their assaults. Hardest hit was 26th Panzer, whose attack stalled from the outset, with a loss of two hundred killed.

Although there was to be more fighting, the tide had clearly turned in favor of the Allies. Clark not only had the airborne reinforcements, but Fifth Army had been bolstered by the arrival of the British 7th Armoured Division (the famed Desert Rats) and the previously uncommitted infantry regiment of the 45th Division.

What had begun as a near disaster had, by a combination of sheer tenacity by the frontline troops, superb gunnery on the part of the Allied navy and the artillerymen ashore, and valiant air support, enabled Fifth Army to hold its ground long enough for reinforcements to arrive and for the Germans to exhaust their resources in unsuccessful counterattacks. When it became clear to Kesselring that there was to be no strategic victory at Salerno, he ordered von Vietinghof to implement a phased withdrawal that would disengage Tenth Army without further serious losses. By 17 September LXXVI Panzer Corps was on the move to the north, while XIV Panzer Corps fought a stiff rearguard action as it disengaged and likewise moved north, stopping along the way to thwart any pursuit by the skillful use of demolitions and terrain.

Fifth Army was equally spent and in no shape for a serious pursuit operation. With the Germans in retreat, the way was at long last open to Naples, which fell to the Allies on 1 October. Clark made a grand entrance into the city, but even he was able to feel only so much elation over becoming the liberator of Naples. Writing after the war in his memoirs, Clark noted that "there was little triumphant about our journey" through the deserted streets of what seemed to be "a city of ghosts."

Fifth Army's baptism of fire had not come without considerable cost. Allied casualties numbered well over 13,000:

	Killed	*Wounded*	*Missing*
British	982	4,060	2,230
U.S.	788	2,814	1,318
Royal Navy	83	43	—
U.S. Navy	296	422	551
Total	2,149	7,339	4,099

Three thousand of the missing were now enemy prisoners. German casualties were comparatively small: 3,472, of which 630 were killed in action.

In British eyes American leadership was still displaying its inexperience. Although units such as the airborne, rangers, and field artillery had performed magnificently, leadership at the top echelon had been less consistent. At Alexander's instigation, the VI Corps commander became the sacrificial lamb for the near disaster at Salerno. Dawley was relieved of command and sent home in his permanent grade of colonel. Although he was far from outstanding as a corps commander, his relief was equally a face-saving gesture on the part of the Allied high command.*

Alexander's generalship at Salerno varied little from his performance throughout the war in the Mediterranean. He failed to influence the outcome of the battle in any but a negative way. Although his task was to ensure that the invasion commander received the optimum support, he

---

*By the time of his relief, Dawley's relations with Clark had become seriously strained. He would not have been Clark's choice to command VI Corps in the first place, and neither was ever comfortable with the other. The night before his relief there was a heated argument in which Dawley caustically referred to "Boy Scouts and boys in short pants," whereupon Clark drove off in his jeep and left the VI Corps commander near the front without transportation.

failed to spur Eighth Army to reinforce Fifth Army more quickly, which it was fully capable of doing. Although the Eighth Army advance north from Calabria was inexcusably tardy, Alexander failed to instill a sense of urgency in Montgomery.* Nor did he move to invest the beachhead with additional support at an earlier moment by committing the 82d Airborne when and where its presence would have made an appreciable difference. Moreover, Alexander failed to address the obvious problem of Clark's flawed invasion plan or even to offer so much as his opinion that he considered it faulty.

Salerno established Mark Clark as a man of exceptional personal courage, but he had a great deal yet to learn about high command. He mistakenly believed he had saved the Allied invasion by his leadership, when in fact it was precisely his inexperience that precipitated most of the problems faced by the invasion force. His relations with Alexander, while always cordial on the surface, never went beyond the formality of a senior-subordinate relationship and frequently led him to ignore Alexander, in the same manner as Montgomery did throughout his tenure as Eighth Army commander. The difference was that Monty had considerable personal rapport with Alexander, while the Alexander-Clark relationship was essentially adversarial.

Nor were Clark's relations with his own American subordinate commanders cause for elation. He related badly to most of them and rarely listened to their advice. As the Italian campaign developed, his relations with Fred Walker, the veteran 36th Division commander, would worsen.

Worst of all, Salerno promoted a continuation of the mistrust between the two Allies that had begun in North Africa. The British remained critical of the American performance, believing that little had changed since Kasserine, the Sicily campaign notwithstanding. McCreery held Clark in utter contempt, and in return the Fifth Army commander

---

*Montgomery was irked by his minor role in Italy and by the fact that his proposals had been ignored by Eisenhower and the AFHQ staff. He responded by halting his army in Calabria on 8 September to regroup, even though Kesselring withdrew virtually all of his units to deal with the threat at Salerno. With only delaying forces opposing Eighth Army, Montgomery could have driven north to Salerno in forty-eight hours; instead, he ignored polite exhortations from Alexander and his chief of staff to speed to the aid of Clark's beleaguered Fifth Army. A group of Anglo-American war correspondents drove ahead of the leading units of Eighth Army, and for nearly one hundred miles they neither heard a shot fired in anger nor encountered a single German soldier. According to one account, they were the first Eighth Army element to arrive at Paestum.

scornfully referred to the 10th Corps commander as a "feather duster." Alexander, who was personally the epitome of an Irish gentleman, revealed his true feelings after the war in a little-known interview with the official U.S. Army historians. With few exceptions, the American generals under his command did not come off well.

For their part, the British had little cause for celebration. The quality of their forces was as mixed as the American forces, and to add insult to injury, Salerno was the scene of one of the most humiliating episodes in the history of the tradition-filled British army: a mutiny. Although little publicized, on 16 September some 700 replacement troops sat down on the beach and refused a series of orders to report to their units. When all entreaties failed, McCreery himself personally intervened and managed to convince the majority to obey. The 192 Tommies who refused, mostly veterans of the 50th Northumbrian and 51st Highland divisions, were court-martialled.* The NCOs who led the rebellion were sentenced to death, but all were soon given a chance to redeem themselves by returning to duty in Italy with suspended sentences. Despite being successfully resolved, the incident became a permanent stain on the honor of the army.

The most important message Salerno should have sent to the Allies was that the Italian campaign was to be a never-ending series of battles in terrain that greatly favored the defender. Salerno imbued Clark with a sense of caution that would later have extremely serious consequences at Anzio. It was a message whose effect subtly but clearly enabled Kesselring and the German army to turn the campaign into a stalemate in central Italy.

---

*The Salerno mutiny had its roots in the failure of the participants to understand that they were being sent to the front to help alleviate a dire situation instead of as ordinary replacements. Most believed their leaders had broken a promise to rotate them home, as their parent divisions had already done. The situation was further exacerbated by the Scots, who resisted being assigned to any unit except a Scottish regiment.

EIGHT

Stalemate at the Gustav Line

DESPITE THEIR INABILITY TO DRIVE THE Allied invasion of Salerno back into the sea, Kesselring and the German army retained considerable cause for optimism. Although outgunned, lacking air superiority, and at the end of a lengthy logistic lifeline, the Germans nevertheless had managed to stifle the invasion landings and in the process had come close to inflicting a major defeat. Most important of all, what happened at Salerno was the proof that Kesselring needed to convince Hitler that his forces could indeed successfully defend central Italy. Had the Allies employed their resources better at Salerno, Kesselring might have drawn a different conclusion and thus altered the entire course of the war in Italy.

Even though the German Tenth Army had voluntarily withdrawn from the Salerno bridgehead and offered little resistance on the road to Naples, it still managed to make the Fifth Army's advance difficult. Kesselring's strategy included creating every possible obstacle to Allied movement, as was vividly illustrated on 27 September when German engineers demolished virtually every culvert and bridge between Salerno and Naples. As Graham and Bidwell point out, "The pace of the victorious advance on Naples was to be determined by the speed at which the engineers could sweep for landmines and bridge the gaps. That was to be the pattern of war in Italy until the bitter end."

Although he had escaped censure for ordering the evacuation of Sicily before receiving Hitler's permission, even Kesselring was no exception to the Führer's penchant for blaming his generals for setbacks over which they had little control. Hitler referred to him as "a dupe among those born [Italian] traitors," and the head of the operations staff of the OKW, General Alfred Jodl, was—like Rommel—no friend at court.

Despite intense pressures from the Allies and from his own high command, Kesselring managed successfully to walk a narrow tightrope between the unrealistic, often wild delusions of Hitler and the realities of
his position as a commander forced to live from hand to mouth in a secondary theater of war.

Italy's defection to the Allies in September 1943 marked a turning
point in Kesselring's relations with Hitler. There was considerable controversy within the OKW over German strategy in Italy, but despite his
own low standing, Kesselring was now able to persuade a reluctant Hitler
to follow his ideas for a strategic approach to the defense of Italy south of
Rome. By November Kesselring's arguments had prevailed, and he was
given command of the newly created Army Group C, which consisted of
von Vietinghof's Tenth Army and a new formation, the Fourteenth Army,
commanded by another Prussian aristocrat, Colonel-General Eberhard
von Mackensen. His father had been a field marshal, and von Mackensen himself was another of the German tank officers who had fought
well in Russia in command of a corps and later of the 1st Panzerarmee.

Kesselring had begun preparations to defend the Gustav Line even
while elements of von Vietinghof's Tenth Army were delaying Allied
troops invading Salerno. Von Vietinghof was one of the new breed of
tough, aggressive armored commanders who had been blooded in Russia
while leading a panzer division under General Heinz Guderian. His supporting cast of field commanders was as able a group as the Wehrmacht
employed in any theater of operations during the war.

In command of XIV Panzer Corps was yet another officer whom the
Allies knew only too well from Sicily, General der Panzertruppen Hube,
who had previously commanded the 1st Panzerarmee on the Eastern
Front under Field Marshal Erich von Manstein. When Hube was reassigned back to Russia in November, his replacement was von Senger.

Lieutenant General Fridolin von Senger und Etterlin was a Bavarian,
a devout Catholic, a lay Benedictine, and a former Rhodes scholar who
had many English friends from his days at Oxford before the First World
War. He was one of a growing number of anti-Nazi generals who fought
not for a regime they despised but for the honor of Germany. His hatred
of Hitler would have doubtless resulted in his removal and court-martial
on more than one occasion had it not been for his outstanding record as a
commander. In Sardinia in September he had openly defied a direct
order from Hitler to execute a large number of Italian officers and soldiers in retaliation for Italy's defection to the Allies.

At division level were some equally tough customers. Commanding the 1st Parachute Division was the able Lieutenant General Richard Heidrich, a portly cigar-smoking veteran of France, Crete, and Russia who was as proud of his resemblance to Winston Churchill as he was of the accomplishments of his soldiers. In Sicily his tiny outgunned paratroop force had single-handedly blocked Montgomery's attempt to break through to Messina during the first week of the campaign.

Others included Major General Ernst-Günther Baade, a brilliant and eccentric veteran infantry officer and a strong Anglophile from his days as an expert rider on the horse circuit in Europe, who was fond of wearing kilts. The aggressive Lieutenant General Paul Conrath was still in command of the Hermann Göring Division. Also present was his eventual successor (in early 1944), Colonel Wilhelm Schmalz, the commander of Kampfgruppe Schmalz, which had fought so well against the British in Sicily.

This, then, was the high-caliber opposition the Allies faced in Italy: veteran infantry, panzer and panzer grenadier, and airborne units commanded by combat-experienced officers, all of whom had long since learned to make do with meager resources.

Even as the German Tenth Army was withdrawing from Salerno toward the Gustav Line, Kesselring was hastening completion of his defenses, which were to be anchored along the mountains overlooking Cassino at the southern end of the Liri Valley. In order to gain the necessary time, the retreating Tenth Army was to delay the Allied advance along a series of natural defensive barriers.

Hube's XIV Panzer Corps was responsible for defending the primary Allied route to Rome along the Liri Valley, while to the east a mountain corps covered the sector from Cassino to the Adriatic coast. It was here that Kesselring planned to establish the main German defenses, which he intended to hold for as long as possible.

We now know that Kesselring's true intentions were not perceived by the Allied high command, which mistakenly believed that the German defense of Salerno presaged a full-scale retreat to the north and a defense in the Apennines centered on Pisa and Rimini, where Allied intelligence had noted the preparation of significant defenses. From Eisenhower on down, the belief prevailed that Rome would soon fall, probably by the end of October 1943.

Sicily and Salerno should have been ample warning of what lay in store for the Allies in Italy. Unless they were to initiate another amphibi-

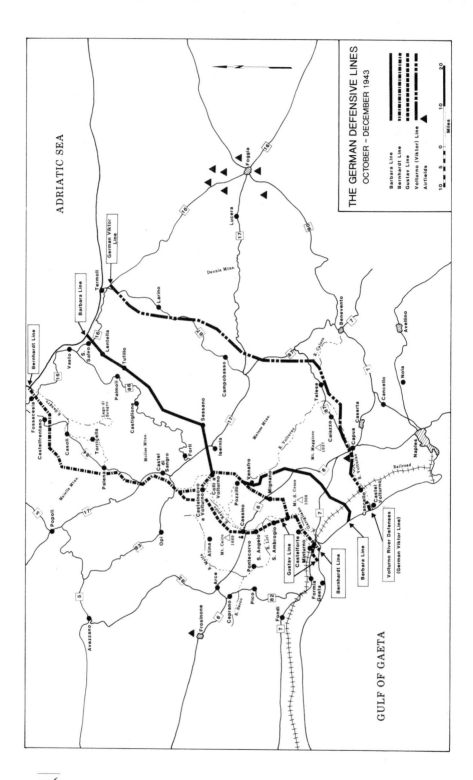

THE GERMAN DEFENSIVE LINES
OCTOBER – DECEMBER 1943

Barbara Line
Bernhardt Line
Gustav Line
Volturno (Viktor) Line
Airfields

10   5   0   10   20
         Miles

ADRIATIC SEA

GULF OF GAETA

Foggia
Lucera
Benevento
Avellino
Nola
Cancello
Naples
Caserta
Capua
Calazzo
Teleso
Mt. Maggiore
1037
R. Volturno
R. Calore
Campobasso
Matese Mtns.
Daunia Mtns.
Larino
Termoli
German Viktor Line
Barbara Line
Lentella
S. Salvo
Vasto
Tufillo
Palmoli
Castiglione
Castel di Sangro
Sessano
Isernia
Forli
Venafro
Pozzilli
Colli a Volturno
Castel a Volturno
Mignano
Mt. S. Croce
1008
Castel Volturno
Railroad
Volturno River Defenses
(German Viktor Line)
Cancello
Barbara Line
Bernhardt Line
Fossacesia
Castelfrentano
Casoli
Torricella
Palena
Maiella Mtns.
Lago di Sangro
Molise Mtns.
Popoli
Opi
Atina
Mt. Cairo
1669
R. Melfa
Pontecorvo
S. Angelo
S. Ambrogio
Cassino
Cassino
R. Liri
Gustav Line
Castelforte
Minturno
Formia
Gaeta
Bernhardt Line
Frosinone
Arce
R. Sacco
Pico
Ceprano
Fondi
Avezzano

86
16
16
8
17
5
83
82
6
7
6
7
7
87
6
6
6
6
17
1
7
9
10
10
16

ous landing north of Salerno, the geography of Italy dictated that the Allies must advance on Rome up the Mediterranean coast, staying to the west of the great chain of mountains that bisects the Italian peninsula from the Alps to the boot in Calabria.

At the Quebec Conference in August 1943 the Combined Chiefs of Staff had at long last resolved the question of when and where the cross-Channel invasion would occur. The target was Normandy, the date would be May 1944, and the campaign in Italy was seen as a vital adjunct to Allied preparations for OVERLORD. Allied strategy centered on keeping the Wehrmacht fully committed in Italy so that its veteran divisions could not be shifted to France to help repel the cross-Channel invasion.

As always, Allied strategy was focused on the capture of Rome. Churchill was emphatic that Rome must fall by the end of 1943, and well before AVALANCHE he warned Alexander that if the liberation of Rome were prolonged, "no one can measure the consequences." Alexander's task thus ran precisely counter to Kesselring's, and speed was of the essence if the Germans were not to be allowed to strengthen their defenses between Naples and Rome. However, before they could test the Gustav Line, the Allies found they first had to get past a series of hastily fortified defensive belts manned by crack German troops.

The mountainous terrain of central Italy was Kesselring's greatest ally. Not only were the mountains themselves formidable obstacles, but the many rivers, the freezing winter weather, the wind, mud, and rain, and the limited road net made any advance against a well-prepared defender a potential nightmare. The mountains had to be negotiated via mule train by sweating, weary soldiers who had to take over the portage of guns, ammunition, and supplies themselves when the trails became too steep even for mules.

Mountains were not the only formidable obstacle to the advance on Rome. No less difficult were fast-flowing rivers which had to be crossed and which made the logistics problems enormous, the execution demanding, and rapid exploitation essential. In Italy the Allies were forced to breach such obstacles during the most difficult time of year. Italian rivers ran mostly across the Allied path; thus the old adage about "one more river to cross" took on a grim reality throughout the campaign.

Ernest J. Dawley's replacement as VI Corps commander was fifty-four-year-old Major General John P. Lucas, an artilleryman who had served with Patton in Sicily as Eisenhower's "eyes and ears." His diary records the hardships faced by the soldiers who fought in Italy:

Rain, rain, rain. Military operations are always conducted in the rain. The roads are so deep in mud that moving troops and supplies forward is a terrific job. Enemy resistance is not nearly as great as that of Mother Nature, who certainly seems to be fighting on the side of the German. . . . This is a heart-breaking business. An advance of a few miles a day, fighting a terrible terrain and a determined enemy, building bridges, removing mines, climbing mountains. The men get punch drunk.

What had been anticipated as an offensive of short duration to capture Rome turned out to be a slow and deadly advance. The first German obstacle was based along the Volturno River, thirty-five miles north of Naples. Here the terrain limited the routes of advance, and von Vietinghof's 60,000 men held a line that ran all the way across Italy from the Mediterranean to the Adriatic. The German anchor was toward the west, opposite Fifth Army, where the XIV Panzer Corps had 35,000 defenders, most of them veteran units from Sicily and, most recently, Salerno. Their mission was to halt the Allied advance along the Volturno River until at least mid-October so that German engineers could complete their fortification of the Gustav Line.

The German Tenth Army's defenses along the Volturno would have been even more difficult for the Allies to break had von Vietinghof not had to deal with a surprise amphibious landing by Eighth Army on 3 October behind German lines at Termoli, on the Adriatic end of the Volturno line. Termoli was an end run by Montgomery to cut behind German lines and block their retreat along Route 16. After the landings by a small force of Commandos, tanks and infantry from Eighth Army were to link up with it.

Von Vietinghof balked at Kesselring's order to shift the 16th Panzer Division to the east to meet this new threat, believing it should remain committed against Fifth Army. Despite the delay in the commitment of 16th Panzer, however, the great potential of the British operation was lost by the advent of vile weather, which delayed the linkup between the amphibious force in Termoli and the main Eighth Army relief force. Orders from Berlin to hold Termoli at all costs led to a vicious battle that nearly destroyed the invaders and nullified the advantage gained by the end run. As it would time and time again, the weather intervened to abet the German defenses of Italy.

The advent of the rainy season had swollen the Volturno and flooded low-lying areas. Roads were turned into quagmires that made vehicular travel virtually impossible. The mud became the greatest ally of the Germans in delaying the Fifth Army offensive until nearly mid-October, when the British 10th Corps and the U.S. VI Corps launched attacks that gained footholds north of the river at heavy cost. The British bore the brunt of the casualties, losing more than 600 men, including over 200 captured.

What was most discouraging and difficult for the Allies was the absence of a visible, attainable objective. Each successful crossing of a river or a mountain led only to yet another series of almost identical obstacles. After the time-consuming and costly operations to gain a bridgehead north of the Volturno, the Allies then faced the hasty defenses of the Barbara Line, which marked the outward boundary of what the Germans called the Bernhard Line, and the Allies the Winter Line. Anchored on the Garigliano River on the west and on a formidable mountain barrier in the center and on the east, the Winter Line was the most serious obstacle the Allies had yet encountered in their march on Rome.

After months of combat, many of the Allied formations were exhausted and in poor shape to sustain an offensive under the conditions they now faced. Worst affected was Eighth Army, where many veteran British units were simply worn out from endless fighting that for most of them dated back to El Alamein the previous year. The Fifth Army after Salerno was in equally rough shape as it struggled to gain a foothold across the Volturno.

Attempts in November to continue the advance toward the Gustav Line lacked sufficient strength even to breach the German defenses along the closer Winter Line, and it was not until early December that the Americans were able to regroup and launch a fresh offensive. A series of bloody battles lasting into mid-December did gain considerable ground but failed to attain the final objective, the Liri Valley and the capture of the town of Cassino.

AS 1943 DREW TO A CLOSE, THE ALLIED high command realized that the capture of Rome was still a distant dream. At that time there were only two roads leading to Rome from the south. The town of Cassino straddled Route 6, the sole interior road to Rome; the other highway to the Italian capital was Route 7, which ran generally along the Mediterranean coast to Terracina, where it crossed the Pontine marshes and the Alban Hills south of Rome. The problem was that the Germans had effectively blocked Route 7, thus preventing Fifth Army from making an end run behind the Gustav Line.

If the hub of the German defenses along the Rapido River could be broken, the terrain to the north along Route 6 would be far less formidable. The Allied offensive in December had been intended to gain at least a foothold in the Liri Valley. It fell short when Fifth Army was unable to penetrate north of the twin obstacles of the Garigliano and Rapido rivers, so Clark's staff began developing a plan for an assault crossing of both rivers.

Alexander was responsible for the conduct of the ground operations in Italy, but it was Mark Clark who felt the greatest pressure to break the growing stalemate. Ambitious and determined to earn a place in history as a great commander, Clark was aware that he had yet to prove his mettle by winning a decisive victory. Salerno had been a near disaster, and in the succeeding three months the Germans had used the weather and the terrain to turn the campaign into a costly stalemate.

Churchill had already complained about the lack of Allied progress in Italy, and, despite a personal liking for the British leader, Clark was no Anglophile. On the contrary, his growing disdain for his British colleagues in Italy began to affect his judgment. He believed that, from Alexander on down, the British intended to take Rome and claim the credit for it at the expense of Fifth Army. The award of the Distinguished Service Cross for gallantry at Salerno, presented to him by President Roosevelt in person, seemed only to intensify a growing obsession that it was his personal responsibility to capture Rome.

By early November, however, Alexander had come to the conclusion that he could not advance to Rome unless the Allies initiated an amphibious end run to draw away the German troops manning the Gustav Line. This operation, code named SHINGLE, was to be a corps-sized amphibious landing by VI Corps eighty miles to the north at Anzio. But as problems mounted over the acquisition of the necessary landing craft and Allied operations became stalled along the Gustav Line, the timetable slipped back to the third week of January 1944.

Both SHINGLE and the river crossings were to be carried out by Fifth Army, and both presented an opportunity for Clark not only to erase British and even some American doubts about his leadership but to capture the prize, Rome. It was to this objective that the Fifth Army planners now turned their attention.

EIGHTH ARMY HAD ENCOUNTERED THE same ferocious resistance along the east coast of Italy that Fifth Army was facing in the west. After the Termoli landings, Montgomery's capture of the important Foggia airfield complex made it possible for Allied airmen to provide close air support within minutes. However, although the Allies were able to penetrate the Gustav Line, any hope of rolling up the eastern flank was lost when the weather grew so bad that Eighth Army became stalled along the flood-swollen Sangro River. Most of the assault bridges constructed by the engineers were washed away, and progress was measured in yards as the Germans fought furiously to prevent the British from breaking through and establishing a bridgehead north of the river.

Montgomery recognized that severing the Adriatic end of the Gustav Line was impossible and would only spend his army in an essentially futile effort. "I am fighting a hell of a battle here . . . [in] a sea of mud . . . and in the most foul conditions you can ever imagine," he lamented. He was dismayed that the Allies "[had] made a sad mess of it" in Italy and believed it was pointless to go on before the weather improved.

Most senior American commanders, including Clark, believed the British were overcautious on the battlefield. Few understood the magnitude of their growing manpower shortages, or realized that by the end of 1943 the British faced a major crisis wherever their troops fought. Four years of global war had stretched Britain's manpower reserves to the breaking point. Most seriously affected was the infantry arm, whose casualty losses were always the highest. In a secondary theater of war like Italy, infantry replacements were not being furnished on a scale even approaching losses. The grim news from the War Office was given to the British commanders by Adjutant General Sir Ronald Adam when he visited Italy in October 1943.

The British drive to the Sangro was Montgomery's last battle in the Mediterranean. For months Churchill, Roosevelt, and the Combined Chiefs of Staff had been wrestling with the problem of reorganizing the Allied high command in England and in the Mediterranean, a theater destined to supply the majority of the senior commanders for OVERLORD. Both Marshall and Brooke desired command of the cross-Channel invasion forces, but neither Roosevelt nor Churchill could afford to part with the men who were the heart and soul of their nation's war effort.

With Marshall and Brooke out of the running, the consensus choice was Dwight Eisenhower, whose appointment was announced on 6 December. Omar Bradley's brilliant performances in North Africa and Sicily had earned him command of the U.S. invasion force, while Patton's lonely exile in Sicily following the slapping episodes would continue until January 1944.

There was considerable wrangling between Churchill and Brooke over the appointment of the British invasion commander. The prime minister avidly favored Alexander, while Brooke maneuvered to secure the appointment for Montgomery. Alexander's less than inspiring performance in the Mediterranean left Brooke convinced that he was unfit for the OVERLORD appointment. He never questioned the gallant Alexander's personal qualities but believed he lacked the ability to perform in a position that required tactical and strategic decisions. Eventually Churchill agreed to leave Alexander in Italy and appoint Montgomery to command the Allied ground forces for the cross-Channel invasion. Lieutenant-General Sir Oliver Leese, the 30th Corps commander, was named the new commander of Eighth Army.

These wholesale shifts of key personnel into and out of the Mediterranean theater took place at a critical moment in the Italian campaign. Admiral Cunningham had returned to London to become the First Sea Lord upon the death of Admiral Sir Dudley Pound. Sir Arthur Tedder had already left to become Eisenhower's deputy, and Coningham would shortly depart to take command of the tactical air support for 21st Army Group. To replace Eisenhower the Combined Chiefs of Staff agreed to the appointment of a British officer, General Sir Henry Maitland Wilson, a six-foot-seven-inch giant of a man whose large ears, not his height, had earned him the nickname "Jumbo."

As the Italian campaign entered 1944, the Allies were basing their hopes for success on the landings at Anzio and the assault crossing of the Rapido south of Cassino.

NINE

The End Run

MARK CLARK'S DISTRUST OF THE BRITISH in general and Lieutenant-General Richard McCreery in particular were major factors in the ill-fated offensive he planned for 20 January 1944 to seize a bridgehead across the Rapido River. He was determined that the main assault be an all-American effort, despite the fact that the opportunities offered by shifting the main effort to the Garigliano River were far more promising.

Clark's intent was to create a diversion by a 10th Corps attack across the Garigliano on the extreme left flank of the Gustav Line and force XIV Panzer Corps to commit its reserves, thus freeing II Corps to assault the Rapido and exploit their success to gain control of the vital Route 6 road junction west of Cassino. By shattering Kesselring's hold on the right flank of the Gustav Line and gaining a foothold in the Liri Valley, Clark would be in a position to continue the offensive north along Highway 6, toward Rome. Most important, the Allied commanders believed that success at Cassino would force Kesselring to abandon the Gustav Line and retreat toward the Apennines.

The key to the success of Clark's plan fell on a single unit, Walker's 36th Division, now assigned to Major General Geoffrey Keyes's II Corps, and perhaps the worst of all possible choices. Not only was the 36th Division exhausted from the failed December offensive, but it had suffered heavy casualties, many of which had not been replaced. Those who had arrived via the American replacement system had yet to experience their first combat. The commander, Major General Fred Walker, believed the operation had scant chance to succeed and was unable to avoid infecting his subordinates with his pessimism.

Walker's fears were fully justified. The site chosen by Clark's planners was along the open floodplain of the valley directly beneath the Cassino massif. There was no cover, and the advance to the river would be under the direct observation (and fire) of the German artillery. The Germans had made any advance here even more difficult by diverting the flow of the river to flood the approach route that the 36th Division was obliged to employ. In plain terms, it meant that virtually all vehicular movement was curtailed and the assault troops would have to approach the river on foot across a swamp, without benefit of cover.

The necessity for thwarting an Allied breakthrough at this key point was not lost on the German commanders. Von Senger had assumed command of XIV Panzer Corps and, along with Kesselring and von Vietinghof, was determined at all costs to prevent an Allied bridgehead across the Rapido. Defending this sector of the Gustav Line was Major General Eberhard Rodt's 15th Panzer Grenadier Division, which had fought superbly in Sicily.

At first glance the Rapido appeared to pose no serious impediments. At the point selected for the assault crossing the river was only fifty feet across. The advantage of narrowness, however, was more than offset by the river's steep banks, its twelve-foot depth, and the torrential speed at which the icy water flowed, often more than ten miles per hour.

Clark's plan called for Ernest Harmon's 1st Armored Division to move up and pass through the Texans and debouch into the Liri Valley once the 36th had secured a bridgehead. The Fifth Army commander's optimism for the operation overlooked the fact that the swampy terrain along both sides of the Rapido was extremely hazardous for the employment of armor.

The exceptionally strong German defense along the outer belts of the Gustav Line ought to have triggered an alarm at Fifth Army. There was absolutely nothing in the German performance to suggest that they had any intention of permitting the Allies to drive them from the Liri Valley. Yet there was an unfortunate and wholly unjustified aura of optimism that led to false assumptions about German intentions.

That false optimism was primarily attributable to the fact that major operations were being planned by inexperienced staff officers, and not by the commanders who had to carry them out. Clark was unable to recognize that the Fifth Army plan for the Rapido-Garigliano operation was fatally flawed. Having decided that the 36th Division would make the main effort, he then attempted to mold the plan to fit this premise. There are few more difficult operations in the military repertoire than an assault crossing under enemy fire. In this instance Fifth Army had not one but two rivers to cross, and at a time when the weather was at its worst.

The British operation went badly from the start. The 46th Division was to assault the Garigliano at Sant' Ambrogio forty-eight hours before the 36th Division, to protect the vulnerable American left flank. At the last moment McCreery postponed the operation for twenty-four hours, to the outrage of the U.S. commanders, who were convinced that this was a prime example of British treachery. McCreery declined to alter his decision, and neither would Clark, who refused Keyes's request to defer the 36th Division assault for a like period. The timetable for Anzio left Clark little choice but to order the operation to proceed. What followed cast a pall of controversy over the career of Mark Clark.

The 10th Corps crossings caught the Germans by surprise. The British brought their artillery forward under the cover of darkness to avoid detection from the German-held heights north of the river. The assault troops of the 5th Division managed to cross the Garigliano in total silence on the night of 17 January. Upriver, the 56th Division launched its attack to the accompaniment of a heavy bombardment, and within forty-eight hours 10th Corps had successfully established a bridgehead several miles deep across a ten-mile front along the lower Garigliano.

Kesselring was then obliged to make his most crucial decision of the Italian campaign: whether or not to commit his only strategic reserve—two panzer grenadier divisions then resting and refitting near Rome—to block McCreery. For some time the Germans had been anticipating an Allied end run into their rear and had been preparing contingency plans to react. There were, however, simply too few formations to meet Kesselring's requirements. If he committed his only strategic reserve to meet the Allied threat on the Garigliano, there would be no forces readily available to counter an amphibious landing near Rome.

Without the slightest hesitation, and against the advice of some of his senior staff officers, Kesselring elected to commit his reserves then and there. In his judgment the threat posed by McCreery's success on the lower Garigliano was so grave that he must react or else risk the collapse of the Gustav Line. Moreover, Kesselring had just been given an erroneous intelligence assessment of Allied intentions by the head of the German Abwehr, Admiral Wilhelm Canaris, who was on a tour of Italy. Unaccountably, Canaris emphatically stated in mid-January that "there is not the slightest sign that a new landing will be undertaken in the near future." At the same moment that Canaris was issuing his confident pronouncement, the Allies were assembling a fleet in the Bay of Naples for an amphibious landing—scheduled for the following week—that the German high command in Italy now believed would not come for at least another four to six weeks.

Had Kesselring known of Clark's intentions, he might not have committed two divisions to the Garigliano sector, especially since Clark's flawed tactical plan had reduced the danger by splitting 10th Corps, so that McCreery was unable to exploit his success. Meanwhile, on 19 and 20 January, the assault crossing at Sant' Ambrogio by Hawkesworth's 46th Division ran into trouble. There were insufficient assault boats, and only a single battalion managed to cross the swiftly flowing Garigliano. Hawkesworth was obliged to extract the battalion to prevent further unnecessary losses.

Having committed himself in advance to a fixed plan for crossing the Garigliano and Rapido rivers, Clark was unwilling to exploit McCreery's earlier success. As Graham and Bidwell point out, there was a fatal flaw in Clark's thinking, which was colored by "his irrational dislike of McCreery and his lack of faith in the fighting power of the 'poor dumb British.' . . . The role of the 10th Corps was to draw in the German Army Group reserves, and no more. The role of the 46th Division was simply to secure the left flank of General Walker's crossing place. After that the Gustav Line battle was to be an all-American show." As a result of these factors, the U.S. 36th Division assault on the night of 20 January 1944 was one of the bloodiest failures of the war.

Rodt's 15th Panzer Grenadier Division manned positions astride the west bank of the Rapido that enabled them to pour a devastating volume of fire on the hapless assault troops of the 36th Division, who had no cover, no artillery support, and insufficient numbers to force a successful crossing of the river.* The operation was a virtual encyclopedia of mistakes that ran the gamut from the lack of coordinated fire support plan to the fact that the infantry and engineers had never even seen one another prior to the assault. River crossing operations require exceptional rapport between engineers and infantry. At the Rapido both groups came under devastating fire from the Germans as they attempted to portage their assault craft across some two miles of marshes. They had to contend not only with the dark but also with uncharted German minefields, which took their toll.

---

*The grim details of this disaster are fully chronicled in Martin Blumenson's fine account of the Rapido operation, *Bloody River.*

The first attempt was repulsed with heavy losses, but Clark was determined to force a crossing and Walker was ordered to renew his assault the afternoon of 21 January. The smoke, fire, and noise were terrifying. Confusion and death were the only constants as the men of the 36th Division were soundly repulsed at the Rapido a second time, with even more severe casualties. Many simply fled the battlefield, while others straggled to the rear as unit integrity disintegrated. Casualties of the 36th Division numbered 1,681, including 143 killed and 663 wounded.* To all who fought there on that day, the Rapido would forever be known as the "Bloody River." Most of the men who were able to cross the Rapido were trapped and rounded up by the Germans. Some 875 men were reported missing, and it was later confirmed that 500 were captured by the 15th Panzer Grenadier Division.

The Rapido-Garigliano crossings were a shambles that left Fifth Army stalled at the mouth of the Liri Valley with little prospect for breaking the Gustav Line in the foreseeable future. Walker was appalled by the severe losses sustained by two of his three infantry regiments, and he fully expected to be sacked by Clark and Keyes "to cover their own stupidity." He was surprised when the Fifth Army commander told him the Rapido failure was partly his own responsibility.†

THE FAILURE AT THE RAPIDO CAME AT THE very moment Fifth Army was about to undertake a major end run by landing VI Corps behind the German lines at Anzio thirty-five miles southwest of Rome. This was the second phase of the Allied plan to escape the growing stalemate and capture Rome.

In the postwar aftermath of the Anzio landings Winston Churchill has been portrayed as the instigator of the ill-fated Allied end run. Although the British prime minister avidly embraced the scheme when first briefed in late December, the architects were actually Alexander and Eisenhower. By early November Alexander had come to the conclusion that there was little likelihood of a breakthrough to Rome by either Fifth or Eighth Army without the assistance of an amphibious end run into the German rear.

---

*These figures do not include losses sustained by engineers and other troops supporting the operation.
†The debacle resulted in a Congressional inquiry of the operation in 1946, after the 36th Division veterans' association called for an investigation of the "fiasco" and of a military system "that will permit an inefficient and inexperienced officer [Clark] . . . to destroy the young manhood of this country and to prevent future soldiers being sacrificed wastefully and uselessly."

On 8 November 1943 Alexander cabled Brooke that it would be necessary to plan for an amphibious operation south of Rome to threaten Kesselring's rear and also threaten, if not actually capture, the Italian capital. Several sites were under consideration, but the primary one was at the twin resort cities of Anzio and Nettuno thirty-five miles southwest of the capital.

Alexander believed the key to this operation lay in the rapid seizure of the Alban Hills twenty miles northeast of Anzio. Also known as the Colli Laziali, this hill mass straddled Routes 6 and 7 (the famed Appian Way), the only road links between Rome and the Gustav Line and the main north-south railroad line. If an Allied force seized and held the Alban Hills, it could block all German reinforcement by road and rail and would likely make Kesselring's position so untenable that he would be forced to retreat to the Apennines in the area around Florence, where the Germans were thought to be preparing their main defensive line in Italy.

The operation was given the code name SHINGLE, and Alexander assigned its planning to Mark Clark's Fifth Army, which would carry it out. SHINGLE's success depended on its conjunction with a major Fifth Army offensive that would place Clark's army in a position to link up with the Anzio force by no later than D plus ten. This, in turn, meant that Clark must crack the Gustav Line and drive thirty miles north at least to the vicinity of Frosinone, a town on Route 6 approximately halfway between Cassino and Rome.

The disaster at the Rapido shattered this premise and later proved to be fatal to the SHINGLE plan. As finally constituted, the task of carrying out the Anzio-Nettuno landings fell to Major General John P. Lucas's VI Corps. Major-General W. R. C. Penney's British 1st Division was to land on the beaches north of Anzio and hold the left flank of the Allied beachhead. On the right, Major General Lucian K. Truscott's U.S. 3d Division was to seize and hold the right flank of the Allied beachhead.

A Ranger force commanded by Colonel William O. Darby (augmented by an airborne battalion) was given the mission of assaulting and securing the vital port of Anzio. While the Rangers were taking Anzio, Colonel Reuben Tucker's 504th U.S. Parachute Infantry Regiment was to parachute into the Alban Hills to establish blocking positions pending the arrival of the main SHINGLE force.

Although an outline plan was developed by the Fifth Army staff, there was no consensus that SHINGLE would ever take place, particularly when it became evident that there were insufficient landing craft available to carry out even a small amphibious operation at Anzio. Virtually all of the available landing craft—particularly the all-important LSTs—were earmarked for transfer to England to support OVERLORD.

The fate of the operation was uncertain until late December, when Churchill became involved and pressured the Combined Chiefs of Staff to delay the return of the landing craft to the United Kingdom. The mounting of SHINGLE depended on Eisenhower's ability to convince the Joint Chiefs of the necessity of retaining sufficient landing craft, something they were loath to approve because of an erroneous perception that the Germans were merely delaying south of Rome and would soon abandon southern Italy and establish themselves from Pisa to Rimini for the decisive battles in the Apennines. There was little enthusiasm for SHINGLE within the Allied naval and air forces, and the operation seemed doomed to oblivion when Clark canceled it on 19 December for lack of landing craft. It was only Churchill's intervention that resurrected SHINGLE.

The operation was part of the turbulent politics that engulfed the Allied camp at this stage of the war. Another controversial plan, to invade southern France in support of the cross-Channel invasion, was also under consideration. An invasion along the Riviera was considered essential by those who saw a pressing need to divert German attention and troops from Normandy during the critical days immediately after the OVERLORD landings.

The southern France landing, code named ANVIL, became one of the most debated Allied operations of the war. Its detractors argued that it was unnecessary, it would require forces needed in Italy, and it would so weaken the Allies that the stalemate in Italy might never be broken. Churchill was particularly worried that the cancellation of Anzio was tantamount to playing into Hitler's hands and leaving Rome in German possession indefinitely.

Churchill was as obsessed with capturing Rome as Clark was, and, never one to pass up an opportunity for action, the prime minister now became the most powerful advocate for an immediate revival of SHINGLE. Even though Churchill would later fight tooth and nail to prevent ANVIL, the need to retain landing craft for that operation was to directly benefit SHINGLE by ensuring that some would remain in the theater indefinitely, at the expense of OVERLORD.

Militarily, SHINGLE was an operation whose size and scope was shaped by outside factors and by a chain reaction of mistakes and faulty assumptions. As we will see, VI Corps became neither fish nor fowl, its mission conditional upon its size, which from the outset was wholly inadequate.

To make matters worse, staff officers, not commanders, were again planning a major battle. Even though he was responsible for carrying out a plan he had no part in creating, Lucas was given only a spectator's role in planning SHINGLE.

Logistically there were sufficient landing craft for a two-division lift plus supporting troops, and it was the navy's judgment that Lucas would have to make do with seven days' supplies on the beachhead, after which the LSTs would be withdrawn and sent to England. Although the period was later raised to ten days, no one answered the most crucial question of all: How long could Lucas hold out with an undersized force against an unknown German reaction, when Fifth Army was bogged down behind the Rapido with no possibility whatsoever of linking up with Lucas within ten days?*

There were major differences of opinion between Alexander and Clark as to what VI Corps was to accomplish after landing at Anzio. Alexander's papers establish beyond doubt that his intention was to strangle Kesselring and open the road to Rome by seizing and holding the Alban Hills. Clark, on the other hand, had been burned once at Salerno and began to view the problem in terms of avoiding another debacle on the scale of AVALANCHE.

By early January 1944 the operation had been resurrected. On 8 January Lucas was informed that SHINGLE would take place on 22 January and "that there would be no more discussion of these points." In his diary Lucas remarked that Alexander also quoted Churchill to the effect that "it will astonish the world [and] it will certainly frighten Kesselring." Like Walker at the Rapido, Lucas believed from the outset that Anzio was an ill-conceived operation that would likely end badly, and he wrote in his diary, "I felt like a lamb being led to the slaughter. . . . This whole affair had a strong odor of Gallipoli and apparently the same amateur [Churchill] was still on the coaches' bench."

The original operations order prepared by Clark's G-3, Brigadier General Donald W. Brann, directed Lucas to seize and retain the Alban Hills. However, both Clark and Brann began to have second thoughts about Lucas's ability to hold the hills with the force at his disposal, along with the obvious necessity of maintaining a twenty-plus-mile logistical lifeline to the beaches. This concern was translated into a modification

---

*The inadequacy of supplies in the beachhead—commitments to return landing craft to the United Kingdom for Operation OVERLORD led the navy to guarantee less than one-third of VI Corps's requirement of 1,500 tons per day—was strongly protested by Clark and led to the retention of additional landing craft.

of Lucas's instructions. On 12 January Brann personally hand delivered a revised operations order which contained a crucial and much-debated change. After establishing a beachhead at Anzio, the new order merely directed Lucas "to advance on the Colli Laziali." Neither a timetable for this advance nor any mention of seizing Rome was contained in Clark's revised order.

It was as if a stone had been lifted from Lucas's shoulders. He now viewed his mission at Anzio in a completely new light. Gone was the obligation to seize the Alban Hills, and in its place was the discretion to conduct the battle on his own terms. The establishment of a beachhead now became Lucas's primary focus. "Much thought had been put into the wording of this order so as not to force me to push on at the risk of sacrificing my corps," he later wrote. "Should conditions warrant, however, I was free to move and to seize [the] Colli Laziali." In effect, Clark was telling Lucas to fight the battle as he saw fit, even though this directly contradicted Alexander's intent that SHINGLE's mission was to capture and hold the Alban Hills.

All of Lucas's subsequent decisions and actions must be viewed in the light of what amounted to Clark's hedging of his bets. Later, Clark left no doubt about what he himself would have done if he were the VI Corps commander. On the seafront in Anzio on D-Day Clark warned Lucas: "Don't stick your neck out, Johnny. I did at Salerno and got into trouble." To add substance to his words, Clark had canceled the airborne landings in the Alban Hills. Tucker's regiment was now scheduled to arrive by LST as ordinary infantry on D-Day.

The divergent opinions of Lucas's superiors obscured any clear definition of what the Allied force at Anzio was to accomplish. To Lucas, Clark's order of 12 January meant that SHINGLE was merely "a 'diversion' to attract enemy troops from the front of the Fifth Army where the main effort was to be made." This would certainly have been news to Alexander, who viewed the operation as anything but a diversion.

Inexorably tied to SHINGLE was the ill-fated Rapido crossing. The success of Clark's plan was dependent on Walker's 36th Division bridging the Rapido and Harmon's 1st Armored driving north along Route 6 to link up with VI Corps, which only then would have the necessary muscle to capture Rome. The stinging setback at the Rapido, however, now made it clear that there would be no such linkup. Although a crucial element of the plan had already failed, no one seems to have asked whether the Allied force of some 36,000 troops was being sent to Anzio merely as a sacrificial lamb.

Even Patton was discouraged by what he heard when he visited Naples before the invasion. He found Clark jumpy, and he worried that Lucas lacked the drive to carry out SHINGLE successfully. According to Lucas, Patton blurted out: "John, there is no one in the Army I hate to see killed as much as you, but you can't get out of this alive."

Time was among Lucas's most pressing concerns. In his opinion there was too little of it to prepare his force adequately, and he was not reassured by the miserable performance of the assault troops during rehearsals held in mid-January and by what he regarded as a lack of cooperation by the navy. "The token rehearsal for the 3d Division [on 19 January] was terrible. Some forty DUKWs [amphibious 2½-ton trucks] and nineteen 105-mm howitzers lost. All because the Navy didn't close on the beach—which they admit."

Foul weather and inadequate time were among the problems faced by both those responsible for planning SHINGLE and the assault troops. Truscott, who was by now a veteran of assault landings, noted that "no single battalion landed on time or in formation . . . [or] on its correct beach." The Allied naval commander of Task Force 81 (the Allied naval force for SHINGLE), Rear Admiral Frank J. Lowry, USN, was so deeply worried by the number of accidents that he declared that it "appeared impractical on the face of it to make an assault [landing at Anzio] without further training." However, as Lucas well understood, there was simply no more time for practice. The army and navy would have learned from their mistakes and do things right on D-Day, or else face potential disaster.

Another question the Allied high command failed to resolve was Kesselring's probable response to the landings. Intelligence showed that several German divisions were then in the Rome area (the same two divisions sent by Kesselring to the Garigliano several days later) and that the Germans could move 20,000 troops into the Anzio sector within twenty-four hours. But would SHINGLE actually force Kesselring to abandon the Gustav Line?

Intelligence estimates prepared before the landings predicted some 14,000 German troops in the Anzio area. By D plus one the Germans could muster another division and as many as three additional regiments. By the day following there might be up to 31,000 Germans opposing VI Corps.

Once again there was unwarranted optimism within the Allied high command that the threat posed by the SHINGLE force would be sufficient to force Kesselring to move to the Pisa-Rimini Line. However, such a premise was valid only if Lucas could move VI Corps into the Alban Hills and isolate the German Tenth Army. And Lucas, of course, now had no intention of doing so. Moreover, this premise neglected to take into account that Lucas would somehow have to keep open his lifeline to the LSTs at the port of Anzio. Without an adequate force to defend both the Alban Hills and his lifeline, Lucas could do one or the other, but not both.

In Sicily 60,000 Germans had held off a force of nearly 500,000 Allied troops; at Salerno they had reacted violently to AVALANCHE; and since then they had made the Allies pay dearly for virtually every yard of ground. Why Kesselring would suddenly abandon Cassino without a better reason than anybody had yet come up with was never seriously considered by the Allied commanders in Italy. Once again, a lesson that the Allies had paid dearly to learn and relearn was about to be ignored.

TEN

The Anzio Beachhead

IN THE EARLY MORNING HOURS of 22 January 1944, Admiral Lowry's Task Force 81 carrying VI Corps arrived off the coast of Anzio-Nettuno. The Allied planners had elected to maximize the possibility of surprise by landing the assault force under the cover of darkness. As Lucas later noted in his diary, "We achieved what is certainly one of the most complete surprises in history. The Germans were caught off base and there was practically no opposition to the landing." Lucas had expected "a fight to get ashore but was not disappointed when I did not get it."

The navy put on a considerable show of force by bombarding suspected enemy positions and supporting the assault with rocket fire which Lucas described as "perfectly terrific." Mounted on LCTs, these improvised rocket ships delivered nearly eight hundred rockets virtually simultaneously in an awe-inspiring demonstration of naval firepower.

Although the Germans had long been expecting the Allies to launch an amphibious end run somewhere near Rome, the SHINGLE landings nevertheless caught Kesselring flat-footed. Even in and around the port city of Naples, where the Allies were amassing their invasion fleet, the Abwehr had failed to detect and report the activities, though Italian vendors were hawking postcards of Anzio on the streets of Naples. The Luftwaffe was equally lax in failing to discover that there was a large fleet being assembled in Gulf of Naples. Reassured by Admiral Canaris, and in the absence of intelligence to the contrary, Kesselring expected the Allies to concentrate their efforts on breaking the Gustav Line.

Guided by beacon submarines, the debarkation was "almost unbelievably smooth and accurate," as Truscott later described it. Darby's Rangers found the port of Anzio lightly guarded, and the scant opposition soon evaporated. German forces in and around Anzio-Nettuno on D-Day numbered less than a thousand troops. A German engineer force sent to Anzio to blow up the mole in the harbor was captured before it could carry out its task.

The SHINGLE landings might best be characterized as a nonevent, or as one of Penney's Irish Guard's officers wrote, "very gentlemanly, calm and dignified." Damage to the Allied fleet was minimal; sporadic Luftwaffe attacks claimed two vessels: an LCI was destroyed by a direct hit, and the minesweeper *Portent* struck an underwater mine. German fighter-bombers attacked targets ashore, but their interference with the SHINGLE landings was minimal. In comparison to the 140 Luftwaffe sorties, the Allied air forces flew over 1,200 on D-Day, attacking road and rail targets in an attempt to seal off the beachhead from enemy reinforcement.

Despite the surprise, Kesselring was not dismayed. He had made plans to react on short notice to any Allied amphibious end run, and within hours the code word for an invasion at Anzio was flashed throughout German-held Italy. The most immediate German concern was to contain the Allied beachhead, and to do so Kesselring called on the Hermann Göring Division and elements of the 4th Parachute Division, both veteran formations. Still under the command of Paul Conrath, the battered Hermann Göring Division had only recently been pulled out of the Gustav Line and was now refitting south of Rome.

On the Allied side, the major problem facing VI Corps on D-Day was the speed with which troops and equipment could be landed. Sand bars and a steep gradient along the British 1st Division beaches to the north of Anzio were particularly troublesome, and the soft sand of the exits stalled many vehicles. An added complication that further delayed the British landings by several hours was the necessity to clear many offshore floating mines. However, the port of Anzio was cleared and ready for LSTs by early afternoon, thus enabling the remainder of the 1st Division to land in the town instead of across the beaches.

By the end of D-Day the Allies had put ashore 36,034 troops, 3,069 vehicles, and large numbers of supplies—90 percent of the VI Corps assault load. Total casualties on D-Day were 13 killed, 97 wounded, and 44 missing or captured.

Lucas had every reason to be pleased with the day's events. Not only had his force gotten ashore unscathed, but VI Corps had attained all of the preliminary objectives for the initial beachhead laid down in the SHINGLE plan. Infantry and reconnaissance elements of the U.S. 3d Division had seized intact all of the bridges spanning the Mussolini Canal, which were considered vital to defending the right flank of the beachhead. One young 3d Division trooper had driven his sergeant in a jeep into the Alban Hills and clear to the outskirts of Rome, and had returned to Anzio without seeing a single enemy soldier. Penney's British 1st Division now controlled some seven miles of the Anzio-Albano road as far as the Moletta River.

It was along the Mussolini Canal that the 3d Division encountered the first serious German resistance. The Hermann Göring Division recaptured most of the canal bridges that night with a tank-infantry force that dislodged the 30th Infantry Regiment. On D plus one the Americans struck back with a regiment-sized counterattack, and by 24 January all of these bridges were again back in Allied hands.

Elsewhere during the first forty-eight hours of SHINGLE, VI Corps expanded its initial gains to carve out a bridgehead seven miles deep that ran from the Moletta River to the Mussolini Canal. The 3d Division, reinforced by Tucker's 504th Parachute Infantry and Darby's Rangers,* had solidified the Allied right flank by taking up positions along the Mussolini Canal and its western tributary. In the British sector a single brigade held the left flank along the Moletta River. Lucas held the remainder of the British 1st Division in corps reserve to repel a certain German counterattack. It was the final calm before the storm.

As the Allies would soon learn, the German reaction to the Anzio landings was a total commitment to containing the invasion. A steady stream of orders flowed down the chain of command as Kesselring sought to counter this new complication before it could get out of hand. Units from as far away as Germany, Yugoslavia, and France were on the move at once. Three divisions in reserve in northern Italy were likewise headed south within twenty-four hours. For the moment Kesselring was content merely to begin the necessary steps to block an Allied advance to the Alban Hills. Later, the German army would demonstrate its furious determination to crush VI Corps.

Within the first twenty-four hours, however, the Luftwaffe began stepping up attacks on shipping and ground targets in an attempt to forestall an expected move by Lucas toward Rome and the Alban Hills. Conrath was directed to establish blocking positions along all roads leading from Anzio to the Colli Laziali. Whatever the cost, the Allies were not to be permitted to establish themselves along this crucial terrain. Pending the arrival of the headquarters of Colonel-General von Mackensen's Four-

---

*Darby's Rangers were attached to the 3d Division, but the 504th Parachute Infantry Regiment were corps troops under the direct control of VI Corps.

teenth Army, the I Parachute Corps was charged with organizing the defense of the Anzio sector.

Kesselring need not have worried that Lucas would make a dash to seize and hold the Alban Hills. The American general had long since made up his mind of the suicidal folly of such a move. As far as Lucas was concerned, there was absolutely no doubt what must be done: VI Corps must be securely established ashore, and no major offensive action would be undertaken until the security of the Allied beachhead was assured.

Lucas's decision played directly into German hands, leaving a surprised but delighted Kesselring in full control of events. The situation along the Cassino front was a stalemate, and there was not even the remotest possibility of the Allies breaking the German grip on the Gustav Line in the foreseeable future. With this in mind, Kesselring was confident that he could detach formations from the Cassino front to reinforce von Mackensen at Anzio.

Lucas was well aware that he must advance at least as far as Cisterna, an important crossroads town on Route 7 fourteen miles northeast of Anzio, and to the vicinity of Albano along the Anzio-Rome highway. German control of Cisterna would thwart a successful advance to the Alban Hills.

To occupy the Alban Hills, VI Corps would have had to advance inland and seize blocking positions at Albano and Cisterna within forty-eight hours after the landings on the Anzio beaches. Although VI Corps was too small to establish and maintain a defensible beachhead and at the same time seize the Colli Laziali, both Cisterna and Albano were attainable objectives. Lucas's failure to press for their capture was to prove his only serious mistake.

Despite their tactical importance, the capture of Cisterna and Albano could not solve the dilemma facing Lucas. As Samuel Eliot Morison points out, seizing the lines of communication on the western side of the hills would still leave the Germans in control of the second rail line and Route 6 to the east. The Allied beachhead would thus be "a mere nuisance to the enemy who might be expected to react violently against it. That was the fundamental weakness of Operation SHINGLE. Either it was a job for a full army, or it was no job at all; to attempt it with only two divisions was to send a boy on a man's errand."

THE FURY OF THE GERMANS' REACTION TO SHINGLE far exceeded the worst Allied fears. By the end of D-Day the Germans had moved 20,000

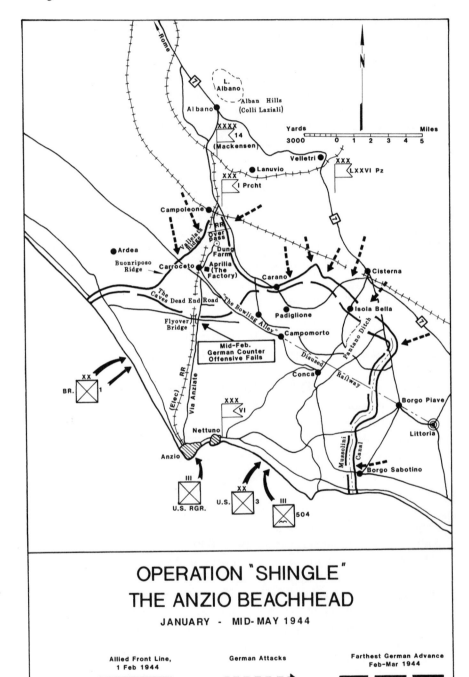

OPERATION "SHINGLE"
THE ANZIO BEACHHEAD
JANUARY - MID-MAY 1944

| Allied Front Line,
1 Feb 1944 | German Attacks | Farthest German Advance
Feb-Mar 1944 |

reinforcements to the vicinity of Anzio, most of them Luftwaffe panzer grenadiers from the Hermann Göring Division and crack paratroopers. In the days that followed, the German buildup continued at a relentless pace. By the end of D plus two the number had doubled to 40,000, and when von Mackensen's Fourteenth Army headquarters assumed responsibility on 25 January there were elements of eight separate divisions in defensive positions. Allied attempts to counter the buildup by heavy air attacks across the entire front had little effect on the German ability to fill the plains surrounding Anzio with troops.

Lieutenant General Ira C. Eaker's Mediterranean Allied Air Forces (MAAF) had done their best to isolate the battlefield, but they could not prevent massive German reinforcements from getting through. While Allied air harassment did disrupt rail and road movements, their interference was little more than a temporary nuisance to the Germans.

The original SHINGLE plan called for VI Corps to be left at Anzio with ten days of supplies, while the landing craft were withdrawn in accordance with the previously established priorities for OVERLORD. As both sides prepared for a major battle, however, there was no further mention of withdrawing the vital LST lifeline between Anzio and Naples.

The Germans were satisfied merely to gain vital time to establish defensive blocking positions, despite a gap of nearly five miles between their main line of resistance and the Allied front lines. However, their reinforcements rose to nearly 70,000 on D plus seven, and it was only a matter of time before von Mackensen initiated a powerful counterattack to drive the Allies back into the sea.

Initially the Allied need for support from naval gunfire and air strikes was negligible. By the time it became urgently needed, the targets were beyond the range of all vessels with lesser firepower than a heavy cruiser, and none of these was available to assist Lucas. Moreover, a new threat soon emerged in the form of deadly radio-controlled glide bombs, which forced Admiral Lowry to retire his support ships at 1600 hours each afternoon.

The Allies now found themselves ashore but with no place to go. The flat plains of Anzio were flanked on the right by the Mussolini Canal, beyond which lay the impassable Pontine Marshes. For nearly thirteen miles these plains are dotted with small villages, isolated farmhouses, and a checkerboard series of secondary roads and small irrigation canals. In a massive effort Mussolini had drained the marshes and reclaimed the bogs that had for centuries made the area a mosquito-ridden hell hole. Il Duce's pride and joy were the canal bearing his name and, in the British sector, the brand new model commune-city of Aprilia* which the Allies soon dubbed "the Factory," so named because from afar the tower in the city center resembled that of a factory smokestack.

To the east, where the British 1st Division was defending the left flank, the country became rough, with a series of steep gullies which reminded its veteran troops of the wadi country of North Africa, with the temperatures often exceeding one hundred degrees in summer and wet in the winter. As both sides would soon learn, the open terrain on the east made any movement during daylight hours a lethal endeavor. The Germans established strongholds in virtually every farmhouse by emplacing antitank guns, automatic weapons, and an occasional tank or self-propelled gun.

Lucas never quite knew what to make of his masters, Alexander and Clark. On D-Day both commanders had visited him at Anzio. Alexander had pronounced himself well satisfied with the landings: "You have certainly given the folks at home something to talk about." What Lucas never knew was that well before the landings Alexander's newly arrived Chief of Staff, Lieutenant-General Sir John Harding, had expressed concern that Lucas lacked the drive to succeed with SHINGLE and had urged Alexander to consider replacing Lucas with someone more forceful. Alexander had been unmoved, and instead told the VI Corps commander: "We have every confidence in you. That is why you were picked." With dry humor Lucas then penned in his diary, "Rather puts it up to me. Pray for sunshine."

This was the day on which Clark issued his warning to Lucas about not sticking his neck out. Lucas well understood that he faced a steadily mounting problem with the great German buildup opposite VI Corps proceeding unabated. He also understood that he was expected to produce results beyond the capability of VI Corps. Unfortunately, Lucas's pessimism ill served him, for although the situation became increasingly gloomy, he had made little attempt to take the offensive when there had still been an opportunity for aggressive action. Now, as things grew worse, he became even more discouraged. Lucas's frame of mind was communicated to his diary: "The strain of a thing like this is a terrible burden. Who the hell wants to be a general."

During the first week of the battle several attempts were made by the two divisions to reach Campoleone and Cisterna, but Lucas ordered no

* Several hundred yards to the west of the Factory lay the village of Carroceto on the Anzio-Rome highway. Paralleling the highway was a rail line. The Factory, Aprilia, and Carroceto were virtually one and the same.

all-out offensive. He now found himself under increasing pressure from Clark, who had changed his mind and was now pressing him to act more aggressively. Alexander too was sending Lucas decidedly mixed signals. During a visit to Anzio on 25 January he called the operation "a splendid piece of work," but after the war he gave the official historians a different version, stating that he was "very much disappointed that Lucas had not pushed out to the Alban Hills."

The 3d Division managed to advance several miles beyond the Mussolini Canal toward Cisterna before Truscott was obliged to regroup to prepare a stronger attack. Truscott believed that the Hermann Göring Division's defenses of Cisterna were too thin to withstand an all-out attack, and he proposed that the 179th Regiment of the 45th Division, the first of the reserve forces to arrive in the beachhead, be attached to the 3d Division. Still acting with ultra conservatism, Lucas declined, and a vital opportunity was lost.

On 25 January the British began an attack, spearheaded by the 24th Guards Brigade, to capture the Factory and advance toward Campoleone. The first of many battles for Aprilia was won by the British, who ejected a regiment of the 3d Panzer Grenadier Division and captured over a hundred panzer grenadiers. The Factory was more than a strong point; it was the key to the road net in and around Carroceto, and both sides were determined to retain possession of this model town of Mussolini's, which had long since been turned into rubble.

A powerful German tank-infantry counterattack was beaten off on 26 January, during which both the Guardsmen and the Germans paid a fearful price. Ambulances and corpsmen could not keep up with the steady stream of wounded, who soon overtaxed the medical aid station. An Irish Guards historian later wrote: "The silent courage of maimed, battered, bleeding Irish Guardsmen lying in the open or, if they were lucky, in some muddy ditch, was a living monument to the strength of the human will in the depths of human misery." Those who fought at Anzio in 1944 were subjected to what sometimes seemed to be endless downpours and numbing cold that froze feet and made existence there under combat conditions a desperate ordeal. As the historian of the Irish Guards has written, "the whole area had for centuries been shunned by sensible men."

As the end of January approached and neither the 1st nor the 3d Division had been able to capture Campoleone or Cisterna, Lucas finally decided the time had come to launch an all-out drive to complement a similar fresh offensive that Clark planned against Cassino on 1 February.

His objective was the Alban Hills, which he intended to seize by means of a double envelopment. Lucas's timing could not have been worse. The VI Corps offensive came at the very moment when von Mackensen was about to launch his own heavy blow against the beachhead. The German commander had massed thirty-six battalions of infantry in the Campoleone-Cisterna salient, supported by large numbers of tanks and artillery.

Both Cisterna and Campoleone were obvious Allied objectives which the astute Kesselring intended to defend to the fullest. The Germans had brought up large numbers of reinforcements the night before the VI Corps offensive. Now filling the previous void around Cisterna were not only the battle-tested units of the Hermann Göring and the 4th Parachute divisions but also a fresh unit, the 26th Panzer Grenadier Division that Kesselring had withdrawn from the Eighth Army front and sped to Anzio. A Polish soldier serving with the Germans managed to escape and attempted to warn the Americans that they were about to advance into a deadly trap, but no one understood Polish, and by the time a translator was located the following day it was too late.

Had Lucas attacked on 29 January, as originally intended, the VI Corps offensive might have turned out much differently. However, he elected to postpone the operation for twenty-four hours to provide time for the British 1st Division and Harmon's newly arrived U.S. 1st Armored Division, to complete preparations for their attack.* The plan called for the British to seize Campoleone, whereupon Harmon's armor would spearhead an attack on the Alban Hills from the direction of Albano.

Now came one of the most humiliating events of the campaign. The 767 men of the 1st and 3d Ranger battalions were given the mission of attacking Cisterna by infiltrating under the cover of darkness along the Pantano Ditch, which ran between two strong points manned by the Hermann Göring Division. The Fosso di Pantano was a dry extension of the Mussolini Canal that provided cover and would enable the Rangers to get within a mile of Cisterna. Both Truscott and Darby believed the Ranger force could create sufficient confusion and panic to ease the main attack by the 15th Infantry and the 4th Ranger Battalion along the Isola Bella–Cisterna road. To aid these attacks Truscott ordered Tucker's

*Except for Combat Command B, the entire 1st Armored Division arrived at the Anzio beachhead between 24 and 28 January. When Harmon reported to the VI Corps command post in Nettuno, Lucas greeted him warmly, "Glad to see you. You're needed here."

504th Parachute Infantry Regiment to advance north along the Mussolini Canal and create a diversion by attacking the German right flank.

Beginning at 0100 hours, the Rangers easily infiltrated German lines and advanced single-file along the Pantano Ditch. Although there were German patrols active in the area, the Rangers believed their presence had not been detected. The lead elements of the 1st Ranger Battalion arrived at the end of the ditch shortly before first light on 30 January. To reach Cisterna they had to advance across nearly one and one-half miles of open terrain. Both battalions deployed in the fields south of Cisterna, but when the 1st Ranger Battalion was 800 yards from the outskirts of the town, they ran headlong into a deadly trap. Three battalions of Germans were in position where none were expected, and they opened fire on the Rangers with self-propelled guns, mortars, and machine guns.

Darby's men fought valiantly but were no match for the much larger German force. Caught in the open and with only shallow ditches for cover, the Rangers found themselves in the jaws of an ambush from which there was no escape. Attempts by the 4th Ranger Battalion and 3d Division infantry units to break through to their position via the Isola Bella–Cisterna road were beaten off as a fierce battle raged throughout the morning. Gradually the Germans tightened the noose against the Ranger force, whose ammunition began to run dangerously low.

The final blow came in the early afternoon of 30 January when the Rangers came under a powerful tank attack. The superior German strength was too much for Darby's men, whose attempts to extricate themselves from the trap failed. The Rangers fought the panzers virtually bare-handed with little more than sticky grenades and a handful of bazookas, yet they managed to knock out or cripple fourteen tanks before running out of projectiles. Time had run out on the Rangers, whose valor simply could not overcome overwhelming opposition.

The Ranger force now ceased to exist. Of the 767 men who took part in the attack on Cisterna, almost all were lost during one of the worst periods of the campaign, which also saw the loss of a British cruiser and a Liberty ship loaded with ammunition. Most of the Rangers were captured by the Hermann Göring Division, which claimed to have taken 639 prisoners. Only six Rangers returned to Allied lines, thus ending one of the most ill-fated small-unit operations of the war.

Darby was devastated by the destruction of his beloved Ranger force. When he learned the extent of his losses, he blamed himself and then broke down and cried. In the aftermath of the Cisterna debacle the re-

maining Ranger battalion was attached first to the 3d Division and subsequently to the 504th Parachute Infantry Regiment. Many of the captured
Rangers were paraded through the streets of Rome, and the Germans
took full advantage of their plight to launch a propaganda campaign that
included gloating pronouncements by Axis Sally.

Within weeks the Ranger force in Italy was formally disbanded and
most of its surviving members returned to the United States, their war
over. When Clark sent the 45th Division to Anzio in the aftermath of the
German counterattacks in early February, Darby was given command of
the 179th Regiment at the height of the great German counteroffensive
later that month.

There was savage fighting across the rest of the 3d Division front on
30 January as Truscott's infantry ran headlong into the newly reinforced
German defenses in front of Cisterna. The attack had begun at 0200
hours but soon ran into trouble. German resistance was stubborn and
the terrain was difficult. Numerous drainage ditches overgrown with wild
briar bushes made night movement of the supporting Sherman tanks impossible and left the advancing infantry without a vital source of fire
support.

The 1st Battalion, 7th Infantry was caught in the open when the Germans fired illuminating flares and began to rain automatic weapons fire
down on the Americans from the protection of nearby knolls. Unable to
advance or retreat, the men of the 1st Battalion were trapped like the
Rangers would be later the same morning and were subjected to continued heavy fire throughout the day.

Their attempts to break out of the trap failed, but they wrested control
of one of the knolls from the Germans and turned it into an American
strong point. This small unit action was typical of the seemingly endless
bloody battles of Anzio, where both sides fought with tenacity and grit
but to little tactical gain.

Truscott reorganized his forces in an attempt to renew the attack on
Cisterna, but after two days of bloodletting he could only get within a
mile of the town. With his reserves fully committed and his losses since
D-Day now over 3,000 plus a third of his tanks and tank destroyers,
Truscott recognized he had no chance of breaking the German defense of
Cisterna. More ominous was the fact that the 3d Division now occupied
terrain unsuitable for stopping a strong counterattack, and Truscott had
to begin preparing to resist the long-awaited German counteroffensive.

The British met a similar fate at Campoleone, which they were unable to capture. After a series of sharp engagements the Sherwood Foresters and a squadron of the 46th RTR managed to advance to the railway line opposite Campoleone Station. But even with the additional support of a tank battalion from Harmon's 1st Armored Division they could not gain control of either the station or the town and its important road net.

Harmon himself came to Campoleone Station in a tank ("A jeep wouldn't have lived long there") to see what could be done to assist the Sherwood Foresters. What he found appalled him:

> There were dead bodies everywhere. I had never seen so many dead men in one place. They lay so close together that I had to step with care. I shouted for the commanding officer. From a foxhole there arose a mud-covered corporal with a handlebar mustache. He was the highest-ranking officer still alive. He stood stiffly at attention. "How is it going?" I asked. "Well, sir," the corporal said, "there were a hundred and sixteen of us when we first came up, and there are sixteen of us left. We're ordered to hold out until sundown, and I think, with a little good fortune, we can manage to do so."

Harmon, who knew good soldiering when he saw it, later wrote, "I think my great respect for the stubbornness and fighting ability of the British enlisted man was born that afternoon."

Although it did not please Alexander, who viewed both Cisterna and Campoleone as vital objectives for the eventual occupation of the Alban Hills, Clark supported Lucas's decision to call off the offensive. Its modest gains had left VI Corps worse off than before the offensive began. Without control of Campoleone VI Corps's left flank had become dangerously overextended. The British salient between Aprilia and Campoleone was a narrow protrusion that now became a defensive liability to General Penney. At Cisterna the 3d Division was not quite as vulnerable, but its new positions were hardly ideal. The end result was a no-win situation for Lucas. "All my eggs are in one basket," he observed, and "we are engaged in a hell of a struggle."

Lucas's decision to return to the defensive to prepare for von Mackensen's counteroffensive brought to a close the first phase of the Anzio campaign. The abortive VI Corps offensive of January 31–February 1 was the one and only attempt by Lucas to capture the Alban Hills. It was also a decisive moment in the war in Italy. Not only was the stalemate at Cassino unbroken, but within days SHINGLE was to become an extension of the same stalemate. Anzio had turned into a colossal liability for the

Allies, who were obliged now to rush reinforcements by sea from the south to meet the threat of the massive German buildup opposite VI Corps. Instead of a stalemate on one front, the Allies now found themselves with the problem of how to extricate themselves from a deadlock on *two* widely dispersed fronts.

French General Alphonse Juin and U.S. Major General John P. Lucas, whose U.S. VI Corps is being relieved by the Corps Expéditionaire Français, Italy, December 1943.
U.S. Army Military History Institute

Major General Fred L. Walker, Commanding General, U.S. 36th Infantry Division.
U.S. Army Military History Institute

Soldiers of a U.S. tank destroyer battalion fire a bazooka at a house they suspect is held by the enemy in the Rapido River area, Italy, 1944.
U.S. Army Signal Corps; George C. Marshall Library

U.S. Fifth Army troops wade ashore from LCI's at Anzio, January 1944.
U.S. Army Signal Corps; George C. Marshall Library

German dead await burial in the Anzio beachhead, 1944.
U.S. Army Signal Corps; George C. Marshall Library

A line of captured German prisoners filing by U.S. infantrymen in foxholes in the Anzio beachhead, 1944.
U.S. Army Signal Corps; George C. Marshall Library

Infantrymen of the 28th Maori Battalion, 2d New Zealand Division, crouch near the bank of the Rapido River during the bombing and shelling of the Benedictine Monastery, 1944.
U.S. Army Military History Institute

Aerial view of the Abbey of Monte Cassino taken during the Allied air attacks, February 1944.
Howard Hammersley; George C. Marshall Library

Left to right: Polish General Odrziezynski, British General Oliver Leese, and Polish General Wladislaw Anders, northern Italy, 1944.
U.S. Army Military History Institute

Foreground: British General Sir Henry Maitland Wilson, Supreme Allied Commander in the Mediterranean, and U.S. Major General Geoffrey Keyes, Commander, U.S. II Corps, Italy, 1944. *At left:* British Lieutenant-General J. A. Clark.
U.S. Army Military History Institute

U.S. Rangers close in on a wooded hill, Italy, 1943.
U.S. Army Signal Corps; George C. Marshall Library

Major General Ernest N. Harmon, Commanding General, U.S. 1st Armored Division, *right,* and Brigadier General Frank Allen, Jr., commander, CCB, with captured German Mark IV tank, Italy, 1944.
U.S. Army Military History Institute

American infantry enjoy a few hands of poker near a German roadblock across a mined street in the Livorno area, Italy, 1944.
U.S. Army Signal Corps; George C. Marshall Library

Soldiers of B Battery, 616th Field Artillery Battalion, U.S. 10th Mountain Division, carry 75 mm howitzer ammunition to be used against German positions in the prewar ski resort of Abetone, Italy, 1945.
U.S. Army Signal Corps; George C. Marshall Library

At 92d Infantry Division Headquarters, Via Reggio, Italy, 1945. *Left to right:*
Generals Alfred M. Gruenther, Mark W. Clark, George C. Marshall, Lucian K.
Truscott, Edward M. Almond, Joseph T. McNarney, and Willis D. Critten-
berger.

U.S. Army Signal Corps; George C. Marshall Library

Lieutenant-General Sir Bernard C. Freyberg, commander
of the New Zealand Division, *left*, being congratulated by
General Mark W. Clark after being awarded the U.S. Legion
of Merit, 1945.

U.S. Army Military History Institute

ELEVEN

Cassino and Anzio: A House Divided

THE STRUGGLE FOR ANZIO ENTERED A NEW and lethal phase in the opening days of February 1944. The failure of the VI Corps offensive of 30–31 January put to rest any notion that SHINGLE was to be a ten-day operation. The Germans had massed well over 70,000 troops in a tight ring across the VI Corps front, and by the second week of the Anzio operation the Allies had been forced onto the defensive. Not only must Lucas fight off the coming German counteroffensive, but without a major infusion of additional combat strength there was little likelihood of regaining the initiative.

In response to the threat posed by the German Fourteenth Army, Lucas was sent, in addition to the 1st Armored Division, two infantry regiments of the 45th Division, the 168th Brigade of Major-General Gerald Templer's British 56th Division, and Brigadier General Robert T. Frederick's Canadian-American 1st Special Service Force.

The expected German counterattack began on 3 February. Lucas was forewarned by Ultra, and by the clandestine efforts of a young Office of Strategic Services (OSS) operative in Rome named Peter Tompkins. A twenty-three-year-old American who spoke fluent Italian and had many friends and contacts in Rome, Tompkins had spent much of his youth in Italy. He entered Rome the day before the Anzio invasion and immediately began to organize what soon became one of the most effective OSS intelligence operations of the war. He recruited watchers who were placed round-the-clock to observe and record all troop movements into and out of Rome. Tompkins also obtained important intelligence directly from a highly placed operative in Kesselring's headquarters. Within days the first of a steady stream of intelligence messages began flowing from

Tompkins's clandestine Radio Rome to the OSS section attached to Fifth Army.

Tompkins's warnings came none too soon, for on 29 January von Mackensen's headquarters journal left no doubt of German aims: "The main mission of the Fourteenth Army is to annihilate the beachhead which the enemy is reinforcing." The same day Tompkins warned the Allies of a deception planned by the Germans to disguise their counter-attack intentions. This was the first of several timely warnings during the next two months.

When it finally came, the German attack fell with stunning force, as both ground forces and the Luftwaffe responded to Hitler's 28 January Order of the Day to "lance the abscess south of Rome."

Von Mackensen's intermediate objectives were the exact reverse of Lucas's several days earlier: first Campoleone and then the Factory, followed by a thrust toward Anzio and the beaches. Penney's 1st Division bore the brunt of the Fourteenth Army counterattacks in the Campoleone sector beginning the night of 3–4 February, when elements of four divisions fell on the narrow British salient with Tiger tanks, infantry, and heavy artillery fire. Campoleone was quickly rendered untenable, and, as it would again and again throughout the campaign, the focus shifted to the Factory, which the Germans reclaimed on 9 February after inflicting nearly 1,400 losses on the British (some 900 of whom became prisoners). Hardest hit were the 1st Battalion, Duke of Wellingtons, the 6th Gordon Highlanders, and the Irish Guards.

The first forty-eight hours were the worst. The British 1st Division was attacked relentlessly, and the front quickly dissolved into a series of small-unit actions between opposing battalions, companies, platoons, and squads. Like the Dutch boy of fable, the British commanders had to counter the very real possibility of a breakthrough with whatever fingers in the dike they could muster. Casualties rose to alarming proportions. In places the German attacks tore gaping holes in the British line, and entire units simply disappeared in the chaos. Three companies of the 6th Gordons were overrun and captured on the morning of 4 February, creating a critical gap, which, however, the Germans were unable to exploit.

In the midst of such confusion it was inevitable that both sides would capture large numbers of prisoners. There were times when the captured became the captors. In one instance a number of Irish Guardsmen were taken prisoner, only to turn the tables on their captors and escape within minutes. Other engagements pitted men and tanks against one another in smaller versions of the larger battle that soon took on unforgettable nicknames, such as "Dung Farm," "Buonriposo Ridge," "Ration Farm," "the Embankment," "the Flyover" and, later, "the Caves."

The German attacks in the Cisterna sector were equally determined but far less successful. To overcome the weakness of his main line of defense, Truscott ordered his tanks and tank destroyers forward to provide the fire support the infantry required to hold their positions. He also massed his artillery so that the firepower of seven battalions could be directed on any target at a moment's notice. Despite Truscott's earlier misgivings, the German attacks against the Cisterna sector never seriously threatened his division, and he observed in his postwar memoirs that "never again during the entire beachhead period was any German attack to endanger the front of the 3rd Infantry Division."

The front itself was virtually impossible to distinguish as the positions of both sides ebbed and flowed according to the local successes of one side or the other. The only constants were the steady German pressure and the growing casualty lists. Among the busiest supporting elements were the medics and the graves registration troops. Many of the dead could not be recovered and remained rotting on the battlefield until the end of the campaign months later. The ferocity of the battles for control of the Carroceto-Factory sector took a grievous toll on both sides. The only winner in the Anzio beachhead in February 1944 was the Grim Reaper, whose image appeared on German propaganda leaflets but who displayed utter impartiality in his choice of victims.

Within two weeks the Anzio beachhead had evolved into a battlefront resembling the trench fighting of the First World War. But what made Anzio different from other campaigns was the close proximity of every Allied soldier and sailor to the fighting. The beachhead was so small that no one in it was safe. The Germans soon brought in the largest guns in their repertoire, including two 218-ton monsters, each mounted on a railway car and capable of firing a 280-mm shell up to thirty-six miles. Allied ships offshore were subjected to frequent bombardment, as were the support facilities located in and around Anzio-Nettuno. Soon nicknamed "Anzio Annie" and "Anzio Express," these giant guns were kept secure in caves in the Alban Hills and only rolled out to fire several rounds at a time. They were then withdrawn into the safety of their caves before the Allied air forces or artillery could react and attack them.

The two railway guns were merely the icing on the cake for the Germans, who employed 372 guns, of which 150 were of calibers over 105 mm. The beachhead was shelled around the clock by these guns and bombed and strafed by the Luftwaffe, who also introduced a deadly new weapon in the form of radio-controlled glide bombs and antipersonnel "butterfly" bombs that claimed numerous victims. Men wounded in combat sometimes lost their lives to incoming artillery in one of the field hospitals. Cooks, bakers, mechanics, medics, dentists, clerks, ordnance and signalmen, engineers, truck drivers, and chaplains all shared a common peril that in the rear areas was sometimes so great that AWOLs and troops resting and recuperating voluntarily returned to the front, where it was considered "safer." Rear area casualties were often high, as on 7 February when a German plane inadvertently bombed the 95th Evacuation Hospital, killing twenty-eight and wounding many more.

At the front the beleaguered British continued to bear the brunt of the German fury and a disproportionately high share of the Allied casualties. The atmosphere across the beachhead was of grim determination to avert another Dunkirk. Mediterranean news reports told of a growing sense of despair, and when these began to appear in the British and American press, an alarmed Winston Churchill urgently cabled Alexander and Allied commander-in-chief General Sir Henry Maitland Wilson for an explanation. Alexander reacted with a rare public display of fury when he visited Anzio in early February and tongue-lashed the correspondents whose "defeatist" attitude, he charged, was detrimental to the Allied effort in Italy.

Churchill was observing the events in Italy with considerable trepidation. Reassurances from Wilson and Alexander notwithstanding, Churchill's frustration at the inability of the Allied military commanders in Italy to break the stalemate and capture Rome led to his now famous remark about Anzio that "I thought we were landing a Tiger cat; instead all we have is a stranded whale." Publicly, the Prime Minister insisted that there was "no justification for pessimism"; privately, he continued to fret.

During the first two weeks of February the Germans attacked repeatedly, again focusing their main attacks on the Factory. To counter the threat to his left flank Lucas rushed reinforcements from the 45th Division to assist the British. The awkwardly shaped Campoleone salient had indeed proven impossible to hold, and during the first ten days of February it seemed as if the entire struggle for Anzio had become this one hellish place, with the Factory subjected to one German attack after another. Despite the numbing regularity of these attacks, the British refused to concede the Factory. The casualties were appalling. The German threat was so grave that the 504th Parachute Infantry, elements of the 1st Armored, and the 45th Division were all committed to help repel the German attacks.

A brief look at the status of the 1st Division provides a glimpse of how badly battered Penney's force was. After two weeks of combat the Division was below 50 percent strength. Of the eleven line regiments,* none could muster over 65 percent, and several were down to 30–40 percent of their authorized strength. The rain and intense damp of February negated direct air support and increased the misery of the troops. Lucas was forced to commit every available resource to aid the beleaguered 1st Division.

By midday on 9 February the Germans were in control of the Factory, even though heavy fighting continued to rage on the right flank of the British 1st Division. This left the British salient hanging by a slender thread in nearby Carroceto. The Scots Guards kept control of the Carroceto railway station until early the following morning, when most of the surviving men were forced to withdraw to the nearby Embankment, which now became the Allied front line. A company of the Irish Guards remained in Carroceto to cover the withdrawal. Near dawn they were overrun by German tanks, parachute troops, and infantry and were never heard from again. The Germans were now in complete control of the two vital points from which they intended to mount the second and decisive phase of their counteroffensive to drive the Allies back into the sea.

The struggle for the Factory was renewed on 11 February by the 45th Division as American forces were baptized into the horror of Aprilia in some of the bitterest fighting of the campaign. Backed by heavy artillery fire, a tank-infantry task force (1st Battalion, 179th Infantry and two tank companies of the 191st Tank Battalion) stormed the Factory, where the fighting became hand-to-hand in the ruins. The Germans defending the Factory were near the end of their tether but managed to launch one more counterattack that drove the latest Allied occupants back to a point some five hundred yards to the south. A second attempt by the 45th Division the following day met with failure.

The Germans had captured important intermediate objectives from which to initiate the decisive thrust they needed to crush the Allied Expeditionary Force. With each passing day Fourteenth Army's strength was bolstered by the arrival of numerous additional infantry, panzer grena-

---

*The reader is reminded that a British infantry regiment in World War II equated to an American infantry battalion. The same applies to tank and artillery units.

dier, parachute, and panzer units, bringing their numbers to a staggering total of 120,000 troops, of which 70,000 were combat forces.* It was now becoming apparent, however, that if Kesselring and von Mackensen were to achieve their object of destroying the VI Corps beachhead, they would have to do so before the Allies could rush additional reinforcements to Anzio. The powerful Allied air interdiction effort was taking a toll on the German fuel supplies in particular. Although both sides could claim at least a moral victory at this point, time was now on the side of the Allies.

Other than in scope, the German plan of attack varied little from their earlier tactics. Two corps would simultaneously attack both wings of the Allied line: the I Parachute Corps was to carry out the main attack down the Albano-Carroceto-Anzio highway, while the LXXVI Panzer Corps carried out a diversionary attack toward Anzio from Cisterna. Von Mackensen believed he could crush the main Allied defenses with overwhelming infantry attacks and exploit the breach with his massed armor.

THE CRUCIAL PHASE OF THE BATTLE FOR ANZIO began near dawn on the morning of 16 February with a massive artillery barrage that filled the sky over the front lines with heavy clouds of smoke and dust from which emerged waves of infantry of the 3d Panzer Grenadier Division and the 715th Infantry Division, heavily supported by tanks. Code named Operation Fischfang (literally, "to catch fish"), the main German axis of advance along the Albano-Anzio highway, the Via Anziate, was intended to drive a massive wedge into the Allied left flank that would eventually carry the attackers clear to Anzio and Nettuno.

The Factory again became the scene of the most intense fighting. There the 45th Division incurred the full wrath of the German break-in attacks that emanated from the protection of its ruins. Although several tanks eventually managed to drive as far south as the overpass known as the Flyover, throughout the five days of this decisive battle von Mackensen's troops were never able to rupture the final defensive line. In the gullies west of Via Anziate and the plains to the east, the British 56th and the U.S. 45th divisions fought them to a standstill despite very heavy casualties. The battles raged first along Dead End Road, approximately a

---

*In World War II the average "tooth-tail" ratio was ten to one; that is, for every combat soldier there were some ten men in logistic/administrative support. The Wehrmacht rarely had such luxury and made do with a far lower ratio, as exemplified at Anzio.

thousand yards north of the Flyover, and later in front of the Flyover itself. Had the Germans broken this final VI Corps defensive line, the entire left flank of the Allied line would have collapsed. Lucas had only a handful of rear area troops left, and with the road to Anzio virtually undefended, the battle would have been lost.

The crisis came on 18 February when von Mackensen renewed his attempt to break the Allied line south of Dead End Road, along the lateral road that passed over the Via Anziate at the Flyover. A bulge was driven into the left flank of the 45th Division, where the armor of the 26th Panzer and 29th Panzer Grenadier joined the 715th Infantry, six battalions of the 114th Jäger Division, and the remnants of the 3d Panzer Grenadier in a last-ditch all-out attack that turned the battlefield into a cauldron.

The Flyover now became the focal point of the battle as the Germans launched a human-wave attack designed to drive the final wedge into the Allied left flank. Defending a two-thousand-yard sector where the Flyover crossed the Via Anziate were the 1st Battalion, the Loyal Regiment, a North Lancashire regiment. After an all-night bombardment the Germans attacked at 0500 hours across a minefield and through the barbed wire protecting the front lines of the Loyals. Throughout the day the battle raged as the sheer size of the German attack threatened to engulf the Loyals. A company of the 6th Gordons and a company of Harmon's Sherman tanks arrived to back up the Loyals, whose front had disintegrated into isolated pockets of defenders fighting hand-to-hand against their attackers.

In a campaign marked by carnage, this engagement was, as British historian Peter Verney recounts, "a charge of the Light Brigade without the horses . . . sheer slaughter." The attackers were cut down by machine-gun and shell fire. Thanks to the bravery of the Loyals the Germans shot their bolt attacking the Flyover and paid for it with grievous losses.

With the weather marginal and Allied air attacks limited to 150 sorties on 18 February, veteran artilleryman Lucas had massed 224 guns, which now directed their fires with devastating results wherever the Germans attempted to advance. Across the front, wave after wave of tanks and infantry hurled themselves on the British and American defenders in a furious and ultimately futile series of attacks that failed to break the Allied line.

A postwar account of the 179th Regiment, which sustained the brunt of the German attacks on 16–17 February 1944, provides a brief glimpse of the hell that was Anzio:

For the first time in its history the 179th's companies and battalions were disorganized, scattered . . . communications cut. . . . The casualties were appalling. Men did trickle back in twos and threes . . . they came back crying, hysterical. Even veteran section leaders, ashen-grey and quaking, broke under the strain: sleepless for days and pinned in their holes by artillery . . . only to find Brobdingnagian steel monsters charging them from all sides, pouring out a deadly fire as they came. . . . Those who lived were only half alive. One haggard, ragged squad leader who came back without a squad, squatted in front on his haunches outside the S-1 tent. . . . Not a sound escaped his lips but for two hours tears rolled down his cheeks unchecked.*

The 157th Regiment suffered grievous losses defending the 45th Division left flank along the Via Anziate, and the 179th and 180th regiments and the 1st Loyals fought with uncommon courage, and in so doing dealt a crippling blow to Hitler's order to smash the Allied beachhead. The cost in human misery was staggering. The statistics for the 179th Regiment showed losses of 55 percent: 142 were killed, 367 wounded, 728 captured or missing, and, most ominous of all, 670 evacuated due to combat fatigue and for psychiatric reasons.

German losses during the five days of Operation Fischfang were 5,389 killed, wounded, and missing, while overall Allied casualties were 3,496. Some German units were gutted by the battle, among them the 715th Division, which on 20 February could muster a mere 185 officers and men. One of 179th's battalions counted more than 500 dead outside its lines, and one of the many German prisoners told his captors that the slaughter at Anzio was worse than anything he had experienced, including Russia.

For the remainder of February the two sides fought and bled in more small-unit actions, the worst of which occurred in the wadi country west of the Via Anziate in what has come to be known as the Battle of the Caves. The 2d Battalion, 157th Regiment, began the battle with 800 men; when the battalion was relieved eight days later by the 2nd/7th Queen's Royal Regiment, 225 were left.

After the German counteroffensive of 16–20 February General Lucas was relieved as commander of VI Corps. However impossible Lucas's

*From Warren P. Munsell, Jr., *The Story of a Regiment* (San Angelo, Texas: Newsfoto Publishing Co., 1946), p. 55.

mission, Alexander was not satisfied with his performance, believing he was too tired and defeatist to continue in command of VI Corps, and he called for his dismissal. That Lucas was soon to be replaced was certain when on 17 February Clark assigned Truscott as the deputy corps commander, ostensibly to assist Lucas but in reality to replace him when the axe fell on 22 February.

Lucas anticipated his fate, noting in his diary: "Message from Clark. He arrives today with eight generals. What the hell." When summoned to Clark's command post that night, he was told by the Fifth Army commander that pressure from Alexander and Lieutenant General Jacob L. Devers,* had led to his removal and replacement by Truscott. "Alexander said I was defeated and Devers said I was tired." Throughout his ordeal Lucas lost neither his composure nor his dignity: "I left the finest soldiers in the world when I lost VI Corps, and the honor of having commanded them in their hour of greatest travail cannot be taken from me."

The relief of Lucas was a classic example of the bankruptcy of the Allied strategy in Italy. Lucas had been given a mission he had no practical possibility of carrying out. He was not popular with the British, particularly General Penney, who believed his leadership was weak and ineffectual. But even Penney, like every other senior Allied commander who fought at Anzio, defended his decision to play it safe.

Although Lucas became the public scapegoat, the lion's share of the responsibility for the mess at Anzio lay with others: Alexander preferred boldness but was unable to provide Lucas with the necessary resources; Clark urged caution from the outset and at one point told Lucas, "You can forget this goddam Rome business." And, finally, Winston Churchill embraced Operation SHINGLE as his very own but was blind to the consequences of sending an inadequate Allied force to Anzio.

Lucas may not have been the ideal commander, but the safety of his corps formed the core of his decision not to race to the Alban Hills. He fully understood that the penalty for failing to do so was dismissal, but he believed he was sacrificed because he had acted prudently. It did not help that Lucas could have done more to help himself, nor is there much doubt that his undue pessimism led him to overcaution. He was overly tentative in failing to capture the key towns of Cisterna and Albano while they were still relatively undefended. However, in the dark days of early

---

*U.S. Lieutenant General Jacob L. Devers was the Deputy Allied Supreme Commander Mediterranean Theater.

February, when there was no certainty that the Allies could retain the Anzio beachhead, it was Lucas who defiantly wrote in his diary, "There are not enough Huns anywhere to drive us off this beach."

Until his death five years later in 1949 at the age of fifty-nine, Lucas never for an instant second-guessed his actions at Anzio. To his mind the decision to launch Anzio had been a mistake from the outset, and, despite having been dealt from a stacked deck, he had acted properly.

THE FRUSTRATION AT ANZIO WAS ONLY half of the crisis that faced the Allies in early 1944. The Rapido disaster had left the Germans in full control of the critical heights in and around the Liri Valley, and it was not until early February that Clark changed his tactics by launching a fresh offensive to capture the town of Cassino. Situated at the base of Monastery Hill astride both the Rapido and the Via Casilina (Route 6), the town had to be captured before Fifth Army could advance along Route 6 toward Rome.

The Cassino massif served as the western anchor of the Gustav Line and was the key to von Senger's defense of the Liri Valley. The ruins of a medieval castle lay directly over the town, and at the top of Monastery Hill stood an ancient Benedictine abbey, one of the holiest shrines of Roman Catholicism. Von Senger had turned Monastery Hill into an integrated position that took full advantage of the terrain both in the valley and atop the heights, but he had assiduously avoided occupying the abbey, in the sincere hope that it would not become an Allied target. A lay Benedictine and devout Catholic, von Senger was instrumental in first persuading and later aiding the abbots to remove the abbey's priceless art and treasures to safety in the Vatican.

The approaches to Cassino lay in full view of the defenders. The plains in front of the town had been flooded, and when Clark insisted on pressing the Rapido crossing even though his most promising option lay with McCreery's 10th Corps, von Senger was able to block a British thrust from the west. However, his task became increasingly difficult after Kesselring was forced to begin shifting units from Cassino to Anzio. Losses were growing and replacements were scarce. Across the Gustav Line the Germans were forced into a catch-as-catch-can approach.

Von Senger's fortunes were bolstered when Lieutenant Colonel Ludwig Heilmann's veteran 3d Parachute Regiment was shifted from the Adriatic sector to replace Major General Ernst-Günther Baade's hardpressed 90th Panzer Grenadier Division, whose units had been decimated defending the Cassino massif. A series of attacks in early February by the U.S. 34th Division threatened both the town and the heights of Monastery Hill. An excellent opportunity to have won what historians have designated the First Battle of Cassino was lost when no effort was made to reinforce the 34th Division. Although the chronic shortage of replacement troops in the Italian theater would have made it necessary to employ British troops under U.S. command, neither Keyes nor Clark showed any inclination to seek help outside II Corps.

Meanwhile the Germans had rushed in reinforcements to fend off this dire threat. Like the battles being fought at Anzio, the ferocious engagements fought in the jagged mountains surrounding Cassino were among the lesser-known horrors of the Italian campaign. Most of the battles of the heights were referred to simply by the numbers shown in meters on the maps of the participants. The Germans cleverly established their defenses on reverse slopes, with mutually supporting fires to cover an attack from any direction.

One of the keys to breaking the German grip of the Cassino heights was Point 593, which exchanged hands several times but ultimately ended back in German hands after a series of bitter battles with Major General Charles Ryder's 34th Division. Although forced to endure unspeakable hardships in the cold and brutal mountains overlooking Cassino, this National Guard division that Alexander a year earlier had pronounced unfit for combat in Tunisia had long since come of age, and was now one of the most battle-tested divisions in the entire U.S. Army. The performance of the 34th Division at Cassino was so outstanding that not only were a private first class and a lieutenant awarded the Medal of Honor, but a British historian later wrote that their exploits "must rank with the finest feats of arms carried out by any soldiers during the war." After suffering enormous losses and with its troops at the very end of their endurance, the division was pulled from the line to rest and refit. Their respite was to be short-lived; in early March they were sent to bolster the defenses of Anzio.

The II Corps had come exceedingly close to breaking the Gustav Line, and in mid-February Alexander and Clark decided to turn the task of finishing the job over to Freyberg's New Zealand Corps. However, the decision to commit the New Zealanders came far too late to take advantage of the earlier gains made by II Corps. It turned out to be a fateful decision that shortly resulted in one of the most hotly debated incidents of the war, the destruction of the Abbey of Monte Cassino.

As Graham and Bidwell record, "no better example could be found of the disadvantages of coalition warfare which handicapped the Fifth Army in Italy time and again." If Freyberg's force had been committed by 9 February, "the battle for Cassino could have been won then and there. Instead an exhausted 2nd Corps held on too long . . . the momentum was lost and the new brooms resorted to the bombing and destruction of the Benedictine Monastery."

At Anzio Clark did not have sufficient forces to carry out the Fifth Army mission; at Cassino in February 1944 he had ample forces to have won the battle if they had not been employed piecemeal. In an unfortunate example of nationalism taking precedence over sound military sense, first McCreery's and later Freyberg's corps were left unused in critical situations where their presence would have been decisive. Had Alexander acted to overrule Clark there would have been time, but rocking the boat was not his style, and the immediate consequence was the bombing of the ancient Abbey of Monte Cassino.

Clark was opposed to bombing the abbey, but in truth it was his own inaction that resulted in Freyberg's request that the monastery be attacked by Allied bombers. The New Zealanders had made little progress against the German strong points guarding the approaches to the abbey, and in the mistaken belief that the enemy was using it to direct artillery fire upon his men, Freyberg insisted upon its elimination. Alexander did not favor the bombing of the abbey, but, like Clark, he was only too conscious of Churchill's growing displeasure over the inability of the Allied armies to break the stalemate in Italy.

That the monastery had never been occupied by German troops was of little consequence, because it formed an essential component of the German defenses overlooking the Liri Valley. Von Senger had established and then violated a self-imposed 330-yard neutral zone around the monastery. As long as it formed a key element in the German defense of Cassino, the abbey's eventual destruction was a certainty. The fact that the instrument turned out to be Allied bombs instead of Allied artillery shells was meaningless.

The sequence of events and the individual actions and responsibilities of the major commanders are complex, but they involved the entire chain of command from Freyberg to Clark, Alexander, and, ultimately, Allied Commander-in-Chief Maitland Wilson. In the end, although adamantly opposed to Freyberg's request, Clark felt obligated to approve any recommendation whose purpose was the saving of lives. In doing so he unleashed a monumental controversy that is still the object of contentious debate more than forty years later.

An unusual quiet hung over the Liri Valley on the clear, bright morning of 15 February when more than two hundred bombers of Major General Nathan Twining's Fifteenth Air Force smashed the Abbey of Monte Cassino to rubble. An almost festive atmosphere existed as spectators, who included combatants, rear area personnel, reporters, and the senior generals of the Allied high command in Italy, watched from across the valley while waves of B-17 bombers dropped their deadly loads. The explosions shattered the morning calm as cheers erupted from the soldiers who witnessed the bombing. At a stroke the jewel of the Benedictines since its founding in A.D. 529 all but disappeared. The monastery seemed to erupt in black-and-white smoke, flames, and flying debris.

Despite its magnitude, the Allied bombing of the abbey was, on the whole, highly inaccurate and did little harm to the thick foundation. Most of the bombs missed the abbey altogether, and it was only the final bombing runs that did any significant damage. But now that all bets were off, troops of the German 1st Parachute Division occupied the abbey that night, turning its ruins to their advantage and considerably strengthening the defenses of Monastery Hill.

Among the missing that morning was Mark Clark, who saw no point in wasting time witnessing an act he personally deplored. On this day he and von Senger shared a common reaction: disgust. When he felt the blast emanating from the dying abbey, a distraught von Senger kept repeating, "The idiots! They've done it after all. All our efforts were in vain."

Even the Allied air commander, Lieutenant General Ira Eaker, had reservations. As his biographer, James Parton, notes, "he had no enthusiasm for bombing the abbey, sharing the views of Clark and Alexander that the ruins would make an even stronger obstacle."

The Germans were presented with a propaganda coup, and they took advantage of it by proclaiming that the Allies had perpetrated a brutal and wanton act of barbarism. The destruction of the abbey was as mistaken militarily as it was costly politically. The New Zealanders were unable to take advantage of the bombing until nearly three days later, by which time it was again too late. When the 4th Indian Division did attack the abbey on 17 February, they were repulsed by the German paratroopers, who inflicted over six hundred casualties.*

---

*Freyberg's New Zealand Corps had not completed its preparations for attacking the monastery when the air attacks were carried out on 15 February. The New Zea-

With the Cassino heights continuing to remain firmly in German hands until May, the bombing of the abbey became a visible reminder of good intentions gone awry. The ensuing controversy sullied the reputations of the Allied military commanders, particularly Freyberg and Clark. Even though American money contributed to the eventual rebuilding of the abbey, to this day the vengeful monks refuse to display signs in the English language.

The bombing of the abbey was the crowning example of the failure of Allied strategy in Italy in 1944. The Allies had not reaped a single tangible military benefit from it, and had instead committed a major blunder. The justification had hinged on "military necessity," which was not served, thus leaving the Allies back where they started.

So ended the Second Battle of Cassino. Other attempts by Freyberg and Clark to capture the abbey and the town of Cassino came to naught in the weeks following the bombing. The Third Battle of Cassino began in mid-March with a two-pronged assault on Fortress Cassino. It was preceded by a thunderous artillery barrage from 900 guns and a massive aerial bombardment of the town, which was pulverized by over 1,000 tons of bombs. The artillery fires began shortly after dawn on the Ides of March and continued hour after hour until some 1,200 tons of shells had been hurled against the town and the Cassino massif.

Again the follow-up ground attacks ended in failure. The 2d New Zealand Division, supported by the New Zealand 4th Armoured Brigade, moved against the town and Castle Hill, while the 4th Indian Division attacked Hangman's Hill some three hundred yards below the abbey. They also launched a tank attack from the vicinity of Albaneta Farm in the mountains to the northwest.

The defenders of all three levels of the Cassino defenses were Heidrich's tough paratroopers, whose tenaciousness and valor were unsurpassed in the war. When the New Zealanders entered the ruins of Cassino town during the afternoon of 15 March, they found its few surviving paratroop defenders groggy and dazed but miraculously still spoiling for a fight. Small pockets of infantry fought each other for control of the

---

land commander ought to have requested a delay until the 4th Indian Division was ready, but he was overly sensitive to Clark's feelings about the bombing and elected instead to take his chances after the bombing, even though a vital ridge complex called Point 593, northwest of the monastery, was now in German hands. For a full description of the complex situation that arose during this attempt to capture the abbey the reader should consult Graham and Bidwell's *Tug of War*, or John Ellis, *Cassino: The Hollow Victory*.

town, with the New Zealanders taking by far the worst of the casualties from snipers.

Some 160 of the 300 paratroopers defending Cassino were crushed to death beneath tons of rubble, in a scene that one German observer above the town described as an inferno. "Dear God, take pity on these men," he thought, while another wrote in his diary, "Today hell is let loose at Cassino. . . . We can see nothing but dust and smoke. The troops who are lying up there must be going mad. . . . The ground is shaking as if there was an earthquake." Survivors later spoke of half-crazed, filthy men stumbling from the shattered ruins only to be obliterated by bombs or shells. "It was like the end of the world."

Very heavy fighting took place for the town, Castle Hill above it, and the abbey itself. Huge mounds of rubble and deep craters made it impossible for the tanks to maneuver in support of the infantry, who often fought hand-to-hand with the one hundred or so paratroopers of the 3d Parachute Regiment who somehow survived the bombing in cellars and bunkers. The paratroopers managed to hold the town against a far larger Allied force long enough for reinforcements to arrive that night.

Although Castle Hill fell to the New Zealanders late on the afternoon of the first day, there was little else to show for the five-day Third Battle of Cassino, which ended in death and stalemate. It was later estimated that it had taken over three tons of bombs for each German paratrooper killed during the battle. Von Vietinghof paid tribute to Heidrich's men when he reported to Kesselring that only the men of the 1st Parachute Division could have held Cassino.

But it fell to Alexander to deliver the ultimate compliment when he wrote to Brooke to explain the latest failure. "Unfortunately we are fighting [against] the best soldiers in the world—what men! I do not think any other troops could have stood up to it perhaps except these para boys."

TWELVE

The Capture of Rome

ON BOTH FRONTS THE STALEMATE DRAGGED ON into the spring of 1944, with neither belligerent posing a serious threat to the other. Across the Anzio front the Allies turned the battle into a holding action. Harmon recalls the "haunting unreality" of the World War I atmosphere, whereby the grim accoutrements of war were juxtaposed with the calm grazing of sheep, cattle, and mules and the determination of Italian peasants to carry on their lives in the midst of the devastation all around them.

The end of the German counteroffensive at the Anzio beachhead had left a dangerous bulge in the front of the Allied lines to the west and northwest of the Flyover, and it was there that the Germans began to focus their efforts. If the western shoulder could be collapsed, von Mackensen believed, the original goal of attacking down the Albano-Anzio road remained a possibility. The key to success remained a penetration beyond the Flyover.

Mark Clark also recognized that the gravest threat to the defense of Anzio was the British sector, and shortly before relieving Lucas he cautioned the VI Corps commander to reinforce his left flank. Lucas needed no prodding from Clark and immediately redrew the areas of responsibility. The principal beneficiary was the hard-hit 45th Division, whose front he shortened considerably, with the British 1st and 56th divisions assigned the defense of the left flank. A regiment of the 3d Division was withdrawn to corps reserve and positioned in the center of the line so as to be able to reinforce if a threat developed anywhere on the front.

If von Mackensen was to regain the initiative, German forces must first control the treacherous terrain along the western shoulder below Buonriposo Ridge. There the desperate Battle of the Caves was fought.

The original 45th Division frontage was so wide that the 2d Battalion, 157th Infantry, was left to guard a two-thousand-yard section of the division's left flank that included the Albano road north of the Flyover. When von Mackensen launched his attack on 16 February, both flanks of the battalion were overrun by tanks and infantry, and the survivors found themselves isolated in the sector known as the Caves. Located near the Moletta River, this was an area of steep, rocky gorges honeycombed with caves in which the Americans were forced to take refuge from the heavy artillery fire.

It was here that the remnants of the battalion made a valiant stand for the entire week of 16 to 22 February. During the last three days of the battle the battalion was completely cut off, and as casualties rose to alarming proportions, hope for relief began to fade. On 20 February the noose grew tighter as fighting raged around the mouths of the Caves, forcing the American commanders on numerous occasions to call friendly artillery fire down on their own positions. The tactic worked, with the Germans suffering heavy losses of 86 killed, 232 wounded, and 84 missing.

The 2nd/7th Battalion, the Queen's Royal Regiment,* ordered to relieve the beleaguered Americans the night of 21 February, became embroiled in bitter and costly firefights and suffered serious losses before breaking through to the 157th's survivors in the Caves. An entire company was lost, and although the survivors of the 157th were relieved, the battle resumed in the same vicious fashion, with new players. The 2nd/7th Queen's suffered the same fate as their predecessors as the German stranglehold made the British situation desperate. Faced with certain annihilation if they remained, they were compelled to abandon the Caves and infiltrate back to friendly lines the night of 23 February.

Losses on both sides were shattering. The already severely debilitated German infantry units were reduced in many instances to mere handfuls of survivors. U.S. losses during the week-long battle were 75 percent of those engaged. Company E, 157th Infantry, was virtually wiped out; only the commanding officer and a platoon sergeant, later killed during the

---

*The 2nd/7th Battalion, the Queen's Royal Regiment, was a territorial unit formed in 1939. Under the British regimental system, the Queen's Royal Regiment was originally "the Queen's (Second) Royal Regiment of Foot." The British territorial army, equivalent to our National Guard, was doubled in 1939, with the result that in some regiments the battalions were divided into two and renumbered; for example, the 7th Battalion was divided into the 1st/7th and the 2nd/7th.

breakout, survived death or capture. In two days the 2nd/7th Queen's lost 362 killed, wounded, or missing. As a postwar U.S. Army account stated, "The battle of the caves did not end the fighting on the left shoulder. It was merely the most important and most costly action in a bloody war of attrition in which whole squads and platoons disappeared without leaving a trace."

Despite staggering losses, von Mackensen seemed determined to carry out Hitler's orders and launch counterattacks until he achieved a successful breakthrough somewhere along the VI Corps front. When the attacks in the Albano-Carroceto-Flyover sector failed, he began planning a series of fresh attacks against the entire Allied right flank from Carano to the Mussolini Canal. The objective was the same: to break open and crush a vulnerable flank, then commit the reserves and execute a tank-infantry thrust to Anzio and Nettuno.

The German strategy of continuous attack was designed in part to keep VI Corps off balance and to delay, if not prevent, the inevitable Allied offensive to capture Rome. Von Mackensen's rationale was that if the beachhead could not be crushed, at least VI Corps must be kept on the defensive for as long as possible.

Up to 29 February the 3d Division had been spared the brunt of the main German attacks, but that day the LXXVI Panzer Corps struck with five divisions. The main attack was aimed at Carano near the junction of the 3d and 45th divisions, a sector defended by Lieutenant Colonel William P. Yarborough's 509th Parachute Infantry Battalion and the 3d Battalion, 30th Infantry.

From behind a heavy screen of smoke the Germans began emerging in a series of infantry attacks aimed at Yarborough's paratroopers, who were emplaced around the village of Carano. As engineers blew gaps in the barbed wire and opened passages through the American minefields, waves of infantry emerged to attack. Despite the heavy volume of return fire and their own severe losses, the Germans overwhelmed a company-sized outpost and began advancing toward the Main Line of Resistance some seven hundred yards to the rear. But there all hell broke loose.

In Lucian Truscott the Germans had more than met their match. The veteran cavalry officer had quickly made his presence felt as the new VI Corps commander. Just as he had when he was the 3d Division commander, Truscott centralized control of the corps and division artillery in order to be able to respond at literally a moment's notice to any threat. Aided by fighters and fighter-bombers, Truscott's artillery, mortars, machine guns, dug-in Sherman tanks, and tank destroyers laid down a steel curtain of deadly gunfire that caused the German advance to falter and then die in its tracks. An awesome total of 66,000 shells were fired in support of the 3d Division. Truscott's foresight had saved the day.

Other German attacks to the east met a similar fate, except at Ponte Rotto, a hamlet on a secondary road southwest of Cisterna. There a tank-armored infantry task force of the 26th Panzer Division drove a wedge a thousand yards deep through the positions of the 3d Battalion, 7th Infantry, before the attack ground to a halt. German probes across the division front continued until 3 March, but it was obvious that they were going nowhere. Nor did their hearts seem to be in these attacks, which, unlike those in the wadi country to the west, obliged them to move across open ground that offered far less cover.

It was the final German effort. Fourteenth Army had paid dearly for its latest failure, with the loss of 30 tanks and over 3,500 men. Henceforth the Germans would return to the defensive to await the inevitable Allied breakout. In fact, six weeks of what must rank as the bitterest combat of World War II had left both sides utterly incapable of carrying out further offensive operations. During those six brutal weeks the inhospitable landscape of Anzio had been turned into a charnel house that spared neither friend nor foe. Twenty-five years later a former British lieutenant returned to Anzio and found that "the place was still a horrible one in which to die."

Kesselring and von Mackensen explored the possibility of a new offensive at the end of March but called it off in early April. Truscott's staff was likewise busy drawing up plans for new offensive operations by VI Corps, but these too never progressed beyond the planning stage. Nothing would happen at Anzio until the Allies attacked Cassino for the fourth time.

Other than local probes, both sides spent the remainder of the winter and early spring constructing fortifications. As it had on the Western Front thirty years earlier, the greatest danger lay in death from artillery fire. Allied troops took extraordinary precautions, some quite bizarre, to protect themselves. Men slept in foxholes under tanks, in bunkers, and some even in large wine vats sunk into the ground to form protective shelters. Some soldiers survived for reasons that defy rational explanation. One morning two U.S. infantrymen who were sharing a foxhole began digging new holes some distance away. Asked if they had been ordered to move, they replied, no, they had simply decided it was time to change their location. Soon after they took up residence in their new foxhole an 88-mm shell crashed into their former position.

Despite the relative inactivity, the casualty rate for VI Corps still exceeded one hundred per day. Weary of what they considered pointless sacrifice, men on both sides began to rebel in small ways. It was widely recognized that one of the fastest ways to die was to go on patrol. Night after night, probes were sent into the no-man's-land that separated the protagonists. In the British sector losses were enormous. As the campaign dragged on, it became common practice for a patrol to find shelter in no-man's-land and then deliberately draw enemy fire. Unable to advance farther, the patrol would then return to friendly lines with a legitimate excuse for failing to carry out its mission.

In preparation for the anticipated breakout, priority was given to a buildup of supplies and the replenishment of VI Corps's battered units. Local skirmishing was carried out only to keep the other side from gaining an advantage.

Liberty ships and LSTs from Naples were the lifeblood of the Anzio beachhead and carried the main burden of resupply, which generally exceeded three thousand tons a day. On any given day the waters off Anzio were filled with Liberty ships, serviced by a fleet of over five hundred DUKWs and LCTs. The excellent work of the engineers had resulted in the creation of considerable dock space in the port of Anzio, which could now accommodate a considerable number of LSTs and LCTs. On their return runs these workhorses became taxis that ferried prisoners and the sick and wounded to Naples.

DURING THE LULL, ALEXANDER'S ABLE CHIEF of staff, Lieutenant-General Sir John Harding, masterminded the plan that was at long last to end the stalemates at Cassino and Anzio. Harding, personally selected for his assignment by Brooke, was a veteran combat commander and a brilliant staff officer of rare ability and tact.

It was Harding who created the strategy for a plan, code named DI-ADEM, to break the Gustav Line. He proposed a sweeping realignment of forces that would concentrate Lieutenant-General Sir Oliver Leese's Eighth Army opposite Cassino for the main attack. With three corps (13th British, 1st Canadian, and 2d Polish), Leese's mission was to unleash a massive force against Cassino. Fifth Army was to be shifted to the Garigliano sector and would be joined there by General Alphonse Juin's*

---

*Many rightly regard Juin as the most able of the senior Allied commanders in Italy. One of the few to fight with honor and brilliance during the fall of France in 1940, Juin was an offensive-minded, brilliant tactician whose earlier plan to outflank

Corps Expéditionaire Français, while the 2d Polish Corps would take over the former French sector on the Eighth Army's right flank. After four failures* Harding intended DIADEM to be a battle of annihilation, not attrition.

Unlike the piecemeal tactics so unsuccessfully employed by Clark, DIADEM called for Eighth Army to concentrate its vast array of firepower, supported by the full weight of the Allied air force, in simultaneous attacks on key points in the German defenses. A major feature of the plan was the concentration of armor at the mouth of the Liri Valley, where Harding intended the breakthrough to occur. Once the Allies were in control of Route 6, the Gustav Line would be effectively cut. Moreover, with the Gustav Line broken, Kesselring and von Vietinghof would lose the capability to plug gaps by the timely shifting of their forces, a tactic successfully employed during the first three battles for Cassino.

Leese would have at his disposal six infantry divisions, three armored divisions, and three independent armored brigades, while on the Garigliano front Clark would have the two divisions of II Corps plus Juin's four divisions. At Anzio, VI Corps was likewise to be reinforced with Walker's 36th Division. With the arrival of Ryder's 34th Division in March, Truscott had a total of six infantry divisions (British 1st and 56th and U.S. 3d, 34th, 36th, and 45th), Harmon's 1st Armored Division, and Frederick's 1st Special Service Force.

The breakout offensive from the Anzio beachhead was to be aimed at the mountain town of Valmontone, which straddled Route 6 fifteen miles to the east. By selecting Valmontone, Harding ensured that the VI Corps offensive would enable Truscott's forces to control all road and rail lines between Rome and Cassino. To add to the Germans' confusion, Harding also conceived what proved to be an exceptionally successful deception designed to convince and worry the German commanders that the Allies were about to initiate another end run into their rear.

DIADEM did not please Clark, who angrily confided to his diary that it was all part of a British plot to rob him and Fifth Army of recognition when Rome finally fell to the Allies. To counter what he believed was British duplicity, Clark—over the strong objections of Truscott—ordered

---

Cassino with his corps, had it been implemented instead of rejected by Alexander, might have averted the bloody confrontations of the first three battles of Cassino.

*The Rapido and the first three battles of Cassino.

VI Corps to be ready to follow any of four courses of action, two of which avoided Valmontone altogether by thrusting northwest toward Rome. When Alexander offered a tepid objection to any but the Valmontone option, Clark pointedly noted that Alexander was "interfering" with his prerogatives as a commander. A more forceful general would long before have brought Clark into line, but Alexander was not about to change his modus operandi at this late stage of the war, and he hedged, leaving the Fifth Army commander with the whip hand.

Truscott favored plan BUFFALO,* a thrust by VI Corps via Cisterna and Cori to cut Route 6 at Valmontone, and he was delighted when Alexander fully backed the scheme when he was briefed at Truscott's headquarters on 5 May. On the following day Clark made his displeasure with Alexander and BUFFALO known in person when he informed Truscott that "the capture of Rome is the only important objective." No matter what Alexander wanted, Truscott was to be prepared to undertake any of the four existing plans.

After the war Clark defended his actions by insisting that the Allies had no chance of destroying Kesselring's two armies south of Rome. Truscott sought to convince Clark that BUFFALO was the only option offering strategic success, and that the seizure of Valmontone would make the capture of Rome inevitable. His arguments, however, were ignored. As Truscott noted in his memoirs, "Clark was obviously still fearful that the British might beat him into Rome."

During April and early May, in one of the most complex maneuvers of its kind ever undertaken, the Fifth and Eighth armies completed the difficult task of realigning themselves for DIADEM without revealing their intentions. Fifth Army was shifted to the Allied left flank north of the Garigliano River and given the mission of turning Kesselring's right flank. The main effort was assigned to Leese's Eighth Army, which was to launch a massive break-in offensive into the heart of the Liri Valley. The success of this redeployment is evident from the fact that despite numerous sources of intelligence, the Germans never detected the Allied preparations. Thanks largely to the realism of the deception operation, Kesselring became convinced that the Allies had finished attacking the

---

*The VI Corps prepared four separate plans for the breakout from the Anzio beachhead and the advance on Rome. Each plan called for a drive to Rome by a different route. Of the four plans, Buffalo came the closest to fulfilling the original aims of both SHINGLE and DIADEM. Although DIADEM and BUFFALO were designed to be complementary to Allied aims, they were completely separate plans.

Gustav Line and would settle for another Anzio-type end run near Rome or in the north near Livorno.

Although DIADEM and BUFFALO were separate plans, their aims were closely linked. As the U.S. official history notes, "General Alexander described the coming offensive in terms of a one-two punch, with the Eighth and Fifth Armies throwing the first punch on the southern front and the Fifth Army's VI Corps the second punch—a left hook from the Anzio beachhead."

It is important to note that Clark and Alexander had vastly different aims. For Clark, Rome was the only object. Alexander, however, intended the focus of DIADEM and BUFFALO to be Valmontone, not Rome. His objective was not the physical possession of a city but rather the destruction of the German Tenth Army, hence his firm backing of BUFFALO as the only option capable of realizing "worthwhile results."

Allied preparations included the most massive buildup of artillery ever undertaken in the war. Some 75,000 artillerymen of 124 battalions, consisting of more than 1,500 guns, were preparing to fire several million rounds of ammunition in support of DIADEM. On 11 May 1944 Kesselring was shocked to learn the inaccuracy of his estimate of Allied intentions when this colossal artillery announced the start of the great DIADEM offensive with thunderous bombardments that one German survivor described as "a blaze of flame down the valley . . . ear-splitting, screaming" that made the ground tremble under its sheer force.

DESPITE THE VAST EDGE IN ALLIED firepower, the first three days of DIADEM were ominously reminiscent of previous failed operations. General Wladislaw Anders's 2d Polish Corps was the first to feel the sting still left in the German tail. Exceptionally well led and highly motivated, the free Poles, like the French, were among the most effective members of the Allied contingent in Italy. The Poles fought valiantly against Heidrich's equally determined paratroopers along the rocky slopes around the abbey, but they took heavy losses in an ill-fated attempt to succeed where others before them had failed.

In the Liri Valley Lieutenant-General Sidney Kirkman's 13th British Corps spent three hellish days establishing a bridgehead across the Rapido. The German Tenth Army commander, von Vietinghof, had concentrated the LI Mountain Corps to repel a main Allied attack which was once again aimed at capturing the abbey. The Germans fought fiercely, aided by a thick fog which caused utter chaos as the leading as-

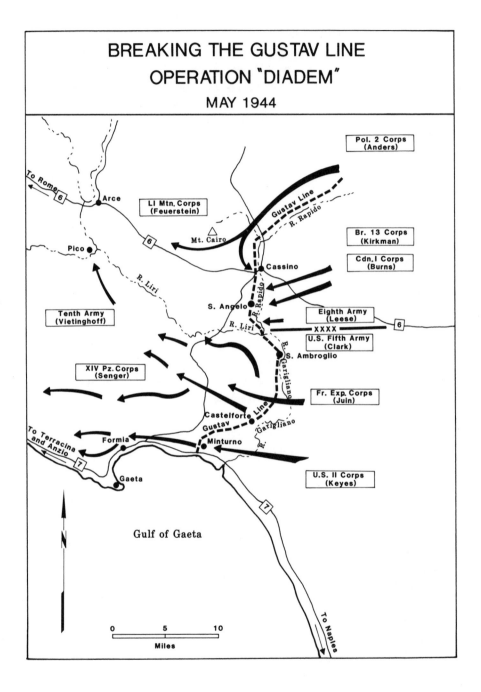

BREAKING THE GUSTAV LINE
OPERATION "DIADEM"
MAY 1944

sault units of the 8th Indian Division became lost and confused. Even the white tape normally so effective at guiding men forward at night became useless; units were forced to creep forward with each soldier grasping the belt of the man ahead to avoid getting lost.

The opening phase of DIADEM thus had all the makings of another "Bloody River," as the Germans took full advantage of the weather and confusion to make life difficult for the 8th Indian Division and the lead units of the 1st Canadian Corps. The Indians found, as the 36th Division had before them, that their greatest problem was emplacing bridges across the Rapido under heavy German fire. Although the assault elements managed to establish a slender toehold across the river, there could be no exploitation until there were bridges for the armor and supporting artillery to cross. Until then the 13th Corps bridgehead remained tenuous at best.

It took three days to gain a firm foothold in the Liri Valley north of the Rapido. The 13th Corps was now poised to join hands with the Poles, provided their second attempt against the abbey and its surrounding heights was successful.

The II Corps was assigned to penetrate the extreme left flank near the mouth of the Garigliano where McCreery's corps had come so close to success in January, only to be denied it by Clark's failure to take advantage of the bridgehead north of the river. Although a regiment of the 88th Division succeeded in capturing an important hill mass north of the river, the main corps attack farther east met bitter resistance from XIV Panzer Corps and stalled.

On the II Corps's right flank, Juin's French troops faced formidable terrain north of the Garigliano, but by dint of a bold plan and highly imaginative maneuvering the French accomplished precisely what Harding intended. In a series of hard-fought battles they not only took the heights dominating the western slopes of the Liri Valley, but by 21 May had driven as far as Pontecorvo on the valley's northwestern rim.

Juin's thrust tore a gaping hole in the right flank of the Gustav Line, which collapsed when the Poles finally succeeded in capturing the Abbey of Monte Cassino on 17 May. With 13th Corps at last on the move into the heart of the Liri Valley, the long-sought breakthrough was realized.

Kesselring was now left with few options and little hope. With Monte Cassino in Polish hands, his right flank in shreds after Juin's attacks, and Leese's armor threatening to thrust clear to Rome along Route 6, he was forced to rush the 26th Panzer and 29th Panzer Grenadier divisions from Anzio, but these proved to be too little and far too late to redeem the situation at Cassino. Their departure in turn severely weakened Fourteenth Army on the Anzio front.

The capture of the abbey by the valiant Poles was the final chapter in the bloody saga of Monte Cassino. Thirteen days of vicious combat to capture this heap of rubble had cost 860 Polish dead and nearly 3,000 wounded. There could be little joy at the sight of the Polish flag flying over the gutted abbey, a dreadful symbol of the carnage of war. Yet across the mountain masses of red poppies had emerged from the now silent battlefield.

Although DIADEM had finally broken the back of the Gustav Line, it was poorly executed, as indeed was the entire conduct of the battles along the Gustav Line since the previous winter. As British historian John Ellis observes in a superb study of the Cassino battles, *Cassino: The Hollow Victory,*

> On the whole both Fifth and Eighth Armies were poorly led during the Cassino battles, where operations were consistently marred by a lack of strategic vision and slipshod staff work. Again and again these two factors combined to produce attacks that were doomed from the start, directed as they were against the strongest and least accessible portions of the German line and against an enemy who resolutely refused to begin the withdrawal so often predicted by the Allies. . . . And so, month after month, they squandered fine divisions in isolated attacks mounted in quite inadequate strength.

The exception to this was the "shining example" of Juin's French Expeditionary Corps to whom the real credit for the success of DIADEM must go.

AT ANZIO, ALLIED STRATEGY HAD called for Truscott to be prepared to open his offensive on twenty-four hours' notice. During the afternoon of 21 May the order came to launch Operation BUFFALO two days later. As at Cassino, the early morning calm of 23 May was shattered by the thunder of more than a thousand Allied guns, tanks, and mortars, most of them aimed at the ruins of Cisterna, the key jumping-off position for VI Corps. At long last the time had come for the Allies to break the stalemate at Anzio. Truscott later described how "the ground quivered and trembled . . . towering clouds of smoke and dust broke through the pall about Cisterna as their [Allied aircraft] bombs crashed into the town and enemy positions. . . . H hour had come and the battle was on."

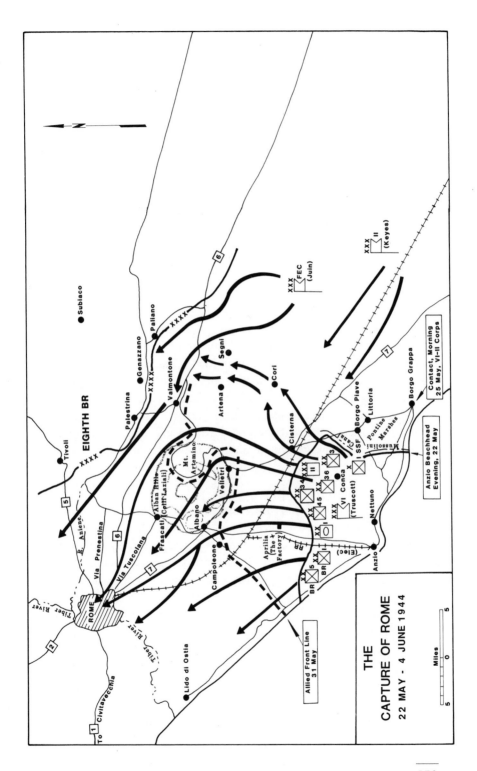

THE
CAPTURE OF ROME
22 MAY - 4 JUNE 1944

Miles
5 0   5

Allied Front Line
31 May

Anzio Beachhead
Evening, 22 May

Contact, Morning
25 May, VI-II Corps

EIGHTH BR

XXXXX

XXX
FEC
(Juin)

XXX
II
(Keyes)

Tivoli

Subiaco

Paliano

Genazzano

Palestrina

Valmontone

Segni

Artena

Cori

Borgo Piave

Borgo Grappa

Littoria

Pontine Marshes

Mussolini Canal

Cisterna

Frascati (Colli Laziali)

Mt. Artemisio

Alban Hills

Velletri

Albano

Campoleone

Aprilia (The Factory)

Nettuno

Anzio

Lido di Ostia

ROME

Tiber River

R. Aniene

Via Prenestina

Via Tuscolana

Via Tuscolana

To Civitavecchia

6

5

6

7

7

6

7

2

1

XXX
VI
(Truscott)

3

I SSF

34

36

45

1

II

VI Conca

X

Eloc

5 BR

BR

To

BUFFALO was essentially an American operation. Alexander had ordered that the two British divisions be given the task of protecting VI Corps's left flank and not be committed to heavy combat. Both the 1st and 56th divisions were spent forces and faced the same replacement crisis that was soon to plague their comrades in Normandy. British manpower was nearing its lowest ebb of the war, and with the priority given to Montgomery's 21st Army Group for OVERLORD, there were insufficient British replacements for the Italian theater.

Alexander's decision undoubtedly delighted Mark Clark, whose obsession with a triumphant American march into Rome had reached its zenith. The spearhead forces were the 3d, 34th, and 45th divisions, the 1st Special Service Force, and the 1st Armored Division, with the newly arrived 36th Division in reserve. By Truscott's reckoning, VI Corps would be in position by 26 May to block the German Tenth Army's retreat north from Cassino along Route 7.

The long stalemate at Anzio may have been over, but the first two days brought few rewards as the Germans stubbornly resisted across the entire front. Cisterna did not fall until 25 May. That same day Clark delivered a bombshell that was to effect the outcome of the Italian campaign. When he returned to his command post, Truscott found the Fifth Army G-3, Brigadier General Donald Brann, bearing bad news. "The Boss wants you to leave the 3rd Infantry Division and the Special Service Force to block Highway 6 and mount that assault you discussed with him to the northwest as soon as you can." In his memoirs Truscott wrote bitterly:

> I was dumbfounded. I protested that the conditions were not right. There was no evidence of any withdrawal from the western part of the beachhead, nor was there evidence of any concentration in the Valmontone area except light reconnaissance elements of the Hermann Göring Division. This was no time to drive to the northwest where the enemy was still strong; we should pour our maximum power into the Valmontone Gap to insure the destruction of the retreating German [Tenth] army.

Clark's pride in his Fifth Army and his desire to focus attention on the American contributions to the campaign were one thing, but at a stroke his order to Truscott—an order based more on vanity than military necessity—destroyed any hope of trapping von Vietinghof's retreating army.

The collapse of the Gustav Line had forced Kesselring to abandon the Cassino front and begin a full-scale retreat on 22 May. If the remnants of the Tenth Army were to make good their escape, they would have to pass through the Valmontone bottleneck at the northern end of the Liri Valley en route to the north and a fresh stand along the Pisa-Rimini Line before VI Corps could block their retreat through Rome. To help keep Route 6 open Kesselring moved the Hermann Göring Division and elements of an infantry division to establish blocking positions until Tenth Army cleared this final obstacle.

The VI Corps losses were heavy, and progress continued to be painfully slow as von Mackensen's stripped-down army fought stubborn rearguard actions across the Anzio front. To demonstrate that their fighting ability had not diminished despite appalling casualties, the German 362d Division, holding out in the shattered town of Cisterna until 25 May against the hammering of the 3d Division, inflicted 2,872 American casualties, including 476 killed.

Elsewhere the 1st Armored and 45th divisions found the going equally tough as they attempted to thrust toward Albano while the two British divisions fortified the corps's left flank. The fighting was so fierce that 1st Armored lost approximately eighty-six tanks and tank destroyers on the first day of BUFFALO.

When Clark announced his decision to switch the VI Corps axis of advance northwest toward Rome,* he masked his true intentions by ordering his chief of staff, Major General Alfred M. Gruenther, to inform Alexander that he was in fact mounting two thrusts, one toward Valmontone and the other toward Rome. His "new" offensive (Operation TURTLE), Alexander was told, would overwhelm an already demoralized enemy in "an all-out attack. We are shooting the works." The VI Corps was also pressing forward with "powerful forces" against Valmontone.

There is no evidence that Alexander was taken in by Clark's deception, but again he declined to exert his authority. To have done so at this stage of the war would likely have been in vain, for, as Martin Blumenson notes: "He had no ground for questioning Clark's judgment on the best course of action in Clark's own zone of responsibility."

The results were altogether predictable: neither thrust was successful,

---

*Operation TURTLE, another of the four VI Corps plans. Under this option, the main effort of VI Corps was switched from the Valmontone Gap to a drive along the Via Anziate to Route 7 west of Albano, and thence up Route 7 to Rome.

and once again a major German force was permitted to escape to fight another day. By stripping Truscott's main attack force for the Valmontone thrust, Clark ensured the escape of Tenth Army. At the same time his new main thrust toward the northwest also failed when the 3d Panzer Grenadier, the 65th Division, and elements from the 4th Parachute Division shattered any hope of a rapid dash to Rome. In fact, the offensive was at a virtual standstill until 30 May, when one of Walker's 36th Division reconnaissance units found a gap that would enable a U.S. force to sidestep the German defenders and gain the Colli Laziali behind the hill town of Velletri.

Even as the 36th Division began to exploit the newfound gap into the Alban Hills, the Germans continued to withdraw elsewhere only grudgingly and after inflicting heavy casualties upon the advancing American infantry and armor. The two fronts had formally linked up the morning of 25 May when a reconnaissance force of the British 1st Division and the U.S. 36th Engineer Regiment encountered a similar force of the 85th Infantry Division along Route 7, thus formally ending the four-month-long siege of Anzio.

The difficult and bitter final days of the Allied drive on Rome were characterized by the same bloodletting and painfully slow advances that were the hallmark of the entire Italian campaign. During the first five days Allied casualties were over four thousand, exceeding those of the great German counteroffensive of 16–20 February.

By the night of 2–3 June the Germans had reached the limits of their ability to delay the Allied advance on Rome, and they began retreating to the north. Only scattered units were left behind to harass, delay, and protect the German rear as the remnants of the Tenth and Fourteenth armies made good their escape. To his credit, Kesselring realized that there was nothing to be gained by fighting for Rome and seeing the city destroyed. He declared Rome an open city and left only minimal forces to cover the German escape.

Mark Clark's obsessive dream became reality on the morning of 4 June when Harmon's armor and Walker's Texans arrived at the outskirts of Rome. By nightfall both divisions were in firm control of the city and of the Tiber River as far as the Mediterranean. The Allied liberators were greeted by cheering, delirious throngs of Romans, who turned their joy at liberation into wild celebrations. The following day Clark made his triumphant entry as the liberator of Rome and was received by the pope. The Allies had won a victory, but at a terrible price.

During the desperate months of the Anzio beachhead the Allies lost 7,000 killed and 36,000 more wounded or missing in action. In addition another 44,000 were hospitalized from various nonbattle injuries and sickness.

Was the price worth the cost? And did Clark squander an opportunity to have ended the frustrating Italian campaign sooner? There are varying opinions about whether VI Corps could have trapped Tenth Army, but there is every reason to believe that Truscott's BUFFALO force would at least have taken a heavy toll on the retreating German forces. Nor could the Germans have prevented VI Corps from seizing the Valmontone Gap. As official historian Sidney T. Mathews writes, "The greatest irony was that if the VI Corps' main effort had continued on the Valmontone axis on May 26 and the days following, Clark could undoubtedly have reached Rome more quickly than he was able to do by the route northwest from Cisterna."

Truscott never wavered in his belief that Clark was dead wrong when he emasculated plan BUFFALO in favor of a direct thrust on Rome. "There has never been any doubt in my mind that had General Clark held loyally to General Alexander's instructions, had he not changed the direction of my attack to the northwest on May 26th, the strategic objective of Anzio would have been accomplished in full. To be first in Rome was poor compensation for this lost opportunity." It was the outspoken Juin who may have best summed up the folly of Clark's fixation with Rome, writing on 30 May that "questions of prestige are shaping events, each one wanting to make the entry into Rome. History will not fail to pass severe sentence."

Perhaps the ultimate irony was that Clark's triumph lasted less than forty-eight hours in the newspaper headlines. On the morning of 6 June 1944 the fall of Rome was all but forgotten as the greatest amphibious operation in history, Operation OVERLORD, the long-delayed, long-debated cross-Channel invasion of Normandy, took center stage.

THIRTEEN

To the Winter Line

EVEN THOUGH IT WAS NOT A GREAT STRATEGIC victory, DIADEM was nevertheless a considerable triumph for the Allies after months of frustrating stalemate at Cassino and Anzio. As we have seen, numerous opportunities that might have shortened the Italian campaign were lost during these months. The Germans had suffered greatly from DIADEM but were far from beaten. The hardest hit was Fourteenth Army, which had absorbed fearful losses from its months of combat at Anzio. Von Vietinghof's Tenth Army was in somewhat better shape, but overall, DIADEM had cost the Germans 38,024 casualties, many of whom would never be replaced as manpower reserves were drained by the Allied invasion of France.

Relatively few Allied troops enjoyed the pleasures of Rome as the war continued unabated north of the Italian capital. Now that the Fifth and Eighth armies were able to engage in mobile warfare, Alexander's army group was in a position to end the campaign once and for all, provided he could retain all of his forces in Italy. The problem was that Operation ANVIL, the invasion of southern France, had become a reality that all too soon would cost Alexander his two best corps.

Churchill and the British Chiefs of Staff were openly critical of the ANVIL plan as it became plain that Eisenhower, the new Allied Commander-in-Chief in Europe, would not be swayed by British arguments that to carry it out would wreck Allied strategy in the Mediterranean. The debate had been simmering for months, and as the date for OVERLORD grew closer, Churchill stepped up his attempts to convince Roosevelt and Eisenhower to cancel ANVIL, which for security reasons had been redesignated DRAGOON. The Prime Minister complained that the operation was unnecessary and that it would be far more useful to leave the Anglo-American invasion force in Italy intact under Alexander.

Eisenhower, whose virtues as a pragmatist had been honed by nearly two years of high command, would have none of it. Time and time again he refused to scrap ANVIL/DRAGOON, despite a chorus of pleas in the days and weeks before the operation, which was scheduled for mid-August. Eisenhower had already compromised by backing away from his earlier insistence on simultaneous landings in both Normandy and the Riviera, and he was determined not to give in to Churchill a second time.

Eisenhower's rationale never changed; he believed the Allies in France required additional ports, particularly Marseilles, and that DRAGOON would serve to protect the right flank of the Allied armies during their broad advance toward Germany. On one occasion shortly before the landings the Prime Minister even resorted to crocodile tears by complaining that the Americans, who now fully dominated the war in Europe, were "bullying" the British and failing to listen to the strategic ideas of their ally.

Of the many problems that plagued Eisenhower during his tenure as the Allied Supreme Commander, none did so more severely than this controversial operation. The more Churchill cajoled and pleaded, the more strongly Eisenhower resisted. On one occasion he returned utterly exhausted from a particularly trying six-hour session with the Prime Minister. In the words of his naval aide, "Ike said no, continued saying no all afternoon, and ended saying no in every form of the English language at his command."

The British case hinged on their Mediterranean strategy and the conviction that too much had already been invested in the Italian campaign to rob it of the potential to end the war in Italy at the very moment when the Germans were in disarray after the fall of Rome. In a cable to Roosevelt on 28 June Churchill pleaded there should be no troops or landing craft pulled from Italy. "Let us resolve not to wreck one great campaign for the sake of another. Both can be won." The Italian campaign, he said, offered "dazzling possibilities," whereas the landings in southern France would "relieve Hitler of all his anxieties in the Po [River] basin" and serve no useful purpose in aiding Eisenhower's forces in northern France.

The American response was firm in its insistence that the invasion of the Riviera go ahead as scheduled. At the behest of Marshall and the U.S. Chiefs of Staff, Roosevelt replied on 2 July, "We are still convinced that the right course of action is to launch 'Anvil' at the earliest possible date," ending with a reminder that "a straight line is the shortest distance between two points." Roosevelt's none-too-subtle admonition was a clear message to the British that the road to Berlin ran through France and western Europe, not Italy and the Balkans.

Why was Eisenhower so insistent on retaining ANVIL, even though it had to be delayed from June to mid-August? Among his reasons was the expectation that the operation would draw off German reserves and protect the southern flank of his armies once they broke free from the Normandy bridgehead.

Moreover, Eisenhower was not optimistic over the usefulness of the Brittany ports, which he correctly believed the Germans would destroy before they could be captured. He may have had political reasons as well, in light of Churchill's latest gambit, which proposed that Alexander's forces drive the Germans from Italy and thus open the way to an Allied drive into Germany via the Ljubljana Gap and Vienna. Eisenhower's distrust of Churchill's Balkans strategy may have caused him to realize that the only way of guaranteeing the priority of OVERLORD was to exercise his authority as the Allied Commander-in-Chief by affirming DRAGOON, thus ensuring that operations in France did not lose emphasis to Italy.

The effects of ANVIL/DRAGOON on the campaign in Italy were enormous. The decision to carry out the operation meant that Alexander was stripped of a considerable part of his resupply capability and a significant proportion of his combat forces, which included Truscott's VI Corps and Juin's Corps Expéditionaire Français, the only mountain-trained Allied force then in Italy. Shortly before the French were reassigned to Lieutenant General Alexander M. Patch's Seventh Army as part of the ANVIL/DRAGOON invasion force, Clark persuaded the visiting General George C. Marshall to award Juin the Distinguished Service Medal. In his memoirs Clark notes that Juin was the first Frenchman in the war to receive an American DSM. It was a well-deserved personal honor for Juin and a recognition of the outstanding contribution by the French.

Not surprisingly, Churchill's strategic ideas were supported by both Alexander and Clark, who perceived the advantages of an amphibious landing in northern Yugoslavia followed by a drive through the Ljubljana Gap to Vienna. The decision to proceed with ANVIL/DRAGOON put an end to this idea and clearly gratified Stalin and the Russians, who had no desire to see the Allies occupying territory that they secretly coveted for themselves.

The principal military beneficiary of the Allied decision to proceed with ANVIL/DRAGOON was Kesselring, who was able to put into practice his plan to relocate the German army in Italy along the Gothic Line in the northern Apennines. Kesselring intended to pursue the same strategy he had followed in northern Italy for the previous ten months: fight strong delaying actions to stifle the Allied advance and then defend for as long as possible along a natural, well-fortified defensive line.

One of the earliest Allied miscalculations had been that the Gothic Line would be the primary German line of defense in Italy. Although preparations for its eventual manning had been ongoing for some time, its defenses were somewhat less formidable than those of the Gustav Line. Nevertheless, the Gothic Line represented a difficult obstacle to the Allied armies.

As had been the case in southern Italy, the Gothic Line was the strongest of a series of defensive barriers designed to slow and then eventually halt the Allies. Located in the mountains north of Florence, the Gothic Line was established in the unforgiving terrain running from Pisa on the Mediterranean, across the Apennines, then southeast to Pesaro on the Adriatic. German engineers had fashioned every conceivable obstacle, from tank traps to concrete fortifications, all of which took advantage of the rough terrain. Here Kesselring intended to stop the Allied advance at least until the winter weather set in, thereby continuing the war in Italy into 1945. In short, German strategy was to be a repeat of Cassino and the Gustav Line.

The German genius for creating obstacles was never more evident than in their retreat north from Rome. While German formations fought delaying actions along several intermediate defensive lines, their engineers destroyed bridges, mined roads, and left diabolical booby traps to maim or kill the unsuspecting. The most visible evidence of the success of this tactic was found in Livorno, when the 34th Division entered the city to find its port in ruins and evidence of sabotage everywhere.

The clever means employed by the Germans made an indelible impression on Clark, who later wrote, "As soon as we mastered one trick we immediately discovered that the Germans had another up their sleeve . . . bars of chocolate, soap, a packet of gauze, a wallet, or a pencil, which, when touched or disturbed, exploded and killed or injured anyone in the vicinity. Others were attached to windows, doors, toilets, articles of furniture, and even the bodies of dead German soldiers. We found over 25,000 of these hideous devices, and many of our lads were killed or injured as a result."

ALEXANDER WAS FACED WITH THE LOSS of seven divisions to ANVIL/ DRAGOON, and although the valuable port of Livorno was captured and opened to supply his forces, the Allied ground commander had no other option except to halt and regroup before assaulting the Gothic Line.

Kesselring claimed that he was once again assisted by the Allied failure to pursue his retreating forces more vigorously. In his postwar memoirs he wrote that in front of Fifth Army "now lay country suitable for motorized forces and tanks; if it chose to press on, the broad high roads to the north lay open. . . . If on 4 June he had immediately pushed forward on a wide front, sending his tank divisions on ahead along the roads, our Army Group west of the Tiber would have been placed in almost irreparable jeopardy, and I might have been induced precipitately to rush back Tenth Army's motorized divisions across the Tiber."

Clark in fact did act aggressively, but on 4 June his focus was on Rome, not the Germans. The Fifth Army commander fully understood that he was in a race against time and would soon lose Truscott's and Juin's corps to ANVIL/DRAGOON. Without success he attempted to persuade Marshall that Juin's force was adequate for the French operation and that VI Corps ought to be left in Italy.

After delaying the Allied advance around Lake Trasimeno, German Army Group C withdrew to another intermediate defensive line along the Arno River near the ancient city of Florence. The Allied pursuit of Army Group C had taken them 175 miles north of Rome to their present position 20 miles south of the Gothic Line. During their deliberate withdrawal the Germans extracted an exceedingly heavy price, inflicting 34,000 casualties. It was at the Arno that the Allies were forced to halt their advance and regroup. Ahead lay another series of epic battles to sever the Gothic Line and drive the Germans from Italy.

THE TIMING OF ANVIL/DRAGOON could not have been worse for the Allied forces in Italy. Literally overnight Fifth Army was reduced to Keyes's II Corps and Lieutenant General Willis D. Crittenberger's recently arrived IV Corps. By contrast, Leese's Eighth Army remained a powerful force, consisting of the 2d Polish Corps, the 1st Canadian Corps, and the 5th and 13th British corps. If he could have kept his army group intact, Alexander believed, he could have thrust through the Gothic Line and driven the Germans from Italy during the summer of 1944. Instead, the loss of seven veteran divisions left Alexander with a force of twenty divisions against Kesselring's twenty-two.

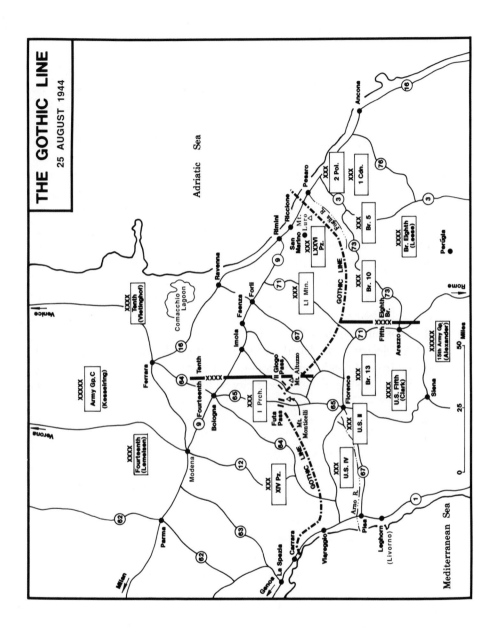

THE GOTHIC LINE
25 AUGUST 1944

Adriatic Sea

Mediterranean Sea

The departure of half his army left Clark with only four divisions, three of which were inexperienced infantry divisions, and the other the 1st Armored Division. Clark also lost a third of his thirty-three battalions of artillery. With even fewer divisions under his command, Clark became more distrustful than ever of his British ally, a feeling reciprocated by Leese, who had not forgotten how the Fifth Army commander had aborted BUFFALO and later stonewalled Alexander's order to give Eighth Army priority along the Fifth Army right flank during the pursuit north of Rome.

Leese not only opposed joint operations with Clark against the Gothic Line but was equally opposed to the idea of having to fight in the mountains on the Fifth Army's right flank. Eighth Army was best known for its set-piece battles and had never adapted well to mountain warfare. Clearly distressed with his role, Leese urged Alexander and Harding to permit him to shift his army to the Adriatic side of the Apennines and attack the eastern end of the Gothic Line.

Unwilling to force Leese to carry out an operation he had no confidence in, Alexander agreed, and for the next three hectic weeks Eighth Army carried out the difficult task of shifting itself across the Apennines to the plains south of Pesaro. The new Allied offensive, Operation OLIVE, called for Eighth Army to launch the main attack along the eastern coast to pierce the Gothic Line and at the same time draw German reinforcements onto its front, while Fifth Army attempted to capture Bologna by driving straight through the Apennines.

At Clark's insistence the British 13th Corps on Leese's left flank was placed under Fifth Army's control, thus restoring a semblance of parity between the two armies. This arrangement robbed Leese of a vital reserve that he would sorely need when he began Operation OLIVE, in particular the two armored divisions, which were unsuited to employment in the mountains between the two advancing armies where Clark planned to employ them. Leese's one remaining armored division, the British 1st Armoured, had not been in combat since North Africa eighteen months earlier and hadn't the slightest concept of how to fight in Italy.

Thanks to excellent deception by the Allies, Kesselring once again failed to detect in advance the time and place of Alexander's offensive. Spearheaded by the Poles, the Eighth Army offensive opened on 25 August on a three-corps front by easily penetrating the Arno Line and driving to the Gothic Line, which was found to be relatively undefended. Kesselring's first reaction was to believe that these attacks were a diversion designed to keep his forces tied up and away from the Riviera, where ANVIL/DRAGOON had taken place virtually unopposed ten days earlier. However, when the Germans captured a message from Leese detailing his plans, Kesselring soon changed his mind and recognized that "the matter on the coast is dangerous."

For once Kesselring failed to benefit from the British penchant for the set-piece battle. His attempt to reinforce the thinly held positions north of the Foglia River with 26th Panzer were not fast enough to prevent the Canadians from driving a wedge into the Gothic Line on 30 August. When the Canadian 5th Armoured Division commander, Major-General B. M. Hoffmeister, detected a noticeable lack of German activity, he elected on his own initiative to commit his division to an all-out attempt to collapse the eastern end of the Gothic Line.

By the afternoon of 30 August the Canadians had penetrated the Gothic Line and occupied important high ground along Monte Peloso and Monte Luro. The timing and boldness of the Canadian attack left the Germans in considerable disarray and helpless to prevent an exploitation, provided it was carried out before they could regroup. In fact, if a drive had been mounted before the Germans could plug the gaps in their secondary line of defense west of Rimini, Eighth Army might have outflanked the Gothic Line entirely and unleashed its armor onto the plains of the Po Valley, with disastrous results for Army Group C.

The 1st Canadian Corps was unable to take advantage of this exceptional opportunity, however, because its commander, Lieutenant-General E. L. M. Burns, had only two divisions and no reserve. Leese had lost confidence in Burns, a fact that led him to refrain from providing a reserve to exploit just such a golden opportunity as the Canadians had now provided him. Leese had unaccountably left the British 1st Armoured Division some hundred miles to the rear, and had provided no plans for its employment on short notice.

Neither Alexander nor Leese had foreseen the sudden success of the Canadian break-in, and both seemed unable to react. Thus, while Burns's two divisions struggled to keep up the momentum of their attack, the best Leese could do was to order 1st Armoured forward. On such decisions do campaigns turn, but as Graham and Bidwell note, this one was utterly inexcusable. Having failed to provide a reserve, Leese, now "condoned by a passive Alexander . . . was guilty of criminal inertia. The door to the enemy position, if not open, was at least ajar," but Eighth Army was helpless to take advantage of it. Nor could Leese have been in the slightest doubt that the Germans would react with their customary speed and fury to eliminate this gravest of threats.

With time critical and 1st Armoured at least twenty-four hours away, Leese certainly could have put together an ad hoc force to assist the Canadians. Graham and Bidwell believe that "a German or American general would have galvanized his staff into immediate action. Any action would have been better than none. Leese did nothing."

The bumbling efforts of the 1st Armoured and the British 5th Corps on the left flank of the Canadians, combined with Leese's inept handling of the battle, cost Eighth Army dearly. Instead of a stunning victory, Eighth Army was soon halted by the weather and the Germans, who, unlike their enemy, had not hesitated when it counted most. An attempt by 5th Corps to dislodge the Germans from the high ground around Coriano failed, and by 3 September the advance had stalled well short of Rimini. Although Eighth Army mounted a fresh offensive that was again spearheaded by the Canadians, the momentum was lost and the OLIVE offensive was over.

The Canadians had fought their finest battle of the war and had handed Leese an opportunity few commanders are lucky enough to receive in war. To them Leese sent a signal of congratulations that said in part, "You have won a great victory. . . . Well done Canada!" The cost in men was borne heavily by the Canadians, who accounted for over 4,000 of the 14,000 Eighth Army losses during OLIVE. The manpower shortage was now biting more deeply than ever, and Leese was forced to break up the 1st Armoured Division and reduce each of his rifle battalions to three companies. As for Burns, his "reward" would shortly be the loss of his command when the Canadian corps was sent to Northwest Europe to join the Canadian First Army in Montgomery's 21st Army Group.

Precious little time remained before the weather would close down the campaign for the second winter. The Germans could not hold their left flank, now anchored on Rimini, and throughout October and early November Eighth Army ground its way across a series of rivers and the soggy plains southeast of Bologna under its new commander, Lieutenant-General Sir Richard McCreery. Along the Lamone River the autumn offensive sputtered and ground to a halt. After a thoroughly undistinguished tenure as Eighth Army commander, Leese was promoted to full general and sent to Southeast Asia as the Commander-in-Chief of Allied land forces.

ON 10 SEPTEMBER CLARK OPENED the Fifth Army offensive with a two-pronged drive by Keyes's II Corps and Kirkman's 13th British Corps aimed at seizing the passes north of Florence. The main German forces protecting the Arno had withdrawn a week earlier to the Gothic Line. Kesselring, as he had with Rome, issued strict orders that the historic city of Florence be spared during the withdrawal. Nothing could be done to save the bridges over the Arno, which were all destroyed except for the famed Ponte Vecchio, where the northern end was blocked by the demolition of nearby buildings.

Clark agreed with Harding that the most exploitable axis of advance lay in the center, through the rocky mountain passes leading to Bologna. Although it offered the best opportunities to break the Gothic Line, the central route also meant that II and 13th corps would have to successfully storm the passes north of Florence. Again opposing Fifth Army was a patched-up Fourteenth Army, now under the command of General der Panzertruppen Joachim Lemelsen, who had replaced the sacked von Mackensen.

Clark decided to make his main attack against Il Giogo Pass guarding the entrance to the Po Valley, thus avoiding the main Gothic Line positions around Futa Pass on Route 64, the main Florence-Bologna highway. During a week of bitter combat Fifth Army fought for the passes while Crittenberger's IV Corps kept pressure on the left flank by attacking von Senger's XIV Panzer Corps.

Through an ULTRA intercept Fifth Army had learned that Hitler had warned Kesselring to expect the primary attack against Futa Pass, and it was Clark's intention to deceive the Germans into believing that this was indeed the case. A fierce diversionary attack against Futa Pass by the 34th Division completely hoodwinked Lemelsen, who failed to perceive his true danger to the east at the less heavily defended Il Giogo Pass. The key to Il Giogo was the capture of the two ridges overlooking the pass. It was here that the decisive battles were fought for Monticelli by the 363d Regiment, 85th Division, and on the opposite ridge by the 338th Regiment, 91st Division, for Monte Altuzzo.

Fifth Army comprised over a quarter of a million men, yet during the battle for the passes the fight was often conducted by companies, platoons, and even squads. The terrain was so rugged that vehicles became useless, and supplies and ammunition had to be carried up treacherously steep slopes on the backs of GIs. The official history describes what the infantry commanders faced as they fought to dislodge the German airborne troops of the 4th Parachute Division:

So cleverly concealed were the Gothic Line defenses that they were almost invisible to the approaching troops . . . [those bearing] the brunt of the fighting at critical points sometimes constituted a platoon or less, seldom more than a company or two. Little clusters of men struggled doggedly up rocky ravines and draws separated by narrow fingers of forested ridges, isolated, climbing laboriously, squad by squad, fighting their way forward yard by yard, often not even knowing the location of the closest friendly unit.

It took the massed fires of artillery, tanks, tank destroyers, and fighter-bomber close air support before the infantry could advance, sometimes mere yards at a time. The battle for Monte Monticelli was considered one of the finest small-unit actions fought by American infantry in the war. When they captured the ridge on 15 September the small surviving force was subjected to fierce counterattacks that continued relentlessly, until by the afternoon of the sixteenth there were only a handful of survivors. One was Private First Class Oscar Johnson, who earned a Congressional Medal of Honor by personally repelling repeated attacks by the desperate German paratroopers for over twenty-four hours.

The unrelenting battering by Fifth Army finally cracked the Gothic Line in a number of places, but the key had been the seizure of the two mountains guarding Il Giogo Pass. Clark lost no time in pressing on toward Bologna by shifting the main axis of attack to Highway 65, where Futa Pass had fallen to II Corps. He well understood that Fifth Army was in a race to break through the mountains and gain a bridgehead over the Po River before winter.

Clark could now recognize how tantalizingly close the Allies were to driving the Germans from Italy. From the heights "I could see for the first time the Po Valley and the snow-covered Alps beyond. It seemed to me then that our goal was very close. . . . We [were] right at the edge of success." So near, yet so far, for as Clark was soon to learn, Fifth Army had nearly shot its bolt. By mid-October it still had not broken free of the northern Apennines overlooking Bologna and the Po Valley. Kesselring knew the Germans in Italy were finished if Fifth Army could get loose in the Po Valley before winter. Berlin agreed and rushed in reinforcements for a last-ditch stand.

To Clark's bitter disappointment the Fifth Army offensive "merely ground slowly to a halt because men could not fight any longer against the steadily increasing enemy reinforcements on our front . . . [it] died out, slowly and painfully, and only one long stride from success." The rains had come, and the conditions facing the troops were a repeat of the abominable winter weather of 1943–44.

During the forty-five days of the battle for the Gothic Line, II Corps alone sustained 15,716 casualties. The troops were exhausted, units were understrength, and the manpower crisis that had for so long plagued the British finally caught up with Fifth Army. Moreover, losses due to combat fatigue had risen to such alarming proportions that Clark wrote to Marshall that "psychiatric breakdown is directly related to the length of time in combat." Clark's ruthlessness in driving his troops to accomplish a mission was well known, but it was now clear even to him that his troops had reached the end of their tether.

The climactic battle took place during the last week of October when II Corps attempted to break through a bulge in the front at Monte Grandi. Attacks by the exhausted infantrymen of the 85th and 88th divisions were bloodily repulsed. It was obvious that further attacks could not break through the final barrier to the Po and would only cause needless casualties. Clark had no choice except to swallow what he afterward considered the bitterest pill of his tenure as Fifth Army commander. Not only was his dream of ending the war in Italy in 1944 shattered, but his men would have to endure a second winter in the mountains. The Fifth Army staff expected that it would at least enjoy the comforts of Florence. They were wrong. An embittered Clark told them, "The men of those divisions are going to spend the winter in the mountains. So is my headquarters."

THE WINTER STALEMATE OF 1944–45 brought a number of changes in command on both sides of the front. On 23 October Kesselring was gravely injured when his staff car collided with a towed artillery piece on a dark road near Bologna. During his three months of recuperation, temporary command of Army Group C was assumed by the able von Vietinghof. In reality, Kesselring's tenure as the German commander in Italy was over in all but name. He was unable to return to his duties until the end of January 1945, and in early March Hitler summoned him to Berlin to take over the crumbling western front from von Rundstedt. The Italian campaign remained in the hands of von Vietinghof.

In early November 1944 the death of Field-Marshal Sir John Dill, the senior British representative in Washington, set off a series of command changes that reached into Italy. Churchill had grown increasingly disenchanted with the outspoken Maitland Wilson and was anxious to find an excuse to move him from the Mediterranean. With Dill's death the opportunity arose, and the Prime Minister ordered Wilson to Washington.

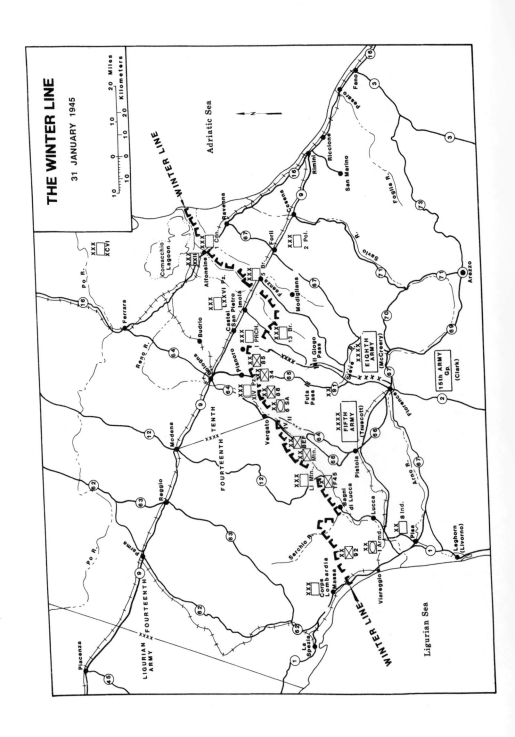

THE WINTER LINE
31 JANUARY 1945

To replace Wilson he named Alexander the new Supreme Allied Commander, Mediterranean Theater.

In December Mark Clark was promoted to the command of the 15th Army Group. Lucian Truscott was summoned from VI Corps in southern France to command Fifth Army and promoted to lieutenant general.

DURING THE FALL BATTLES IN the Gothic Line, the Allies had come within a hair's breadth of ending one of the most brutal campaigns fought by the Allies in World War II. For a fleeting moment the opportunity had been there for Leese to gain immortality by winning a famous victory. But Leese was a pale imitation of his predecessor, Montgomery, and during Operation OLIVE had ignored a fundamental principle of any commander on the offensive: be prepared to exploit success.

Clark's Fifth Army had fought with bulldoglike tenacity, but he could not win the war of attrition without a steady stream of replacements, which simply were no longer available to the Italian theater. In the end he came very close, and unlike Leese he had achieved the most he could expect from the forces at his disposal.

In Northwest Europe Eisenhower's Allied Expeditionary Force had broken the stalemate in Normandy and pursued the battered German army to the Siegfried Line. But winter slowed operations, and Hitler staved off the collapse of the Third Reich until the spring of 1945 by launching his great counteroffensive in the Ardennes. The Allies' failure to end the war in the west in 1944 guaranteed the continuation of the campaign in Italy. Until they could resume the offensive in April 1945 the Allied armies in Italy were forced to endure a miserable sojourn on the Winter Line. Ahead lay the bitter battles of the Po Valley.

FOURTEEN

The Final Days

THE WAR IN ITALY DRAGGED ON into the spring of 1945. As 1944 drew to a close, the end still seemed nowhere in sight. Now entering its seventeenth month, the campaign in Italy truly became the "forgotten front."

The winter hiatus gave both sides time to prepare for the final confrontation of the war. The Apennines became the source of a logistical chain that stretched from the United States to Naples and Livorno, and from there mainly by road to the Fifth Army. In the mountains motorized warfare ended, and most frontline units were resupplied not by truck but by mule train. Fifth Army employed fifteen companies of Italian troops, with nearly 3,900 pack mules, to help sustain the Allied soldiers manning the Winter Line.

Supplies were stockpiled, units retrained, and the numerous depots, hospitals, and other facilities vital to the support of an army in the field were established. Huge supplies of ammunition were assembled and heavy 8-inch artillery units arrived, as did the elite 10th Mountain Division, the only unit of its type created by the U.S. Army during the war. Trained in Colorado, the division was commanded by a World War I Medal of Honor winner, Major General George P. Hays, and consisted largely of college-educated troops who knew how to ski and function in snow and ice. Many were former members of the National Ski Patrol.

There was very little combat until February, when Truscott ordered IV Corps to carry out several limited offensives to gain better ground for the start of the spring offensive. In their first combat the vaunted 10th Mountain Division attacked at night up steep, icy slopes, completely surprised the Germans, and won several key positions leading to the Po Valley. Their success so alarmed Kesselring that he was obliged, against his wishes, to commit the 29th Panzer Grenadier Division to prevent any further breaches in the Winter Line.

By the time Clark launched 15th Army Group on its final offensive of the war, his force had truly become an international one. At one time or another the forces of sixteen nations were under Mark Clark's command.* In northern Italy these comprised the 2d Polish Corps, a South African armored division, a Brazilian infantry division, and an Italian force that grew to 150,000 by war's end. The Poles almost revolted when the results of the Yalta Conference became known, and it took all of Clark's persuasion to convince General Anders not to withdraw his corps from further fighting alongside the two allies who had betrayed them. Also serving in Fifth Army was the famed all-Nisei 442d Regimental Combat Team, whose soldiers were among the most highly decorated of any unit in the U.S. Army. Their exploits included those of a future United States senator, Second Lieutenant Daniel K. Inouye, whose heroism in single-handedly wiping out a German machine gun nest in April 1945 despite serious wounds earned him a Distinguished Service Cross.

BY THE SPRING OF 1945 EISENHOWER'S armies had driven into Germany and cut off the Ruhr, trapping the 300,000 men of Field Marshal Model's Army Group B. The war was nearly over, but there remained one final bloodletting between the two army groups in Italy. The splendid exploits of the 10th Mountain Division paved the way for Truscott to open his offensive on Bologna from the left flank, along the axis of Route 64.

Both Kesselring and von Vietinghof wanted to avoid the destruction of Army Group C and designed a series of withdrawals, first to the natural defensive barrier of the Po River, and, when the Allied armies could no longer be contained, further delays until they reached the safety of the Alpine passes. With no reserve and the loss of several divisions sent to Germany to be consumed in the final defense of the Reich, von Vietinghof had no other options. The choice was stark: either reposition Army Group C, or else face certain annihilation when the final Allied spring offensive got under way.

Signs of German desperation abounded. Resupply became a night-

*Representatives of sixteen nations fought for the Allied cause in Italy: Americans, British, Canadians, Poles, Brazilians, South Africans, Rhodesians, Indians, Pakistanis, Greeks, Italians, French, Moroccans, Tunisians, Algerians, and New Zealanders.

mare. The Allied air forces ruled the skies, and bombed and strafed anything that moved. Bridges were smashed to prevent supplies from getting
through, and rail lines were interdicted. The Germans were forced to
erect bridges underwater, invisible to Allied airmen, whose aggressiveness left no German on the ground safe from air attack.

Army Group C also had to contend with a dramatic rise in partisan
activity in northern Italy. These paramilitary forces became increasingly
effective, attacking targets of opportunity and ambushing Germans whenever and wherever the opportunity arose. In return, the SS routinely shot
hostages in retribution.

Von Vietinghof and the new Tenth Army commander, General der
Panzertruppen Traugott Herr, were like doctors attempting to apply a
gauze bandage to a severed artery; they could stop the bleeding temporarily, but in the end they could not prevent the death of their patient.
Nevertheless, even in its death throes the German army in Italy ably
fought bitter rearguard actions during the final battles of the war. To the
end the German army never lost its pride as a fighting force.

The Germans were dazed by the intensity of the Allied blows when
they finally fell, first on 9 April from Eighth Army, and then, five days
later, from Fifth Army. Supported by massive artillery bombardments
and the offensive-minded airmen of Ira Eaker's air forces, the Germans
could not withstand the powerful pressure that squeezed them from two
directions without letup. From his bunker in the ruins of Berlin Hitler
refused von Vietinghof's request to withdraw Army Group C.

Clark had done his best to reduce the role of Eighth Army to that of a
supporting bystander. His Anglophobia seems to have been magnified
when McCreery was appointed to command Eighth Army, and Clark attempted to impose on Eighth Army the same strategy that Alexander and
Montgomery had used with Seventh Army in Sicily. And, like Patton before him, McCreery pretended to conform to Clark's plan while actually
carrying out the offensive in such a way that Eighth Army remained a
major factor in the Allied drive.

Hitler's insane delusion that somehow he could still pull Germany's
chestnuts from the fire even as the Third Reich was literally collapsing
around him was partly the result of a secret overture to the Allies by
General Karl Wolff, the head of the SS in Italy. Wolff's representative
and the head of the OSS in Switzerland, Allen Dulles, secretly met over
a period of weeks and worked out tentative terms for an armistice in
Italy.

The top Nazis had all duped themselves by the belief that they could convince the West to join forces with Germany to deal with their real enemy in the war, Stalin and the Red Army. Hitler ordered von Vietinghof to hang on in Italy for at least another two months in order to buy time for an arrangement with the Allies. Defeatism would not be tolerated.

Under relentless pressure from the 15th Army Group the Germans could not hold the Winter Line and were forced to begin retreating toward the Po. Bologna was bypassed as II Corps drove toward the river, while to the west IV Corps brushed aside all resistance as five divisions debouched up the coast toward Genoa. The die-hard veterans of the 1st Parachute Division fought their last battle of the war against the equally tenacious Poles, but Bologna finally fell on 21 April.

McCreery's plan was superbly executed by Eighth Army. The task facing the new Eighth Army commander was far more difficult than that faced by Truscott's Fifth Army. The Po River valley consists of numerous rivers sandwiched between marshes and the natural obstacle created by Lake Comacchio. The final Allied offensive raged for sixteen days before the end came in Italy.

With the Allies loose on the plains of the Po and the Germans under attack on the ground and from the air, the wide and swift river became an impassable barrier to their retreat. Most of the bridges across the Po were destroyed, and some 100,000 German troops found themselves boxed in and forced to surrender. Those who succeeded in retreating across the river were soon run to ground as the Allied spearheads now swept away all before them. McCreery had sent the 6th Armoured Division on a dash to cut off the Po, and they responded with a brilliant drive that left the Germans on the Eighth Army flank with nowhere to go. The wreckage and litter of a defeated army dotted the battlefield.

Von Vietinghof may have been a colorless soldier, but he had courage. Like many other senior officers of the Wehrmacht, he too defied the lunatic orders of Hitler by ignoring the Führer's decree that he hold in place to the bitter end. For his temerity he was immediately relieved of command and ordered arrested by none other than Kesselring himself. It was a meaningless gesture because the war in Italy was all but over. It merely remained for the Allies to mop up the remnants of Army Group C and arrange for their formal surrender.

The Wolff-Dulles negotiations culminated in the formal signing of unconditional surrender documents at Alexander's headquarters in the royal palace at Caserta on 29 April. On 2 May 1945 all German forces in

Italy were ordered to lay down their arms. In the north the cease-fire was carried out on 4 May by von Vietinghof's personal emissary. For the final act of the Italian campaign he had chosen General Fridolin von Senger, who reported to a grim Clark, who was flanked by his two army commanders, McCreery and Truscott. In perfect English the defender of Cassino saluted and said, "As the representative of the German Commander-in-Chief, South-West, I report to you as the Commander of the 15th Army Group for your orders for the surrendered German Land Forces."

So ended the Italian campaign. The cost in human misery had been staggering. The numbers of dead and homeless Italians can only be guessed, but for those who fought in Italy there are more precise figures. Allied forces there ranged from a low of 400,000 to a high of approximately 500,000. Overall Allied casualties were 312,000, of which 189,000, 60 percent, were sustained by the U.S. Fifth Army. Of these, 31,886 were killed in action. Most were Americans (19,475 killed; 109,642 overall casualties). Of the British and Commonwealth troops who served under Fifth Army, 6,605 were killed out of a total of 47,452 casualties. French losses were 5,241 killed of 17,671 total casualties. The battles along the Gothic and Winter lines cost the Brazilians 275 dead and overall casualties of 2,411. The free Italian forces suffered 290 killed of a total of 1,570.

Total German losses in Italy have never been accurately calculated, but it is known that army casualties totaled 434,646. Of these, 48,067 were killed in action and another 214,048 were reported missing. Most of the missing were never accounted for and were presumed dead.

The butcher's bill aside, Italy was devastated by the war and its economy was shattered. With the exception of Rome, which received only minor damage, devastation lay wherever there had been fighting. The German scorched-earth policy ensured no less, and the warring parties completed the cycle.

There was little rejoicing in Italy when V-E Day finally came in Europe. The Italian campaign had lasted twenty months and carried the Allies from the boot in Calabria to the foothills of the Alps. Along the way they had fought the bitterest battles of World War II, along an eleven-hundred-mile axis* in some of the most forbidding terrain on the planet. From the Salerno landing in September 1943 to the final surrender on 2 May 1945, the Italian campaign consumed 602 days.

---

*Road miles from Cape Péssaro on the southeastern corner of Sicily to the Alps.

EPILOGUE

IN THIS BOOK I HAVE PRESENTED a general overview of the battles and campaigns fought in the Mediterranean theater of operations during the period between El Alamein and the end of the war in May 1945. The focus has been on North Africa, Sicily, and the long campaign fought on the mainland of Italy. My intent has been not only to illuminate how these campaigns were planned and led by the generals on the battlefield, but also to present in microcosm some of the elements of modern warfare.

The advent of the twentieth century saw the introduction of the airplane as a weapon of war and the improved use of naval vessels in the evolution of amphibious warfare. Yet the basic weapons of the Mediterranean campaigns were the rifle, the machine gun, and the artillery piece, all of which had been in various forms of development and usage since the invention of gunpowder. Although the technology of war has made incredible advances in this century, in Sicily and Italy the mule was often far more effective than the internal combustion engine.

However, when all is said and done, and despite the important role of technology throughout the war, the one common thread is that victory and defeat on the battlefields of Tunisia, Sicily, and Italy were mainly the result of Allied control of the air and sea and of that greatly misunderstood word *logistics*.

The term *logistics* has as many definitions as Napoleon had maxims, but reduced to its simplest form it has been defined as "the practical art of moving armies and keeping them supplied." The industrial might of the United States was able to produce and sustain a two-ocean war. The German forces in the Mediterranean were at the end of a lengthy logistical chain that eventually made a continuation of military operations in North Africa impossible.

In Sicily and Italy the Germans partly made up for their logistical shortfall by skillful and creative improvisation. Whether it was developing an efficient ferry service across the Strait of Messina or taking advantage of the terrain and whatever edge the Allies would give them to delay an Allied advance, the Wehrmacht performed with skill and commendable bravery.

The German presence in the Mediterranean was never more than a sideshow, and Hitler's employment of the Wehrmacht in North Africa was nothing short of criminal. Other than buying a short delay of several months, an entire army was needlessly sacrificed to Hitler's stubbornness during a critical stage of the war. During the period covered by this narrative the Germans fought defensively to protect their southern flank and to keep the maximum number of Allied forces tied up fighting in a secondary theater of war. Allied grand strategy, such as it was, existed for the same ostensible purpose, and it is fair to question just who was doing what to whom.

Allied strategy in Italy never seemed to be to win, but rather to drag out the war there for as long as possible and in so doing to keep Army Group C from being dispersed to fight on other fronts—particularly in France, where it was feared these formations might have made the difference between success and failure when OVERLORD was finally carried out in June 1944.

Alexander never had a mandate other than to take Rome, and at critical points in the campaign he was denied the men and the logistical assets needed to conclude the campaign. The most important instrument of transport became the LST, the workhorse that almost single-handedly kept open the lifeline between the Anzio beachhead and the giant logistical support base of Naples. There were never enough of these versatile craft to support theaters of war in both Italy and Northwest Europe.

The other factor that determined the outcome in Italy was the leadership of the armies that fought there. In Kesselring the Germans had a master of the art of defense, a commander who, for all his blindness to the evil of the regime he served, was highly regarded by his adversaries. His British biographer, Kenneth Macksey, has written: "Of what other general can it be said that, over a period of two and a half years, he fought a virtually incessant delaying action against desperate odds, managed to impose his will upon strong-minded and sceptical subordinates, and yet emerged unscathed by serious rout, leading his men in fighting to the last gasp."

For all his personal courage and other soldierly qualities, Alexander was an unimaginative strategist. His loose-reins style of leadership may have been conducive to enhancing the egos of a coalition of senior Allied commanders, but when it was most needed it was found wanting. Alexander may have been Churchill's favorite general, but among his peers he was regarded as a lightweight who required propping up by a strong chief of staff. In the desert Brooke had sent him McCreery, and in Italy he orchestrated the assignment of Harding, one of the outstanding British soldiers of the war.

Eisenhower's role in the Italian campaign was cut short by his appointment as Supreme Allied Commander. Starting in North Africa, where his inexperience in the art of high command was often painfully evident, he showed increasing signs of maturity that came to full fruition with the campaign in Northwest Europe, and there he earned a permanent entry in the pages of history. His attitude toward Allied strategy in the Mediterranean reflected both his own role as a commander and the policies of his superiors in Washington. While he was the Allied Commander-in-Chief in the Mediterranean he disapproved of ANVIL, but when he changed hats he fought tooth and nail to retain the operation.

The war in Italy frustrated Montgomery, who railed without effect against what he regarded as the stupidity of fighting a war of attrition instead of winning it outright. There is little doubt that he breathed a sigh of relief at the news of his return to the United Kingdom to command Allied ground forces for the cross-Channel assault. His replacement, the colorless Leese, was a good corps commander who demonstrated that he was well out of his depth commanding a field army.

The Polish and French commanders in Italy—Anders and Juin—were both outstanding soldiers, and both would have made able army commanders had their forces been of sufficient size to have earned them a higher place in the Allied command hierarchy. On the U.S. side, Lucian Truscott served with distinction as a division, corps, and army commander.

General Mark Clark was a man of many contradictions. A dedicated but overly ambitious soldier, he entered the campaign with no experience of high command, but he learned quickly. Unfortunately his education was sometimes a costly exercise for those under his command. The near disaster at Salerno, the fiasco at the Rapido, and the first two battles for Cassino were prima facie evidence of this, as was his decision to dismember Operation BUFFALO at the very moment when Truscott stood on the verge of a major victory. Like Eisenhower, Clark matured on the job, but unlike his longtime friend, he too often let his ego and his Anglophobia overshadow his better judgment.

Dawley and Lucas were examples of men who were perceived to have failed, yet in each instance their alleged failures were linked to the acts of their superior, Clark. Lucas in particular became a sacrificial victim for a dreadful mess not of his own making. The failure of Anzio to become anything more than just another bloody campaign was really the fault of Churchill, Alexander, and Clark.

In North Africa the U.S. Army learned valuable lessons that were put to good use in Sicily. The American troops in Italy fought with the same distinction as the rest of the Allied multinational force. Those who fought there, no matter what nationality, will always remember Italy as a tunnel which never seemed to have any light at the end of it.

In the years to come the debates will continue about the value of the campaigns fought in the Mediterranean theater of operations. Many theories abound as to how the Allies ought to have fought there. However, the major partners in the Allied coalition never fully agreed on a mutually acceptable strategy. Modern wars are as much about political motivations as they are about military victory on the battlefield.

Whatever the reasons, the war in the Mediterranean was the longest sustained series of campaigns fought by the western Allies during the Second World War. On this basis alone it deserves our attention for the lessons it offers to those willing to learn from the past.

ESSAY ON SOURCES

THE LITERATURE OF THE WAR IN THE Mediterranean is vast but fragmented, and those interested in further reading about the various campaigns and battles will find a select list of recommended books cited below.

TUNISIA

There are two excellent general accounts of the war in the Mediterranean: John S. D. Eisenhower, *Allies: From Pearl Harbor to D-Day* (New York: Doubleday, 1982), recounts the war up to the D-Day landings in France in June 1944. Charles MacDonald's acclaimed *The Mighty Endeavor: American Armed Forces in the European Theater in World War II* (New York: Oxford University Press, 1969) covers the entire period from American entry into the war to V-E Day.

There have been relatively few books written about the Tunisian campaign, but the following are a good cross-section of official and unofficial accounts. The best account of Kasserine Pass is Martin Blumenson, *Rommel's Last Victory* (Boston: Houghton Mifflin, 1967). The official histories are: I. S. O. Playfair, "History of the Second World War," in *The Mediterranean and Middle East*, vol. 4 (London: H.M.S.O., 1966), and George F. Howe, "U.S. Army in World War II: Mediterranean Theater of Operations," in *Northwest Africa: Seizing the Initiative in the West* (Washington, D.C.: G.P.O., 1957). Also of interest are Kenneth Macksey, *Crucible of Power: The Fight for Tunisia, 1942–1943* (London: Hutchinson, 1969), and W. G. F. Jackson, *The North African Campaign, 1940–43* (London: Batsford, 1975). Ernest N. Harmon, *Combat Commander* (Englewood Cliffs, N.J.: Prentice-Hall, 1970), and Omar N. Bradley, *A Soldier's Story* (New York: Henry Holt, 1951), are useful memoirs.

SICILY

References to the Sicily campaign appear in well over a hundred books, but little has been written in the form of campaign histories. The official U.S. Army account is Albert N. Garland and Howard McGaw Smyth,

Sicily and the Surrender of Italy (Washington, D.C.: G.P.O., 1965). The British version is merely window dressing to the Italian campaign in C. J. C. Molony, *The Mediterranean and Middle East*, vol. 5 (London: H.M.S.O., 1973). The Canadian official history is G. W. L. Nicholson, *The Canadians in Italy, 1943–1945* (Ottawa: Queen's Printer, 1967). For a recent unofficial comprehensive account of Sicily, see Carlo D'Este, *Bitter Victory: The Battle for Sicily, 1943* (New York: E. P. Dutton, and London: William Collins, 1988).

The best of the naval accounts are Samuel Eliot Morison, *Sicily-Salerno-Anzio* (Boston: Little, Brown, 1954), and the official British naval history, S. W. Roskill, *The War at Sea*, vol. III, pt. 1 (London: H.M.S.O., 1960). An excellent short account of the Sicily campaign is in Hanson W. Baldwin, *Battles Lost and Won* (New York: Harper and Row, 1966). British journalist Hugh Pond also wrote a brief account in *Sicily* (London: William Kimber, 1962).

The exploits of the 82d Airborne Division in Sicily are described in Clay Blair, *Ridgway's Paratroopers* (New York: Dial Press, 1985), an account of American airborne operations in World War II, and James M. Gavin, *On to Berlin* (New York: Viking, 1978). Possibly the best memoir of both Sicily and the Italian campaign is Lucian K. Truscott, *Command Missions* (New York: E. P. Dutton, 1954). Major General John Frost recounts the British airborne operation at Primosole Bridge in *A Drop Too Many* (London: Buchan and Enright, 1982). An excellent history of airborne operations, including those in Sicily and Italy, is Gerard M. Devlin, *Paratrooper!* (New York: St. Martin's Press, 1979).

The air war in the Mediterranean has been poorly served. The U.S. official history is Wesley F. Craven and James L. Cate (eds.), *Europe: Torch to Pointblank, August 1942 to December 1943* (Chicago: University of Chicago Press, 1949). The RAF is covered in Sir John Slessor, *The Central Blue* (London: Cassell, 1956). The best account of the RAF in World War II is John Terraine, *The Right of the Line: The Royal Air Force in the European War, 1939–1945* (London: Hodder and Stoughton, 1985). Lord Tedder's memoirs, *With Prejudice* (London: Cassell, 1966), offer a view of the air war from on high.

THE ITALIAN CAMPAIGN

The best overall account of the Italian campaign is Dominick Graham and Shelford Bidwell, *Tug of War: The Battle for Italy, 1943–45* (New York: St. Martin's Press, 1986), a provocative examination of a controversial campaign written by two superb British military historians and former Royal Artillery officers who both served in Italy during the war. Other general accounts of the campaign include G. A. Sheppard, *The Italian Campaign, 1943–1945* (New York: Praeger, 1968), and the official histories. The U.S. Army official history appears in two works: Martin Blumenson, *Salerno to Cassino* (Washington, D.C.: G.P.O., 1969), and Ernest F. Fisher, Jr., *Cassino to the Alps* (Washington, D.C.: Center of Military History, 1984). The British official history of the Italian campaign is covered in three volumes by C. J. C. Molony, *The Mediterranean and Middle East*, vols. V, VI, pt. 1 (London: H.M.S.O., 1984), and vol. VI, pt. 2, due out shortly.

Other official histories are the Canadian (Nicholson, *Canadians in Italy*) and volumes written by the Indian, New Zealand, and South African historical offices.

SALERNO

Mark Clark's memoirs contain his highly personal version of the Italian campaign in *Calculated Risk* (New York: Harper and Row, 1950). See also: Blumenson, *Salerno to Cassino;* Morison, *Sicily-Salerno-Anzio;* Truscott, *Command Missions;* Gavin, *On to Berlin;* Fred Walker, *From Texas to Rome: A General's Journal* (Dallas: Taylor Publishing, 1969); Des Hickey and Gus Smith, *Operation Avalanche: The Salerno Landings, 1943* (London: Heinemann, 1983); Hugh Pond, *Salerno!* (London: William Kimber, 1962); and W. G. F. Jackson, *The Battle for Italy* (London: Batsford, 1967).

CASSINO

See Martin Blumenson, *Bloody River* (London: Allen and Unwin, 1970); John Ellis, *Cassino: The Hollow Victory* (New York: McGraw-Hill, 1984); David Hapgood and David Richardson, *Monte Cassino* (New York: Congdon and Weed, 1984); and Fred Majdalany, *The Battle of Cassino* (London: Longmans, Green, 1957).

ANZIO

See Martin Blumenson, *Anzio: The Gamble that Failed* (New York: J. B. Lippincott, 1963; Dell paperback edition, 1986); Wynford Vaughan-Thomas, *Anzio* (New York: Holt, Rinehart, and Winston, 1961); W. G. F.

Jackson, *The Battle for Rome* (New York: Scribners, 1969). Two excellent accounts of British operations are Peter Verney, *Anzio: An Unexpected Fury* (London: Batsford, 1978), and Desmond Fitzgerald, *A History of the Irish Guards in the Second World War* (Aldershot: Gale and Polden, 1949). Peter Tompkins relates his exploits in Rome in *A Spy in Rome* (New York: Simon and Schuster, 1962). A fine account of the fall of Rome is Raleigh Trevelyan, *Rome '44: The Battle for the Eternal City* (London: Hodder and Stoughton, 1981). Harmon's memoirs, *Combat Commander*, provide a bitter remembrance of Anzio, as do his two articles in the *Saturday Evening Post* in 1948. Truscott's *Command Missions* likewise presents a thorough account of his role at Anzio. A good short account is in the American Forces in Action series: John Bowditch III, *The Anzio Beachhead* (Washington, D.C.: Department of the Army, 1947).

GOTHIC AND WINTER LINES

Very little has been written about the last eleven months of the Italian campaign. Readers interested in learning more should consult the relevant official history or Douglas Orgill, *The Gothic Line* (New York: Zebra Books, 1986). See also Brian Harpur, *The Impossible Victory: A Personal Account of the Battle for the River Po* (London: William Kimber, 1980).

GERMAN AND ITALIAN ACCOUNTS

A controversial but excellent account of the war from the German side is David Irving, *Hitler's War* (London: Hodder and Stoughton, 1977; also published in a two-volume paperback edition by Macmillan [Papermac, 1983]). Kesselring's biography is by Kenneth Macksey, *Kesselring: The Making of the Luftwaffe* (New York: David MacKay, 1978), and his memoirs are *Kesselring: A Soldier's Record* (New York: William Morrow, 1954). Von Senger's memoirs are published in English in *Neither Fear Nor Hope* (New York: E. P. Dutton, 1954). The best book dealing with Mussolini and the fascist period is F. W. Deakin, *The Brutal Friendship: Mussolini, Hitler and the Fall of Italian Fascism* (New York: Harper & Row, 1962). Two excellent biographies of Mussolini are Laura Fermi, *Mussolini* (Chicago: University of Chicago Press, 1961), and Denis Mack Smith, *Mussolini* (London: Weidenfeld and Nicholson, 1981). Those interested in Rommel may wish to consult B. H. Liddell Hart (ed.), *The Rommel Papers* (New York: Harcourt, Brace, 1953), or Ronald Lewin, *Rommel as Military Commander* (New York: Random House, 1968; or Ballantine paperback edition, 1970). Another short but useful account of the German side of the war in the west is Siegfried Westphal, *The German Army in the West* (London: Cassell, 1951). For the story of the German army in World War II see Matthew Cooper, *The German Army* (London: Mac-Donald and Janes, 1978).

BIOGRAPHIES AND MEMOIRS

Virtually all of the major Allied figures who served in the Mediterranean have written their versions of events. In addition to those previously cited, the following are of interest: George S. Patton, Jr., *War as I Knew It* (published in various U.S. and British hardback and paperback editions), and Martin Blumenson, *The Patton Papers*, vol. II (Boston: Houghton Mifflin, 1974); Dwight D. Eisenhower, *Crusade in Europe* (Garden City, N.Y.: Doubleday, 1948); and B. L. Montgomery, *Memoirs of Field-Marshal the Viscount Montgomery of Alamein* (Cleveland and New York: World Publishing, 1958).

Biographies include Stephen E. Ambrose, *The Supreme Commander: The War Years of General Dwight D. Eisenhower* (Garden City, N.Y.: Doubleday, 1970), and Merle Miller, *Ike the Soldier: As They Knew Him* (New York: G. P. Putnam's Sons, 1987). Nigel Hamilton portrays Monty in *Montgomery: Master of the Battlefield, 1942–1944* (New York: McGraw-Hill, 1984), the second volume in his masterful trilogy of the life of Field-Marshal Montgomery. The only biography of Field-Marshal Earl Alexander is Nigel Nicholson, *Alex: The Life of Field Marshal Earl Alexander of Tunis* (London: Weidenfeld and Nicholson, 1973). Biographies of Mark Clark, Alan Brooke, and Ira Eaker are, respectively, Martin Blumenson, *Mark Clark* (New York: Congdon and Weed, 1984); David Fraser, *Alanbrooke* (New York: Atheneum, 1981); and James Parton, *"Air Force Spoken Here": General Ira Eaker & the Command of the Air* (Bethesda: Adler and Adler, 1986). There are many biographies of Churchill, but I recommend Martin Gilbert, *Road to Victory: Winston S. Churchill, 1941–1945* (London: Heinemann, 1986; also published in the United States).

INTELLIGENCE AND ULTRA

Readers interested in learning more about intelligence, deception, and the uses of Ultra intelligence can consult F. H. Hinsley et al., *British In-

telligence in the Second World War, vols. 2 and 3, pt. 1 (London: H.M.S.O.); Ronald Lewin, *Ultra Goes to War* (London: Hutchinson, 1978, and New York: Pocket Books, 1981); and Ralph Bennett's recent superb account, *Ultra and the Mediterranean Strategy* (New York: William Morrow, 1989). Accounts of the "man who never was" are in two books by the Royal Navy intelligence officer who helped mastermind the operation, Ewen Montagu, in *The Man Who Never Was* (New York: J. B. Lippincott, 1954), and *Beyond Top Secret Ultra* (New York: Coward, McCann & Geoghegan, 1978). A useful investigative report of the operation is Roger Morgan, "The Man Who Almost Is," in the British magazine *After the Battle* (No. 54, 1986). See also J. C. Masterman, *The Double Cross System* (London: Yale University Press, 1972).

Index

Note: Military units are listed alphabetically by country affiliation, with numbered subheadings listed in numeric order, for reader convenience.